Cic

ON ACADEMIC
SCEPTICISM

Cicero

ON ACADEMIC SCEPTICISM

Translated, with Introduction and Notes, by

Charles Brittain

Hackett Publishing Company, Inc.
Indianapolis/Cambridge

06   07   08   09   1   2   3   4   5   6   7

For further information, please address
  Hackett Publishing Company, Inc.
  P.O. Box 44937
  Indianapolis, IN 46244-0937

  www.hackettpublishing.com

Cover design by Listenberger Design Associates
Interior design by Elizabeth Wilson
Composition by Agnew's, Inc.
Printed at Edwards Brothers, Inc.

Library of Congress Cataloging-in-Publication Data

Cicero, Marcus Tullius.
    [Academica. English]
    On academic scepticism / Marcus Tullius Cicero ; translated,
  with introduction and notes, by Charles Brittain.
      p. cm.
    Includes bibliographical references and index.
    ISBN 0-87220-775-7 (cloth) — ISBN 0-87220-774-9 (pbk.)
    1. Knowledge, Theory of—Early works to 1800. 2. Scepticism—
  Early works to 1800. I. Brittain, Charles. II. Title.
  PA6308.A2B75 2006
  186'.2—dc22
                                                            2005019197

Contents

Preface

I started work on this translation in the autumn of 1996 while teaching a seminar on Academic scepticism. It seemed plausible then that a new translation aimed at philosophical readers might help to make this fascinating subject more accessible—and I assumed that after five years' work on it in connexion with my dissertation, and with Reid's excellent commentary to help me, the text would present few difficulties. Nearly ten years later, and after three sets of radical revisions to my translation, I hope I wasn't mistaken on both counts. The *Academica* is a difficult work; but it is a vital text for students of ancient scepticism and interpreters of Cicero.

It is hard to acknowledge all the debts I have piled up in the interval. I am very grateful to my friends Gail Fine, Scott MacDonald, John Palmer, Hayden Pelliccia, Karin Schlapbach, Danuta Shanzer, and Cristiana Sogno for their direct and indirect help with my work on Cicero. I am glad to recognize the enduring generosity of my colleagues at Cornell, and of the university for awarding me a year's leave. I owe a similar debt to the members of the B caucus in Classics at Cambridge, and to Corpus Christi College, Cambridge, which furnished me with the peace and beautiful surroundings required to finish this book during a visiting fellowship in 2004–5. I also owe a great deal to the remarkable patience and support of Brian Rak, my editor at Hackett. My greatest debt, however, is to Harriet, Sophie, and Helena Brittain, for their delightful company and nearly inexhaustible sympathy.

The final version of the translation is the product of a revision based on the detailed criticism provided by a number of scholars and friends: by David Mankin and Tobias Reinhardt on the text, Terry Irwin on the notes, and Julia Annas, Jonathan Barnes, Tad Brennan, John Cooper, Michael Frede, Brad Inwood, David Sedley, Gisela Striker, and Robert Wagoner on the translation. It is a great pleasure to acknowledge how much I owe to their exacting standards and wonderful generosity.

This book is dedicated to the memory of Heda Segvic: *inquisitor ardentissimus veritatis.*

Cambridge, 19 May 2005

Introduction

Cicero's work on Academic scepticism has been unduly neglected in modern times. One reason for this is that it is only in the last two or three decades that historians of philosophy have begun to recover the significance of this tradition of scepticism, both as a sophisticated philosophical position in its own right and as the intellectual parent of the better-known Pyrrhonist sceptical tradition.

A second reason is the complexity of the work itself. In part, this is due to Cicero's purpose, which was to explain and defend his own philosophical position to the general Roman audience he was trying to create. He took this to require not just an adversarial context—a dialogue with an Academic sceptic responding to dogmatic criticism—but also the presentation of the rather complicated and controversial evolution of the sceptical Academy. As a result, the work contains several layers of debate. The most prominent layer is the Stoic-Academic arguments of the third and second centuries BCE, but these are overlaid by the dispute between Antiochus and the Academics in Cicero's youth (90s–80s BCE), and filtered through a set of near-contemporary Roman interlocutors (62/1 and 45 BCE). And within each layer there are several distinct strata—the first, for instance, includes at least two distinct Academic responses to three sets of Stoic criticism.

A further difficulty facing a modern reader is one that Cicero could not have anticipated: we no longer have his work in its entirety. What we now have are fragments from two quite distinct editions—a first, two-book edition, consisting of the lost *Catulus* and the extant *Lucullus* (the latter abbreviated as '*Ac. 2*'), and a revised second, four-book edition, the *Academic Books,* of which we have only about half of Book 1 ('*Ac. 1*').[1] And since the fragmentary Book 1 doesn't fit together very easily with the extant *Lucullus* (see below), the modern reader starts in the middle of a debate whose terms are lost.

The complexity of the work, however, is philosophically rewarding, once the various layers of debate are untangled so that the

---

1. Elsewhere the *Lucullus* is sometimes referred to as the '*Academica Priora*'—i.e., the 'early edition of the *Academica*'—and the *Academic Books* as the '*Academica posteriora*'—i.e., the 'later edition'. In this translation, I use 'the *Academica*' to refer to the two editions or their surviving parts as a whole, and the abbreviations '*Ac. 2*' for the *Lucullus* and '*Ac. 1*' for Book 1 of the *Academic Books.* A list of abbreviations is given on pages xliv–xlv.

interlocutors' arguments can be seen in their appropriate historical contexts.

I: The Historical Context
Cicero

Cicero's work on Academic scepticism forms part of a sequence of philosophical dialogues written in 46–44 BCE, the last few years of his life. By this time he was one of the most prominent political figures in Roman society, as well as its most celebrated forensic orator, and an influential writer on rhetorical and political theory.[2] He had started out with the disadvantage of coming from a provincial—though aristocratic—family from Arpinum, about one hundred miles southeast of Rome; but by 63 BCE his oratorical skills had won him enough popularity and influence to secure the consulship (the chief political office in Rome, won by election and held for one year). His consulship was marked by the controversial suppression of the 'Catilinarian conspiracy' (see *Ac.* 2.62–63).[3] When Pompey and Caesar gained control over the political process, this was used to force Cicero into exile in 58 BCE. He returned a year later but was unable to play the leading political role he desired in the tumultuous years leading up to the civil wars. After Julius Caesar's assassination in 44 BCE, Cicero tried to marshal republican opposition to Antony but failed, and was eventually murdered in the proscriptions of 43 BCE.

His personal motives for turning to philosophical writing are explained in *Ac.* 1.11 (cf. *Ac.* 2.6): the political situation—under the dictatorship of Julius Caesar, which meant that there was little role for public speaking either in the law-courts or in the senate—had driven

---

2. For further information about Cicero's life, see C. Habicht, *Cicero the Politician* (Baltimore 1990); on his speeches and rhetorical writings, see J. Powell and J. Paterson, 'Introduction' in their *Cicero the Advocate* (Oxford 2004), pp. 1–57, and the essays in J. May (ed.), *Brill's Companion to Cicero: Oratory and Rhetoric* (Leiden 2002); on his philosophical writings, see J. Powell, 'Introduction: Cicero's Philosophical Works and Their Background', in J. Powell (ed.), *Cicero the Philosopher* (Oxford 1995), pp. 1–35.

3. The Catilinarian conspiracy was an attempt to overthrow the government by force, led by Catiline, a disaffected and heavily indebted aristocrat. Cicero believed that he had saved the republic; but many thought that the threat was exaggerated and criticized Cicero's role in persuading the senate to execute the conspirators he had exposed in Rome. His political opponents characterized this as the extrajudicial murder of Roman citizens; see Habicht 1990, pp. 31–48.

him to an enforced period of 'leisure'.[4] Since he could not satisfy his
desire to serve (and influence) the Roman public in the traditional
way, he decided to try to educate his fellow-citizens by turning to
philosophical writing in Latin. This was a relatively novel form for
Latin literature, whose utility is debated in *Ac.* 1.3–12.[5] The problem
was not so much that educated Romans were not interested in philosophy, but that the intellectual elite was effectively bilingual in Latin
and Greek, and philosophy was regarded as something best done in
Greek (as history and rhetoric had been until recently). But Cicero believed—correctly, as it turned out—that Latin could be put to use as a
medium for philosophical thought, and so set out to naturalize Hellenistic philosophy into his native culture. (This explains the emphasis in the *Academica* on philosophical terminology: the interlocutors
are actively forging a new vocabulary.)[6]

Cicero was well placed to perform this service because he had
both the rhetorical skill to bring off the new form and the philosophical training it required. His philosophical teachers had included the
Epicurean Phaedrus (who taught him in his youth; see *ad Fam.* 13.1);
the Academic Philo of Larissa (whose lectures he heard in Rome in
88–87 BCE; see *Brutus* 306); the Stoic Diodotus (who taught him logic
in the 80s; see *Ac.* 2.115); the renegade Academic Antiochus of Ascalon
(whose lectures he attended in Athens in 79–77 BCE; see *Ac.* 1.14); and
the Stoic Posidonius (see *Tusc.* 2.61)—i.e., most of the leading Greek
philosophers of his age. He had also maintained his interest in philosophy throughout his political career, as we can see in his earlier
writings from the 50s BCE, which included three works modeled to
some extent on Plato: *On the Orator,* drawing very loosely on Plato's
Phaedrus, and his political works *On the Republic* and *On Laws,* inspired more directly by Plato's *Republic* and *Laws.*

4. *Ac.* 1.11 mentions the death of his daughter Tullia as another stimulus to writing; but, although it led to the composition of his (lost) *Consolation,* this occurred in
February 45 BCE, after his first philosophical dialogue, the *Hortensius,* had already
been completed.

5. The intellectual context of Cicero's work in philosophy is examined in E. Rawson, *Intellectual Life in the Late Roman Republic* (London 1985), pp. 282–97.

6. See e.g., *Ac.* 2.17–18 on the Greek terms *katalêpsis, enargeia,* and *phantasia,* and *Ac.*
1.25 on *poiotês.* The English–Latin–Greek Glossary shows Cicero's Latin glosses for
Greek technical terms (explicit glosses are in bold letters). For further information
on Cicero's translations of Greek philosophical terminology, see J. Powell, 'Cicero's
Translations from Greek', in Powell, *Cicero the Philosopher,* pp. 273–300. The best
study of the development of his philosophical terminology is H.-J. Hartung, *Ciceros
Methode bei der Übersetzung Griechischer philosophischer Termini* (Hamburg 1970).

His plan to 'put philosophy on display to the Roman people' (*Ac.* 1.18; cf. *Ac.* 1.3) probably started off as a project for three books: the (lost) *Hortensius* (completed in 46) and the *Catulus* and the *Lucullus*— i.e., the two books of the first edition of the *Academica* (finished by May 45). His intention with this trilogy was to advocate the study of philosophy in the first volume, and explain his own philosophical position as an Academic sceptic in the other two (see *DND* 1.6, *Div.* 2.1, and *Tusc.* 2.4).[7] But by the time he had started work on the *Academica* in early 45 BCE, he was already thinking of the larger sequence of works he eventually produced: *On Ethical Ends, Tusculan Disputations, On the Nature of the Gods, On Divination,* and *On Fate.*[8] In this larger sequence, the *Academica* has the additional function of covering 'logic' or epistemology, while the later works dealt with 'ethics' and 'physics', the remaining 'parts' of Hellenistic philosophy (cf. *Ac.* 1.19, 2.116).

Cicero's choice of the adversarial dialogue as the appropriate form for the exposition of philosophy to his fellow-citizens was at least partly influenced by his own philosophical position as an Academic sceptic.[9] The Academics construed their philosophical activity as a revival of the critical investigation of dogmatic presumption pursued by Socrates in the Platonic dialogues (see *Ac.* 1.44–46).[10] Their

7. The development of Cicero's plans and his writing of the *Academica* are lucidly explained in M. Griffin, 'The Composition of the *Academica.* Motives and Versions' in B. Inwood and J. Mansfeld (eds.), *Assent and Argument* (Leiden 1997), pp. 1–35. The *Hortensius* had the same protagonists as the *Catulus* and the *Lucullus* and a similar setting and fictional date. Its alleged effect on Hortensius is alluded to in *Ac.* 2.61.

8. Cicero also wrote his works *On Friendship* and *On Old Age* in this period, as well as *On Duties* and several technical works on rhetoric. By the summer of 44 BCE he was also heavily engaged in political work, including the writing of the brilliant *Philippic Orations* against Antony that led to his death.

9. Cicero had declared himself a follower of the Academics in his earliest work from the 80s BCE (*Inv.* 2.9–10). Some scholars believe that he became a follower of Antiochus after his time in Athens in the 70s, and only returned to scepticism in the 40s BCE. Some support for this view comes from his sidelining of the sceptical Academics in *Leg.* 1.39 and the description of his advocacy of the Academy in the works of the 40s as 'unexpected' in *DND* 1.6 (cf. *Ac.* 2.11) and as an 'abandonment' of the Antiochian 'Old Academy' in *Ac.* 1.13. But the first passage is explicable as a function of his aims in that work, while the latter two concern the subjects Cicero chose to write about rather than his beliefs. See W. Görler, 'Silencing the Troublemaker: *De Legibus* I.39 and the Continuity of Cicero's Scepticism', in Powell, *Cicero the Philosopher,* pp. 85–113, replying to J. Glucker, 'Cicero's Philosophical Affiliations', in J. Dillon and A. Long (eds.), *The Question of "Eclecticism"* (Berkeley 1988), pp. 34–69.

10. Cicero emphasizes the Socratic nature and origins of the Academics' methods in *Fin.* 2.1–4, *DND* 1.11, *Tusc.* 2.9, and *Or.* 3.68, 3.80, and 3.107. In fact, the Academics

task was to protect the rational standards philosophers claimed to ad-
here to by subjecting the positive theses and arguments of their contemporaries to critical examination (see *Ac.* 2.7–9 or *DND* 1.11). Hence
they characterized their position primarily by their method of argument 'on either side' of philosophical questions, rather than by any results it tended to produce (see *Ac.* 2.60).[11] Perhaps unsurprisingly, the
usual result of searching for the truth by this method was the realization that neither side had conclusive rational support: neither case
amounted to knowledge, though one view might seem more 'persuasive' than the other in the light of the available evidence. (The Academics disagreed about the implications of finding one thesis more
'persuasive' than another—see Section II below. But Cicero followed
the earlier Academics in construing 'persuasive' views as claims they
might accept provisionally, but to which they were not rationally committed; see *Ac.* 2.127–28 and 2.141.)

The format of adversarial dialogue thus allows Cicero to introduce a range of philosophical views without compromising his stance
as an Academic or imposing his own authority on the reader. Each
side is subjected to a critical examination, and the debate is left un-
settled by the interlocutors. One implication of this method is that
Cicero takes both (or all) sides seriously and invites his readers to do
the same. This means that we should be cautious in inferring Cicero's
views directly from the arguments he presents as an interlocutor in
the *Academica* (or elsewhere): the purpose of the dialogue is to investigate the arguments for *and* against Academic scepticism, not to show
that one side is right.[12]

---

employed several different methods, since Arcesilaus used the technique of cross-
examination depicted in the Socratic dialogues (*Ac.* 1.45), while Carneades developed what became the standard form of arguing both for and against a thesis
(*Ac.* 2.7). The latter is the form Cicero uses in most of his dialogues. Cicero points
out in *Fin.* 2.4 that a third Academic method, of arguing against a thesis proposed,
but not defended, by a student—the method he employs in the *Tusculan Disputations*
and *On Fate*—is not genuinely Socratic, because, unlike the other techniques, it
leaves one side without an advocate.

11. It was the dogmatic opponents of the Academics who liked to identify them in
terms of the notorious conclusions their arguments led to—e.g., that nothing can be
known and it is irrational to hold philosophical beliefs. See, in addition to *Ac.* 2.59,
e.g., Plutarch *Stoic Contradictions* ch. 10 1036a (a Stoic characterization of the Academics) or Sextus *PH* 1.1–4 and 1.226–30 (a Pyrrhonist characterization). Cicero always
characterizes them as engaged in a positive search for the truth or its best approximation by means of argument on either side.

12. This caution is more clearly applicable in dialogues such as *On Divination*,

The structure of the dialogues

The primary purpose of his use of the dialogue form is thus to allow Cicero to present a rather complicated series of philosophical debates stretching over 250 years. But since they can be rather hard to keep track of in the surviving parts of the two editions, it is a good idea to start with a chronological sketch of these debates. This will allow us to reconstruct the general structure of the original editions, by aligning the various interlocutors to the relevant philosophical schools and arguments.

The first layer of arguments comes from the Stoic-Academic debates about epistemology from the third and second centuries BCE. There are roughly four historical stages to this debate, each meeting the previous criticisms and providing new counterarguments:

1) Zeno, the founder of the Stoa, made and defended his novel epistemological claims (see *Ac.* 1.40–42) in the period from c. 300 to 270.[13] They were attacked by Arcesilaus, the initiator of the sceptical turn of the Platonic Academy, during his lifetime, though probably after Zeno's retirement, in the period from c. 275 to 240 (see *Ac.* 2.16, 2.76–77, 1.43–46).

2) Zeno's views were reformulated and defended against Arcesilaus' criticisms by Chrysippus in the period from c. 240 to 210 (see *Ac.* 2.93–96, 2.143).

3) Chrysippus' defence of the Stoa was elaborated by his student Diogenes of Babylon and attacked with renewed vigour by the Academic Carneades in the period c. 170–150 (see *Ac.* 2.16, 1.46; cf. 2.87, 2.93, 2.98).

4) Carneades' arguments were opposed by Diogenes' student Antipater (see *Ac.* 2.17 and fr. 1), and the nature of his scepticism

---

where Cicero's role as an interlocutor is to criticize the Stoic thesis that the art of divination allows the gods to communicate with us; see M. Schofield, 'Cicero For and Against Divination', *JRS* 76 (1986), pp. 47–65. In the *Academica* his views as an interlocutor in *Ac.* 2.64–146 seem to support the general authorial claims made in *Ac.* 2.7–9. But this does not imply that Cicero himself holds *all* the views his character argues for. (Elsewhere, for instance, he is much more sympathetic to Antiochus' historical claims than one might think from *Ac.* 2.112–46.)

13. For fuller information about the dates and philosophical activities of the philosophers mentioned here, see the Glossary of Names. The general Index lists references to each philosopher in the dialogues.

was disputed by his own Academic students, notably Clito-machus and Metrodorus of Stratonicea, in the period c. 140–110 (see *Ac.* 2.16, 2.78, 2.148).

The second layer of arguments is the result in the early decades of the first century BCE of the intra-Academic disputes about the most consistent form of scepticism, initiated by Clitomachus and Metro-dorus. There seem to have been three main stages to this narrower and more internecine debate (though the details remain extremely controversial):[14]

5) Philo, the Academic leader or 'scholarch', abandoned the rad-ical scepticism of his teacher Clitomachus and adopted a form of mitigated scepticism in the decade of 100–90 BCE (see, e.g., *Ac.* 2.78).

6) Philo's new position was criticized and rejected by two of his students in the late 90s: Aenesidemus, who reworked rad-ical Academic scepticism into a new (or revived) form of Pyrrhonism;[15] and Antiochus, who abandoned scepticism and founded a syncretic school reviving the doctrines of the Old Academics and Peripatetics, but relying on Stoic epistemology (see *Ac.* 2.68–71 and Section II below).

7) Under pressure from these critics, Philo abandoned mitigated scepticism for a form of naturalistic fallibilism, bolstered by a new interpretation of the history of the Academy. This posi-tion was set out in his 'Roman Books' in 88/7 BCE, and criti-cized by Antiochus and other still sceptical Academics through the 80s (see *Ac.* 2.11–12, 2.18, 1.13).

The final layer of arguments is that of the Roman interlocutors in Cicero's dialogues, which are set in 62/1 and 45 BCE, i.e., after the

14. The outline given here is defended, e.g., in C. Brittain, *Philo of Larissa* (Oxford 2001). Some scholars argue that stages [5] and [7] constitute a single Philonian po-sition; see D. Sedley, 'The End of the Academy', *Phronesis* 26 (1981), pp. 67–75, reaf-firmed recently in J. Glucker, 'The Philonian/Metrodorians: Problems of Method in Ancient Philosophy', *Elenchos* 25.1 (2004), pp. 99–153.
15. The date, and sometimes fact, of Aenesidemus' defection from the Academy is also disputed; see F. Decleva Caizzi, 'Aenesidemus and the Academy', *Classical Quarterly* 42 (1992), pp. 176–89, and J. Mansfeld, 'Aenesidemus and the Academics', in L. Ayers (ed.), *The Passionate Intellect* (London 1995), pp. 235–48.

deaths of all the Greek philosophers listed above. So the next task is to see how the interlocutors' positions in the surviving parts of the two editions align with these views.

As indicated above, the **first edition** of the *Academica* consisted of two books, called the *Catulus* and the *Lucullus* (of which the latter is our *Ac.* 2). The fictional date for both books is 62 (or possibly 61) BCE, the year after Cicero's consulship and suppression of the 'Catilinarian conspiracy' (see *Ac.* 2.62), and nearly twenty years before their date of composition.[16] The dialogues are set on two consecutive days in the seaside villas of Catulus (in the *Catulus*) and Hortensius (in the *Lucullus*; see *Ac.* 2.9).[17] The conversation in the *Lucullus* takes place outside, in the sunshine of a portico within sight of the sea (*Ac.* 2.9).[18] The interlocutors are a group of prominent Roman political leaders who share an interest in learned and intellectual conversation. Two—Catulus and Lucullus—were famous, if not entirely successful, generals; the other two—Hortensius and Cicero—derived their political prestige from their success as forensic orators.[19] But, with the exception of Cicero, whose influence was at its peak at this time, all were nearing the end of their political (and actual) lives.[20] Elsewhere Cicero

16. The fictional date is fixed by the allusion to Cicero's consulship in 63 BCE and by Catulus' death in 61 BCE. Some of the joking references in the dialogue to troublesome tribunes—i.e., the people's representatives who had authority to disrupt legislation by the governing consuls—may refer to Cicero's friend Cato (his opponent in his speech *For Murena*, from 63 BCE); see *Ac.* 2.63 and 2.97. But the seditious tribune of *Ac.* 2.144 is probably Clodius (who had Cicero exiled in 58 BCE).

17. Hortensius' villa was at Bauli; Catulus had two villas in the area of the bay of Naples, one at Cumae and one at Pompeii (*Ac.* 2.80). The interlocutors arrive by boat (*Ac.* 2.9); Cicero and Lucullus depart by boat to their local villas (*Ac.* 2.147–48). These seaside villas were summer houses for the Roman aristocracy.

18. The location and view of the sea are mentioned at *Ac.* 2.9, 2.80–81, 2.105, and 2.147–48. Cicero explains his frequent use of the sun as an example (*Ac.* 2.82, 2.105, 2.116, 2.123, 2.126, 2.128) by reference to its radiance as he speaks at *Ac.* 2.126.

19. Lucullus' generalship is praised in the prologue (*Ac.* 2.1–4; cf. *Ac.* 2.11 and 2.61); Catulus' was no doubt lauded in the prologue of the *Catulus*. Hortensius had a bigger role in the *Catulus*, where his oratorical abilities were probably highlighted. The reference to his memory in *Ac.* 2.2 is an implicit plaudit of his speaking ability, and his acknowledgment that he 'exceeded his brief yesterday' (*Ac.* 2.10) is probably an in-joke—he and Cicero often argued legal cases together, and Cicero usually spoke last.

20. Lucullus lived from c. 115 to 57/6 BCE; Catulus from c. 115 to 61 BCE; Hortensius from 114 to 49 BCE; and Cicero from 106 to 43 BCE.

acknowledges that his interlocutors were considerably less learned in philosophy than he made out in the dialogue—his picture of aristocratic leisure is somewhat idealized (*Ac.* 2.5–6).[21] But he takes pains to stress that their arguments are derived from other people—Lucullus insists that he is repeating Antiochus' arguments from memory (*Ac.* 2.10, 2.12, 2.28, 2.49, 2.61); Catulus gives only his father's view (*Ac.* 2.11–12, 2.148); and Hortensius denies having any philosophical expertise (*Ac.* 2.9; cf. *Ac.* 2.61).

The structure of the surviving *Lucullus*, the second book of the first edition, is straightforward. Aside from the prologue in praise of Lucullus and defence of Cicero's philosophical writings (*Ac.* 2.1–9), the general machinery of dialogue is exhausted by a very short mise-en-scène (*Ac.* 2.9–10), a brief intermezzo (*Ac.* 2.63), and a final paragraph giving a concise record of the interlocutors' reactions (*Ac.* 2.148).[22] The bulk of the work is taken up by a long speech by Lucullus (*Ac.* 2.11–62) and Cicero's reply (*Ac.* 2.64–147). The vital thing for the philosophical reader, however, is to note that the interlocutors represent distinct perspectives on the epistemological debates set out above. The general debate is clear:

- Lucullus represents Antiochus directly, and hence, given Antiochus' epistemology, the Stoics.

- Cicero represents the Academics in general.

But we can see from some comments in the work that the characters advocate more specific views:

- Cicero champions the Academic position of Clitomachus (*Ac.* 2.66, 2.78, 2.112–13).[23]

21. Cicero explains the need for a second edition with new speakers to his friend Atticus by noting that Lucullus, Catulus, and Hortensius were "prominent men, of course, but not at all literati" of the sort he represented (*ad Att.* 13.12.3), or characterized "not, indeed, by lack of education, but a recognized unfamiliarity with those subjects" (*ad Att.* 13.16.1). In another letter he is less kind: "the arguments were more philosophical than anything anyone would think they could ever even have dreamed of" (*ad Att.* 13.19.3).

22. Cicero added the prologues praising Catulus and Lucullus to the two volumes a month after the dialogues had been written; see *ad Att.* 13.32.3.

23. Clitomachus' view is set out in Section II below. The references are to passages where Cicero either accepts *in propria persona* the views that distinguish Clitomachus from Philo's mitigated scepticism (*Ac.* 2.66, 2.112–13) or states his agreement with the former as against the latter (*Ac.* 2.78).

- Catulus promotes his father's Academic view, which seems to be the one held by Philo before he wrote the Roman Books (*Ac.* 2.11–12, 2.18, 2.148).[24]

- Lucullus advocates Antiochus' view over the Stoics', where the two disagreed (e.g., *Ac.* 2.28).

- Hortensius *may* have represented the Stoics' views over Antiochus' where the two disagreed (but there is no hard evidence for this in the extant *Lucullus*).[25]

- None of the interlocutors agreed with Philo's view in the Roman Books (*Ac.* 2.11–12, 2.18).

The outlines of the lost *Catulus* can be tentatively reconstructed from the cross-references to 'yesterday' in the extant *Lucullus* and what we know of the second edition.[26] The bulk of the work was probably taken up by two competing historical accounts, opposing Antiochus' and an Academic view of the history of philosophy, as in the extant *Ac.* 1. Part of that Academic history was a critical report on Philo's Roman Books by Catulus (see the cross-references at *Ac.* 2.11–12, 2.18; cf. *Ac.* 1.13), and at least a brief exposition of his father's mitigated scepticism (see *Ac.* 2.59, 2.78, 2.148). The historical introduction was followed by some initial—perhaps Stoic—anti-sceptical arguments given by Hortensius (see *Ac.* 2.10, 2.28), to which Cicero responded with a battery of arguments against the veridicality of the senses (see *Ac.* 2.10, 2.42, 2.79; cf. *Ac.* 2.17, 2.19).[27] This is not much to

24. Catulus' father's view is not explicitly identified with Philo's mitigated scepticism in the dialogue. But the older Catulus disagreed with Philo's Roman Books view (*Ac.* 2.11–12, 2.18) and accepted the rationality of assent in the absence of knowledge (*Ac.* 2.148), which is the view that characterizes Philo's mitigated scepticism (*Ac.* 2.78).

25. One reason for this suspicion is Cicero's original decision to replace the 'Antiochian' interlocutors of the first edition with an avowed Stoic and a professed Antiochian; see note 29 below.

26. The fragments of the lost Books 3 and 4 of the second edition *Academici Libri* correspond word for word, in most cases, with the extant *Lucullus*. Since this is firm evidence that Cicero's rapid restructuring of the work did not involve a complete rewriting of the arguments, we can infer that Books 1 and 2 probably corresponded very closely to the lost *Catulus*.

27. The references in this paragraph give all the cross-references in the *Lucullus*, except for an implicit one at *Ac.* 2.13–15, where Lucullus suggests that Cicero has already appealed to the Presocratics (presumably in much the same way as he does in *Ac.* 1.44–45).

go on, but it suggests that what we have lost is less important for our understanding of the principal epistemological debate in the *Lucullus* than one might have feared. The real loss is perhaps the *Catulus'* more detailed information on the intra-Academic disagreements about mitigated scepticism and Philo's Roman Books.

In the **second edition** Cicero recast the original two books into four *Academic Books* (*Academici Libri*), of which a substantial portion of Book 1 (*Ac.* 1.1–46) and some thirty-six fragments are still extant. The revision was motivated by Cicero's realization that the characters he had chosen in the first edition were unsuitable for the technical philosophical arguments the dialogue contained.[28] He spent the month of June 45 BCE worrying about the changes, but completed the revisions in a single week.[29] Aside from the restructuring into four books, the principal alteration is a new set of interlocutors—Varro and Atticus replaced Lucullus, Hortensius, and Catulus (Cicero retained his own role). The advantage of selecting Varro was that he was a remarkable scholar with a wide range of interests, including philosophy (see *Ac.* 1.9), and also an acknowledged follower of Antiochus (cf. *Ac.* 1.7).[30] Atticus—a close friend of Cicero—seems to have been included to make the debate more conversational: since his philosophical inclinations were Epicurean, it seems unlikely that he played a more significant role in the lost parts of the dialogue than he does in *Ac.* 1. A second alteration in the new edition was to the fictional date, which moved to 'recently' (*Ac.* 1.1)—i.e., spring 45 BCE, after the death of Cicero's daughter, Tullia, and his composition of the *Consolation* (*Ac.* 1.11). The new dialogue is set in Varro's villa by the Lucrine lake (*Ac.* 1.1 and fr. 13), close to Cicero's at Cumae and the settings of the first edition.

The general structure of the second edition is fairly clear from the surviving fragments:

28. See the letters to Atticus (*'ad Att.'*) cited in note 21 above.
29. See *ad Att.* 13.18 and 13.19.3–5. His first idea was to switch from Catulus, Lucullus, and Hortensius to Cato, a Stoic, and Brutus, a follower of Antiochus; see *ad Att.* 13.16.1 and Griffin 1997, pp. 20–27. But Atticus persuaded him to make another change to Varro, to whom a book from Cicero was due.
30. Varro's Antiochian sympathies are also mentioned in the dedicatory letter Cicero sent to him (*ad Fam.* 9.8). Augustine's summary of Varro's 'On Philosophy', in *City of God* 19.1–3 is our main non-Ciceronian source for Antiochus' ethics. The differences between Varro's and Lucullus' interpretations of Socrates (see *Ac.* 1.15–17 and 2.15 and Section II below) may stem from Cicero's knowledge of Varro's disagreement with Antiochus on this issue.

- Book 1: Varro presents Antiochus' history of philosophy in *Ac.* 1.15–42; Cicero gives a sceptical Academic alternative, of which only *Ac.* 1.44–46 survives.

- Book 2 contained a series of sceptical arguments by Cicero against the veridicality of the senses, probably taken from his replies to Hortensius in the lost *Catulus;* see fr. 3 and fr. 6–11.

- Book 3 corresponded fairly closely to the main part of Lucullus' speech in the first edition (*Ac.* 2.19–60); see fr. 13 and 16–19.

- Book 4 corresponded very closely to Cicero's speech in the first edition (*Ac.* 2.66–146); see fr. 20–31.[31]

The main problem for readers of the surviving parts of the *Academica* is thus not that we cannot see roughly how the two dialogues worked. It is rather that our two principal fragments—*Ac.* 1.1–46 and the *Lucullus*—do not fit together very precisely. For this reason, the fragments of the *Academic Books* are preceded in this translation by the extant *Lucullus.* (Most of the philosophical arguments in the latter are self-standing, though readers may find it useful to consult *Ac.* 1 in order to understand the context of the arguments appealing to conflicting views of the history of philosophy.)

II. The Philosophical Context
Academics vs. Stoics

The central questions of the *Academica* are set out in the debate between the sceptical Academics and the Stoics over the attainability of knowledge.[32] The Stoic theory of knowledge represented a radical shift in post-Socratic epistemology, since it offered an empirically-based route to the kind of wisdom Socrates and his immediate followers had sought. Its basis was three novel claims made by Zeno, the

31. Cicero's Greek sources for the two editions seem to have been [a] for Lucullus' and Varro's speeches, some unspecified works by Antiochus (not his *Sosus,* as *Ac.* 2.12 shows), and [b] for Cicero's speeches, several works by Clitomachus (see *Ac.* 2.98, 2.103), probably supplemented by an Academic doxographical work (supplying the basis for *Ac.* 2.114–46).

32. Two excellent general accounts of this debate are M. Frede, 'Stoics and Skeptics on Clear and Distinct Impressions', in M. Burneat (ed.), *The Skeptical Tradition* (London 1983), pp. 65–93, and G. Striker, 'Sceptical Strategies', in M. Schofield, M. Burnyeat, and J. Barnes (eds.), *Doubt and Dogmatism* (Oxford 1980), pp. 54–83.

founder of the Stoa, set out in *Ac.* 1.40–42.[33] First, Zeno proposed a
new psychological theory: to form a belief of any kind is to give one's
assent to one's occurrent thought or 'impression' (*phantasia*) about the
matter. Second, he claimed that some of our perceptual impressions
are 'cataleptic' (*katalêptikê*), i.e., self-warranting in such a way that assenting to them constitutes an apprehension or grasp (*katalêpsis*) of
their objects.[34] And, third, he argued that we ought to restrict our assent to just cataleptic impressions, i.e., that it is irrational to assent to
inadequately warranted, noncataleptic impressions, that is, to form
(true or false) 'opinions'. Since there are cataleptic impressions, re-
stricting our assent to them allows us to attain secure and stable
knowledge, because our beliefs will then be constituted entirely by apprehensions ultimately warranted by perception.

The centre-piece of the Stoic theory is Zeno's definition of the
cataleptic impression. The standard formulation of this definition is
that a cataleptic impression is one that [a] comes from what is, and [b]
is stamped and impressed in accordance with what is, [c] in such a
way it could not come from what is not (see Diogenes Laertius *Lives*
7.46, Sextus *M.* 7.248). The precise meaning of this definition was debated in the Stoa, but we can see from Cicero's various translations—
notably at *Ac.* 2.18, 2.77, and 2.112—that he tended to take it in roughly
the following way (the way Chrysippus made more or less canonical).
An impression is cataleptic if [a] it is true, [b] it is caused in the appropriate way for correctly representing the state of affairs that is its
object, and [c] its truth is warranted by the inimitable richness and detail of the representation guaranteed by its causal history.[35] Zeno's

33. See M. Frede, 'Stoic Epistemology', in K. Algra, J. Barnes, J. Mansfeld, and
M. Schofield (eds.), *The Cambridge History of Hellenistic Philosophy* (Cambridge
1999), pp. 295–322, and J. Annas, 'Stoic Epistemology', in S. Everson (ed.), *Epistemology* (Cambridge 1990), pp. 184–303.
34. The term *katalêptikos* ('cataleptic') is often plausibly translated as 'cognitive'
elsewhere. In this translation of the *Academica,* however, the phrase Cicero uses to
render it into Latin is translated by the potentially misleading English term 'apprehensible', for reasons explained in Section III below.
35. One controversy is about the interpretation of the phrase 'what is'. Some Stoics took this to mean 'from a real object' in [a], and hence something like 'from anything except the relevant real object' in [c]. On this view, the first clause rules out
'vacuous impressions', i.e., ones caused by imagination, etc., rather than an external object; see Sextus *M.* 7.244–45, and D. Sedley, 'Zeno's Definition of *phantasia
katalêptikê*', in T. Scaltsas and A. Mason (eds.), *Zeno of Citium and His Legacy: The Philosophy of Zeno* (Larnaka 2002), pp. 137–54. Since Cicero replaces 'what is' with
'something true' at *Ac.* 2.112, and standardly construes the third clause as 'can't be

idea was thus that some of our thoughts or impressions, and particularly our perceptual impressions under normal conditions, constitute an immediate grasp of facts. The content of such impressions represents their objects so accurately that it could not be mimicked or reduplicated: that kind of detailed and accurate representation only occurs when the state of affairs represented actually obtains, i.e., when the impression 'can't be false' (*Ac.* 2.57–58).

Academic criticism of Stoic epistemology is centred, unsurprisingly, on Zeno's definition of apprehension. The Academics argued that if this definition was correct, nothing could be apprehended, and hence, since all knowledge depends on apprehensions, nothing could be known at all. Their basic tactic, from the time of Arcesilaus onwards (*Ac.* 2.77, Sextus *M.* 7.154), was to grant that conditions [a] and [b] were often met, as Zeno claimed, but to argue that condition [c] was never obtained. We can see from our text that the Academics followed two main lines of attack. One line depended on the existence of metaphysically indiscernible—or, at any rate, experientially indiscriminable—objects, such as twins, pairs of eggs, statues, etc. (*Ac.* 2.54–58, 2.84–86; cf. Sextus *M.* 7.408–10).[36] Any one of these, they argued, could be mistaken for another, no matter how good or accurate one's impression of it was. The second depended on abnormal states of mind, such as dreams, illusions, drunkenness, and fits of madness (*Ac.* 2.47–53, 2.88–90; cf. Sextus *M.* 7.402–8). In any of these states, they argued, we can have false impressions with the same representational detail and causal effects on us as waking impressions under normal conditions. So in either case, the Academics argued, whether the nature of the objects or of our minds was at fault, it was always possible to have a false impression with exactly the same phenomenal content as a true impression [a] that also met condition [b]. But if that was right, no true impression could be self-warranting in virtue of the way in which its content was represented, so condition [c] was never obtained. Hence, if the Stoic definition is correct, there is no apprehension, and thus no knowledge of any kind.

---

false' (e.g., at *Ac.* 2.23, 2.57–78) this cannot be his general interpretation; see Frede 1999, pp. 300–313. A second controversy is discussed with reference to Antiochus, below.

36. The qualification allowing that the objects of our impressions may always be discernible in principle, as the Stoics claimed they must be (*Ac.* 2.54), is stressed at *Ac.* 2.40. At *Ac.* 2.56 and 2.58 the Academics also allow that any pair of our impressions themselves may be discernible. But in either case, they argue, such differences are irrelevant if they are not available to our minds, i.e., if they are indiscriminable, consciously or otherwise, by us.

Cicero gives schematic versions of this 'core' Academic argument at *Ac.* 2.40–42 and 2.83, which can be paraphrased as follows:

[1] Some impressions are true (a Stoic view).

[2] False impressions are not cataleptic (Zeno's condition [a]).

[3] If the phenomenal content of a true impression is potentially indiscriminable from that of a false impression, it is not cataleptic (Zeno's condition [c]).

[4] The phenomenal content of any true impression is potentially indiscriminable from that of some false impression (the Academic argument).

[5] So there are no cataleptic impressions.

So if the Academics are right about [4], on the Stoic view, nothing can be known.

The Stoics responded with a detailed defence of apprehension. They adduced two general considerations against the first line of Academic argument—from the indiscriminability (*aparallaxia*) of true and false (or, more accurately, of cataleptic and noncataleptic) impressions. The first was a metaphysical claim that no two things could be identical (*Ac.* 2.50, 2.54–56). But this was supplemented with an experiential or phenomenological claim, that our ability for cognitive discernment can improve with practice: their view was not that people could always automatically discriminate between any two similar impressions or objects, but that the expert or 'sage' could learn to do this consciously in relevant fields (*Ac.* 2.20, 2.56–58). The Stoic response to the second line of Academic attack—depending on abnormal states of mind—was the related claim that our impressions in such states lack the 'perspicuity' or clarity of normal (cataleptic) perception (*Ac.* 2.51–54). But in this case, the idea is that the causal effect of such impressions on our minds is weaker, and hence that we automatically react to them with less confidence at the time, even if we are not conscious of the difference until we recover (*Ac.* 2.52).

Arcesilaus and later Academics also supplemented their 'core' epistemological argument with a second argument drawing on Zeno's conception of rationality.[37] Since the Stoics thought it possible to build a

---

37. The Stoic theory is examined in M. Frede, 'The Stoic Conception of Reason', in K. Boudoris (ed.), *Hellenistic Philosophy* II (Athens 1994), pp. 50–63.

body of stable and infallible knowledge—on the basis of perceptual apprehensions and the conceptions our mind naturally forms from them as it becomes rational (see *Ac.* 2.22 and 2.30–31)—*only* if one is not confused by false or weakly supported beliefs, they argued that it was irrational to have mere opinions, i.e., to assent to noncataleptic impressions. This gave rise to the controversial 'corollary' to the core Academic argument, set out by Cicero at *Ac.* 2.66–67 (cf. Sextus *M.* 7.155–57), and debated, e.g., at *Ac.* 2.78.

[5] If there are no cataleptic impressions (as the Academics have argued), and

[6] it is irrational to assent to noncataleptic impressions (as the Stoics hold), then

[7] it is irrational to assent to any impressions at all.

Here the Academics pointed out to the Stoics that if the Academic argument [1]–[5] against condition [c] of the definition of the cataleptic impression is successful, the Stoics are committed to the conclusion that it is rational to suspend assent universally [7], i.e., to form no beliefs at all. The Stoics, of course, denied premise [5]. But they also developed a famous counterargument, known as the 'inactivity' (*apraxia*) argument: life—or in other versions, a good or happy life— is impossible without assent, because action requires belief, and to believe something is to assent to an impression (see *Ac.* 2.24–25 and 2.37–39).[38] (The Academic responses to this argument are considered below.)

These are, in brief, the central arguments examined in Cicero's work. Lucullus' speech in *Ac.* 2.11–62 gives a large number of Stoic arguments in defence of their theory and against the Academics; and Cicero (the dialogue character) does the reverse in *Ac.* 2.64–146.

Academics vs. Academics

The presentation of the arguments in the *Academica* makes it easy to assume that the Academics themselves were committed to the negative conclusions of [1]–[7] above: to be an Academic sceptic seems to consist precisely in maintaining that nothing can be known ([5]) and that it is irrational to have any beliefs ([7]). But, as the parallel version in

---

38. The reports of Arcesilaus' responses to the inactivity argument in Plutarch *Against Colotes* ch. 26 1122, and Sextus *M.* 7.158 give some idea of the forms Chrysippus' versions of it probably took.

Sextus *M.* 7.150–57 shows, the original purpose of these arguments was to point out the unwelcome conclusions the Academics thought the Stoics were committed to in virtue of their epistemological theory and some (supposed) facts about the content of perceptual impressions. We can infer that the Academics themselves were committed to those conclusions only if there is good reason to think that they accepted the Stoic epistemological framework their arguments depend on—the Stoic theories of thought, belief, perception, apprehension, rationality, etc.— or had other, independent grounds for maintaining their conclusions.

This is the vital question for an understanding of Academic scepticism, and one that remains extremely controversial. There are two sources of difficulty here. One is that our sources for Arcesilaus and Carneades disagree radically about the form and extent of their scepticism.[39] The second derives from the philosophical methods of the earlier Academics, which were explicitly 'dialectical' or ad hominem. This means that we know a reasonable amount about some of the arguments they deployed, but very little about their motivation. (Hence the first problem.) So we know that Arcesilaus and Carneades defended [5] and [7] against Stoic objections, e.g., by introducing several kinds of 'practical criterion' (see below), but it is not clear whether these defences were intended to give their own theories or just to further the dialectical debate.[40]

For the present purposes, however, it is not necessary to resolve these questions in the cases of Arcesilaus and Carneades, since it is clear from the *Academica* that later Academics, at least, had widely divergent views about theses [5] and [7] and about the grounds for accepting them.[41] And given that the later Academics also disagreed

---

39. In the case of Arcesilaus, for instance, some sources see him as a radical sceptic along the lines adopted by later Pyrrhonists, who therefore does not accept [5]; see Sextus *PH* 1.232–33 and Diogenes Laertius *Lives* 4.28. But others see him as a straightforward proponent of conclusions [5] and [7]; see Cicero, e.g., at *Ac.* 1.44–45, and *Ac.* 2.67 and 2.77. The latter group tends to regard Carneades' introduction of 'persuasive impressions' as a significant improvement in the consistency of Academic scepticism; see, e.g., Cicero *Ac.* 2.32–36, Numenius fr. 27.14–19 (Des Places), and Augustine *Against the Academics* 2.12.

40. For strong 'dialectical' readings, showing the critical or anti-Stoic function of these arguments, see Striker 1980 and, on Carneades, J. Allen, 'Academic Probabilism and Stoic Epistemology', *Classical Quarterly* 44 (1994), pp. 85–113. A nondialectical reading is given by M. Schofield, 'Academic Epistemology', in K. Algra, J. Barnes, J. Mansfeld, and M. Schofield (eds.), *The Cambridge History of Hellenistic Philosophy* (Cambridge 1999), pp. 323–51.

41. The range of views on Arcesilaus' scepticism is canvassed in C. Brittain,

about which position Arcesilaus or Carneades had preferred, it is more useful to focus here on the later views, which are the ones advocated or examined directly in Cicero. (These views are, perhaps unsurprisingly, themselves the subject of continuing controversy, so readers are advised to take the following sketch as merely one way to reconstruct the philosophical differences between the later Academics.)

The easiest way to discern the different forms of Academic scepticism is by looking at the Academics' disagreements about the appropriate response to the Stoic 'inactivity' argument. The Stoic objection takes the form of a practical *reductio* of the Academic corollary argument ([5]–[7] above): if the Academics were right, action would be impossible; but it is not, so (either premise [6] or) premise [5] must be mistaken. The *reductio* form seems to leave the Academics three options. They can

i) reject the connexion between assent and action that the objection presupposes, and so maintain [5]–[7];

ii) accept the objection and reject premise [6]—the irrationality of holding opinions—and hence reject the conclusion in [7]; or

iii) accept the objection and reject premise [5], and hence reject [7].

We can see from Cicero's text that something roughly corresponding to each of these options was adopted by an Academic at some point in the school's evolution.[42]

The first option is the position of **Clitomachus**—or, as Cicero puts it, Clitomachus' interpretation of Carneades. On this view, the correct response to the inactivity argument is [i] above: the Academics deny that action presupposes assent and are thus free to maintain universal inapprehensibility and suspension of assent. The philosophical basis for this position is set by two distinctions, the first between different kinds of impressions (*Ac.* 2.99, 2.103), and the second between two kinds of 'assent' (*Ac.* 2.104).

'Arcesilaus', in the *Stanford Encyclopedia of Philosophy*. On Carneades, see J. Allen, 'Carneades', in the *Stanford Encyclopedia of Philosophy*, and R. Bett, 'Carneades' Pithanon: A Reappraisal of Its Role and Status', *Oxford Studies in Ancient Philosophy* 7 (1989), pp. 59–94.

42. The correspondence is inexact because the second option—the mitigated scepticism associated with Philo and Metrodorus—does not argue that action as such requires assent, but only that a happy or good life requires that one have some opinions (see below). So this is a response to the second version of the inactivity objection.

The first distinction distinguishes between two aspects of any impression on the Stoic theory: its objective status, i.e., whether it is cataleptic or noncataleptic (and if the latter, true or false), and its subjective force on the person having it, i.e., whether it strikes them as plausible or persuasive, or not. Following Carneades, Clitomachus argued that the Academic arguments to show that all impressions are noncataleptic ([1]–[5] above) are only relevant to the question of an impression's objective status: we cannot tell whether any of our impressions are true, because all of them are noncataleptic. But that does not mean that we cannot discriminate between our impressions at all (cf. *Ac.* 2.32–36). Some of them leave us with no prima facie inclination to accept them or act on them at all; but some of them are, at least initially, 'persuasive'. The 'persuasive' status of the latter is the product of both the internal characteristics of the relevant impressions—e.g., the clarity and detail with which they represent a purported object or state of affairs—and the context in which we have them—e.g., in apparently good perceptual conditions, or when they present a state of affairs that coheres well with our other impressions. But these conditions are not sufficient to secure the truth in the way the Stoics want to, since any or all of them are replicable in other circumstances when the impression in question is false (premise [4] above).[43]

To meet the Stoic inactivity argument, however, it is not enough just to identify a set of criteria for discriminating between impressions on the basis of their subjective characteristics. For the Stoic account of action requires assent, and, in their theory, to assent to an impression is simply to take it to be true. On this view, assent is an all-or-nothing affair: either you assent and so form a belief about the subject represented by your impression, or you fail to assent (suspend judgment) and so fail to form any view about the subject. It is thus beside the point whether the impression you act on is in fact objectively true or false, cataleptic or noncataleptic, or subjectively certain or just persuasive, etc.—these features constitute constraints on the rationality of your assent, not conditions for assent as such.

It is at this point that the second distinction, between two kinds of assent, comes into play. Following Carneades and Arcesilaus, Clitomachus argued that the Stoics' unitary notion of assent or belief fails to account for much of our cognitive experience. It seems clear that some of our actions are not the product of distinct acts of assent: we can act unconsciously or from habit, as animals act even on the Stoic

---

43. Carneades' arguments for the first distinction are set out more extensively in Sextus *M.* 7.166–89 and *PH* 1.226–29; see Allen 1994.

account; and we can also act deliberately without assent, for instance when we follow an unendorsed hypothesis in conditions of uncertainty (cf. *Ac.* 2.100, 2.109). Hence, Clitomachus argued, we should distinguish between 'assenting' to an impression in the Stoic sense and 'approving' it in one of these latter ways, i.e., acting on it *as if* we took it to be true. The Academic thus gives his *approval* to the impressions he acts on—he 'follows' persuasive impressions—but does not assent to them (*Ac.* 2.104).[44]

This sketch of Clitomachus' account of how the Academic might act without assent raises some important questions for both Stoics and Academics about human psychology and the nature of assent, action, and belief. The vital point for the present purpose, however, is to see that Clitomachus used this 'practical criterion' (i.e., truth-indifferent mechanism for rational action) not just to defend the Academics from the Stoic inactivity argument, but also to explain their advocacy of universal inapprehensibility and suspension of judgment ([5] and [7] above). For, on his account, the Academic will follow persuasive impressions in order to act both in ordinary life and in the course of philosophical arguments (see *Ac.* 2.32 fin. and 2.104 fin.).[45] Hence, when the Academics draw their notorious conclusions about the unattainability of knowledge and the irrationality of forming beliefs, they are maintaining only that these conclusions are currently 'persuasive': they are not committed to the truth of these views or of the arguments that support them. But in that case, the Clitomachian Academics do not *believe*, e.g., that nothing can be known, or, at least, they do not believe it in the sense implied by Stoic assent. It is perhaps unclear how we should (or even can) make sense of this position, but it is plain that Clitomachus did not subscribe to the form of dogmatic, negative scepticism suggested by his advocacy of [5] and [7].[46] For this reason, it is appropriate to call this Academic position 'radical scepticism'.

44. Carneades' reasons for making the second distinction are examined in Bett 1989; cf. R. Bett, 'Carneades' Distinction Between Assent and Approval', *Monist* 73 (1990), pp. 3–20.

45. The methods for assessing the persuasiveness of impressions in each case are different. Perceptual impressions are 'persuasive' when they meet various tests on the perceptual conditions and their coherence with the subject's other beliefs (*Ac.* 2.32–36), whereas philosophical theses become 'persuasive' as a result of argument on either side (*Ac.* 2.7, 2.60).

46. The consistency of the radical scepticism of Clitomachus (and in most modern accounts, of Carneades and Arcesilaus) remains controversial. See the discussion of the parallel question in the case of Pyrrhonism in M. Burnyeat and M. Frede (eds.), *The Original Sceptics: A Controversy* (Indianapolis 1997).

We can get a better idea of the implications of Clitomachus' radical scepticism by contrasting it with the more familiar position suggested by option [ii] above, which was adopted by **Philo** and (probably) **Metrodorus**.[47] The difference between these two Academic positions is set out by Cicero in connexion with an argument Carneades is reported to have occasionally used in place of the corollary argument (*Ac.* 2.59, 2.67, 2.78; cf. *Ac.* 2.112). The new argument replaces premise [6] above—positing the irrationality of assent to noncataleptic impressions (in agreement with Zeno)—with a new premise ([8]), giving the following argument:

[5] if there are no cataleptic impressions, and

[8] it is sometimes rational to assent to noncataleptic impressions, then

[9] it is sometimes rational to hold opinions.

Clitomachus thought that Carneades used this argument merely to point out to the Stoics the disastrous consequences for their epistemology of the Academic arguments for [5]: a genuinely wise person (the ideal of rationality) must either suspend all assent or hold opinions—and in either case, the Stoics need to radically revise their conception of rationality. But other Academics, apparently following Philo and Metrodorus, took this new 'corollary' argument to be a statement of Carneades' own position and adopted it themselves (*Ac.* 2.78; cf. *Ac.* 2.59).

The second position—which we can call 'mitigated scepticism' to distinguish it from Clitomachus'—accepts inapprehensibility, but maintains that it does not follow that we should reject all assent. Hence, these Academics reject the conclusion that it is irrational to assent to anything [7]. But they also characterize the beliefs they do form as 'opinions' to mark the fact that, despite their rational grounds for holding them, they are explicitly rational *beliefs*, i.e., they do not

---

47. Metrodorus' role in the development of mitigated scepticism is unclear. Cicero's evidence (*Ac.* 2.16, 2.78) seems to be incompatible with our other brief reports in Philodemus *History of the Academy* 26 and Augustine *Against the Academics* 3.41, which erroneously suggest that his view was closer to Philo's subsequent position in the Roman Books; see Brittain 2001, pp. 214–15. Glucker 2004 (pp. 118–33) argues that the mistake was Cicero's, even though he was Augustine's source and Philodemus' text is fragmentary.

amount to apprehensions (cf. *Ac.* 2.148).[48] If this is right, the mitigatedly sceptical position is one that advocates forming reasonable beliefs in conditions of uncertainty—and since, in their view, conditions are always uncertain owing to the nonexistence of cataleptic impressions, it also claims that reasonable beliefs are the best we can hope to attain. (This is the principal form of Academic scepticism that we find described—and often misascribed to Carneades and Clitomachus—in later ancient sources such as Sextus Empiricus, Plutarch, Aulus Gellius, Favorinus, and Photius, as well as in most modern criticism until the late twentieth century.[49])

The difference between this position and Clitomachus' is difficult to discern in practice, because both groups used the same criteria for evaluating impressions and philosophical theses. So both groups use the subjective 'clarity' of their perceptual impressions and their coherence with other impressions to grade their degree of 'persuasiveness' (*Ac.* 2.32–36), and both use the Academic method of arguing on either side of philosophical questions to examine which are more 'persuasive' (e.g., *Ac.* 2.60). But they differ in that the mitigated sceptics will assent to persuasive impressions or claims when the evidence supporting them is sufficiently strong—and they assume that persuasiveness under the appropriate conditions does provide *evidence* for the truth (cf. Sextus *M.* 7.435–38). It is not easy to determine the precise conditions that must be satisfied before assent is warranted, but we have at least one case in the *Academica* that satisfies them: the thesis of universal inapprehensibility (see *Ac.* 2.148).

A more detailed outline of the mitigatedly sceptical position associated with Philo and Metrodorus would need to explain how, e.g., its conceptions of rationality, evidence, and assent differ from those of both

48. The textual crux at the end of *Ac.* 2.148 leaves it theoretically open for interpreters to deny that Catulus and other mitigated sceptics rejected the universal suspension of assent (*epokhē*). But it is clear from the immediate context, as well as from *Ac.* 2.59 and 2.78 and the usage of later Academics, that holding an opinion is incompatible with *epokhē*. See Brittain 2001, pp. 76–82; A. Long and D. Sedley, *The Hellenistic Philosophers* (Cambridge 1987), vol. 2, p. 451; and M. Burnyeat, 'Antipater and Self-refutation: Elusive Arguments in Cicero's *Academica*', in B. Inwood and J. Mansfeld (eds.), *Assent and Argument* (Leiden 1997), pp. 277–310, esp. pp. 300–309.
49. Mitigated scepticism is ascribed to 'the Academics' in general by Aenesidemus in Photius *Library* 212 170a, Gellius in *Attic Nights* 11.5, Favorinus in Galen's *The Best Teaching-Method* ch. 1, and the anonymous *Prolegomena to Plato's Philosophy*, chapter 7. Sextus Empiricus ascribes it to 'Carneades and Clitomachus' in *PH* 1.226–31 and *M.* 7 passim, especially 7.435–38.

radical Academic sceptics and Stoics.[50] But the fact that they take the thesis that nothing can be known ([5]) to be a paradigm for rational belief or 'opinion' itself indicates the depth of their disagreement with more radical sceptics like Clitomachus. Their view implies, after all, that they have bought into the Stoic theories of psychology, impressions, perception, etc., because they think that they have adequate *rational* grounds to believe that the Stoic definition of apprehension is correct even though its conditions can never be met. The arguments Carneades had used to show that Stoic epistemology is no more warranted than any other view have now become arguments that show it to offer a substantially correct conception of what knowledge would be like, if there were any. Their position is heavily parasitic on Stoicism—they are 'Stoics fighting Stoics', as one dissident radical Academic put it.[51]

An alternative to mitigated scepticism was offered by the third option above, which **Philo** took in his (lost) **Roman Books.** The evidence for this position is severely circumscribed—what we know of the Roman Books is just what can be gleaned from *Ac.* 2.18, a parallel passage in Sextus *PH* 1.235, and a few hints in *Ac.* 2.11–12 and 1.13. But it seems clear that Philo's principal epistemological claim in this work was that the Stoic definition of apprehension was mistaken. The error Philo identified was the third clause of Zeno's definition guaranteeing that a cataleptic impression 'can't be false' ([c] above). The precise implications of this diagnosis are controversial. But Antiochus' criticism suggests that Philo argued that an impression is sufficient for apprehension just when it is true, accurately stamped and impressed on our minds—the first two clauses of Zeno's definition—and we assent to it (see *Ac.* 2.18). The fact that we might always have been mistaken, as the Academics had consistently argued against the Stoics, is irrelevant: in such a case we have an accurate grasp of the object or state of affairs represented by the impression. Of course, given the Academic arguments for the indiscriminability of true and false impressions, any impression we in fact assent to may be false, so our knowledge-claims are always fallible. But that does not mean that we do not apprehend anything, but only that we should be cautious about when we assent and modest in our assertions of knowledge.[52]

On this interpretation, the third position—Philo's 'fallibilism'—constitutes a radical rejection of the Academic corollary argument,

50. I have tried to give this in Brittain 2001, chapter 2.

51. Aenesidemus, in Photius *Library* 212 170 a 14–22. See note 15 above.

52. See J. Barnes, 'Antiochus of Ascalon', in M. Griffin and J. Barnes (eds.), *Philosophia Togata* (Oxford 1989), pp. 51–96, esp. pp. 71–74 and 85; and Brittain 2001, chapter 3.

since Philo holds neither that there are no cataleptic impressions ([5]) nor that one should suspend assent universally ([7]).[53] It is thus easy to see why his innovations were vehemently rejected by Antiochus (*Ac.* 2.18), and why they surprised or irritated Academics like Heraclitus (*Ac.* 2.11) and Catulus senior (*Ac.* 2.12, 2.18). This no doubt explains the short shrift given to them in the *Academica*. But if this interpretation is correct, we can also see how Philo's abandonment of scepticism about apprehension or knowledge constituted not just a major (and perhaps welcome) innovation in epistemology but also a serious attempt to revive the critical Academic method of Arcesilaus and Carneades. His new view did not reject the traditional Academic anti-Stoic arguments; rather, it reinterpreted them as properly dialectical, i.e., as criticism of the Stoics' unwarranted claims instead of arguments in favour of an 'Academic' position.

Antiochus vs. the Academics

Antiochus is a central figure in the *Academica*, since he is acknowledged as the source for both the anti-Academic arguments of Lucullus in *Ac.* 2.11–62 and the history of Platonic philosophy and its revision by the Stoics in *Ac.* 1.15–42.[54] Although the details of his philosophical position remain difficult to work out (see below), its main lines are fairly clear. He defected from the sceptical Academy under Philo (see *Ac.* 2.69–71) in order to reclaim the Platonic heritage that he thought they had betrayed. His method was syncretic: rather than reverting to Plato's dialogues, he chose to emphasize the significant elements of the Platonic heritage shared by most of the dogmatic philosophical schools.[55] Hence the rather surprising claims

53. If the reconstruction suggested above is right, Philo must also have rejected [6], the claim that it is irrational to hold opinions, since his fallibilism implies both that it is rational to assent and that one may always end up with an opinion when one does assent.

54. Lucullus stresses that his speech from *Ac.* 2.13–60 reports Antiochus' arguments directly at *Ac.* 2.10, 2.12, and 2.61. He mentions his elision of some of Antiochus' original argumentation at *Ac.* 2.49, and probably alludes to a similar elision in *Ac.* 2.30. Varro's speech in *Ac.* 1.15–42 is introduced as a presentation in Latin of Antiochus' view at *Ac.* 1.13–14; this is confirmed by him at *Ac.* 1.35, and by Cicero at *Ac.* 1.43.

55. See Barnes 1989. Antiochus' syncretism is confirmed by Cicero's relentless jibes in *Ac.* 2.112–46, pointing out the explicit disagreements between the Stoics and Old Academics or Peripatetics—e.g., in epistemology (*Ac.* 2.69–70, 2.112–13—cf. *Fin.* 5.76—and 2.143) and ethics (*Ac.* 2.132–4—cf. *Fin.* 5.77–85—and 2.134).

that are distinctive of his position—that the Old Academics and the Peripatetics shared a single Platonic philosophy (see, e.g., *Ac.* 1.17–18), and that the Stoics advocated the same view, although they made a few 'corrections' to it (see, e.g., *Ac.* 1.43).[56]

The latter claim, however, makes understanding Antiochus' own position rather difficult, despite the fairly detailed account of his interpretation of the Old Academic, Peripatetic, and Stoic views in *Ac.* 1. For it is not clear from that account whether Antiochus means us to take the original 'Platonic' position, a Peripatetic revision of it, or its Stoicized 'correction' as authoritative. The nature of this problem is clear from the case of ethics, where we have external evidence for Antiochus' views from other sources. Varro lists six main Stoic 'corrections' of Old Academic ethics in *Ac.* 1.35–39. But we can see from *Ac.* 2 and *Fin.* 5 that Antiochus accepted four of them wholeheartedly—that is, he agreed with the Stoics in rejecting the Platonic distinction of the soul into rational and nonrational parts, and he saw the implications of this for some further Old Academic views about virtue and emotion. But he rejected the two remaining corrections—Zeno's demotion of 'bodily' and 'external goods' to the status of 'indifferents', and his consequent reworking of 'appropriate actions'. Or rather, as Varro puts it, he characterized them as misconceived but essentially terminological innovations (*Ac.* 1.37).

The problem is worst in the case of physics, where we have very little external evidence for Antiochus' views. Varro mentions only two Stoic 'corrections' here—the mind is corporeal and constituted by fire (*Ac.* 1.39)—and both are to Peripatetic or Old Academic views that are not mentioned in the original 'Platonic' exposition. We do not have direct evidence to determine whether Antiochus accepted these or not (though he probably did), since Cicero's criticism highlights only the disagreements between dissident Peripatetics and the Stoics (*Ac.* 2.119–21). A second problem in this case is that we do not have independent evidence for Varro's account of 'Platonic' physics. The 'Platonic' doctrines of 'force', 'matter', and god are surprisingly close to the views the Stoics adopted. It is unclear whether this is evidence

56. The essential unity of the Old Academics and Peripatetics is stressed repeatedly in *Ac.* 1 and 2. Antiochus' near identification of the Stoic position with this 'Platonic' view is most clear at *Ac.* 1.43 and 2.16, *DND* 1.16, and *Fin.* 5.74. (The Old Academics include all of Plato's institutional followers until Arcesilaus; Aristotle and Theophrastus were the Peripatetics whom Antiochus was most concerned to include in his heritage.)

that Antiochus was right about the near identity of Stoic and Old Academic views, at least on this topic, or a sign that his history is a fabrication, retrojecting Stoic physics into the late Old Academy.[57]

The problem of interpreting Antiochus' own view is less immediate in the case of 'logic' or epistemology, since we have an argued defence of his epistemological position in Lucullus' speech in *Ac.* 2.11–62. Antiochus clearly rejected 'Platonic' rationalism and anti-empiricism in favour of a more or less Stoic epistemology, since that is almost without exception the source of Lucullus' wide-ranging arguments against the sceptical Academics.[58] Their Stoic origin is explicit in the case of the central arguments about the possibility of apprehension and the necessity for assent, where it is acknowledged by Lucullus or noted by Cicero.[59] But it is also clear from Lucullus' use of definitions or arguments advocated elsewhere only by the Stoics that Antiochus drew even the details of his attack on the Academics from Stoic sources.[60] The main lines of these anti-Academic arguments—the rebuttal of the Academic 'indiscriminability argument' and the deployment of the Stoic 'inactivity argument'—had probably been established by Chrysippus in response to Arcesilaus.[61] But later

57. The authenticity of Varro's account is supported by D. Sedley, 'The Origins of Stoic God', in D. Frede and A. Laks (eds.), *Traditions of Theology* (Boston/Leiden 2002), pp. 41–83, followed by J. Dillon, *The Heirs of Plato: A Study of the Old Academy (347–274 BC)* (Oxford 2003), chapter 4. It is doubted by many scholars, e.g., W. Görler, 'Älterer Pyrrhonismus, Jüngere Akademie, Antiochos aus Askalon', § 52 'Antiochus aus Askalon und seine schule', in H. Flashar (ed.), *Die Philosophie der Antike 4: Die Hellenistische Philosophie* (Basel 1994), pp. 938–80, at pp. 949–51, and G. Reydams-Schils, *Demiurge and Providence: Stoic and Platonist Readings of Plato's Timaeus* (Turnhout 1999), pp. 128–32.

58. There is some question about Antiochus' views on Platonic 'Forms'. Since they do not play any role in his epistemology in *Ac.* 2 or in *Fin.* 5, it seems likely that he thought that Aristotle's critique had fatally undermined them (*Ac.* 1.33); see Barnes 1989, pp. 95–96.

59. The Stoic basis for Lucullus' principal arguments is noted by Lucullus himself at *Ac.* 2.17 and 2.28 on apprehension, and by Cicero, e.g., at *Ac.* 2.67 on the corollary argument, *Ac.* 2.77 on the indiscriminability argument, *Ac.* 2.85 on the indiscernibility of impressions, *Ac.* 2.107–8 on assent, and *Ac.* 2.112 on the arguments as a whole.

60. The arguments from perception, conceptions, memory, the arts, virtue, and wisdom in *Ac.* 2.19–24, for instance, all rely on the Stoic definitions of these epistemic states.

61. The inactivity (*apraxia*) argument is ascribed to the Stoics in Plutarch *Against Colotes* chs. 26–29 1122–24; Plutarch also notes Stoic responses to the indiscriminability (*aparallaxia*) argument in *Common Conceptions* ch. 36 1077c–e. There is no

Stoics had been forced to supplement them in response to Carneades' new arguments, including his revised 'corollary argument' (*Ac.* 2.67; cf. 2.59), and his advocacy of 'persuasive impressions' as a practical criterion (*Ac.* 2.32, 2.104; cf. 2.33–36). The most prominent of these later Stoics in our text is Antipater, whose anti-Academic work is cited several times by Lucullus.[62] But direct parallels with a short exposition of the views of the 'Younger Stoics' in Sextus *M.* 7.253–60—a group that may include Antipater—show that Antiochus was far more indebted to the later Stoics than Lucullus admits.[63]

Perhaps a more interesting question is whether Antiochus contributed anything significant of his own to the tradition of anti-Academic arguments. There seem to be three main candidates here, aside from the historical arguments considered below.[64] The first is his revision of an argument by Antipater—trumpeted by Lucullus in *Ac.* 2.28–29, and dismissed by Cicero in *Ac.* 2.109–10—to the effect that it is essential for a philosophical system to apprehend its 'principles', especially its constitutive ones concerned with the 'criterion of truth' and 'the final good'. This looks unpromising, not merely because the Academics clearly had a good answer to it, but because its premises were probably unoriginal.[65] The second is his argument against Philo's redefinition of apprehension in the Roman Books—which postdates his known Stoic sources—claiming that apprehension or knowledge presupposes the epistemic security guaranteed by Zeno's definition (*Ac.* 2.18). But this argument can hardly be original if Antiochus

---

direct evidence that Chrysippus initiated these standard Stoic arguments, but it seems very likely from the context; cf. note 38 above.

62. *Ac.* 2.17, 2.28; cf. *Ac.* 2.109 and fr. 1.

63. Antiochus' direct debt to the Younger Stoics is obvious at *Ac.* 2.14 = Sextus *M.* 7.258; *Ac.* 2.33 = *M.* 7.260; and *Ac.* 2.28 = *M.* 7.257.

64. A further candidate is Antiochus' objection that the Academics presuppose the truth of their impressions while arguing that it is unavailable to us in principle (*Ac.* 2.111; cf. *Ac.* 2.33). But the basis for this argument seems to be already present in the Younger Stoics at Sextus *M.* 7.259.

65. The argument relies on two premises: first, that the Academics cannot 'teach' (cf. *Ac.* 2.60), and, second, that philosophical 'schools' or 'systems' are individuated by certain doctrines. The second was probably drawn from a debate amongst Hellenistic historians of philosophy attested in Diogenes Laertius *Lives* 1.18–20; see R. Polito, 'The Sceptical Sect: Reception, Self-definition, Internal Conflicts' (forthcoming). The first is not directly attested in earlier anti-sceptical writing, but is pervasive in later reports of anti-sceptical argument, which suggests that it was a commonplace; see, e.g., Plutarch *Stoic Contradictions* ch. 10, and Galen *The Best Teaching-Method* chs. 3 and 5 (cf. Sextus *PH* 2.1–11).

interpreted that security in the way the Stoics had, since establishing the definition of apprehension was something Zeno had initiated (*Ac.* 2.77, 1.41) and with which Antipater was explicitly credited (*Ac.* 2.17).

The final case, however, suggests that Antiochus may not have construed the definition as the Stoics had. For among the series of arguments against Carneades' 'practical criterion' (*Ac.* 2.32–36), we find the idea that the 'distinctive mark' of a cataleptic impression might be a 'sign' of its truth (*Ac.* 2.33). This suggests that Antiochus took the third clause of Zeno's definition to point to a feature of cataleptic impressions that is immediately *available* to the subject, which is an 'internalist' interpretation modern commentators have sometimes proposed, but one that Chrysippus and the Younger Stoics did not accept.[66] If so, Antiochus may have thought that we assent to cataleptic impressions because we *infer* from this phenomenal 'sign' or feature that they are true. This is not an original view as such, since it is precisely the way Carneades wanted to force the Stoics to go (Sextus *M.* 7.160–65), and the way the later Academics had gone on their own account. But the implications of this 'internalist' view for the Stoics are disastrous, because the cataleptic impression is no longer a *natural* and *automatic* 'criterion of truth', as they had argued. The result is either that we need another criterion to judge when an impression has the relevant feature, which leads to a regress, or that we are stuck with evaluating the 'evidence' of our impressions for coherence, which leads to mitigated scepticism.[67]

The unity of the Academy

The frequent appeals to historical precedent and authority may strike a modern reader as a curious, or even unattractive, feature of the

66. The orthodox interpretation does not make the 'clarity and distinctness' of a cataleptic impression, in virtue of which it 'can't be false', something that is in principle available to the perceiver (although it may be to experts or the Stoic sage, with practice); see *Ac.* 2.57 and Frede 1999, pp. 313–16. Versions of the 'internalist' interpretation are given by Annas 1990 and ascribed to Antiochus (via his Academic training) by G. Striker in 'Academics Fighting Academics', in B. Inwood and J. Mansfeld (eds.), *Assent and Argument* (Leiden 1997), pp. 257–76.

67. See Striker 1997, pp. 262–65 and 270–72. It is not clear that Antiochus intended the 'internalist' interpretation of the third clause of Zeno's definition of apprehension. The term 'sign' (*signum*)—like his remarks on our 'confidence' in our impressions—is ambiguous, since it may refer to a natural sign, which does not require interpretation to function. Lucullus' use of the word may also be a mere variant of his more usual term 'mark' (*nota*).

Academica. There are several plausible ways to explain these appeals. We might see them as a reflection of the instinctive classicism of ancient philosophers (see, e.g., *Ac.* 2.75)—the reflex that led to the canonization of Socrates and Plato—or as an indication of the institutional disputes of professional teachers, each eager to profit from a distinguished heritage (e.g., *Ac.* 2.69–70). We might also take them to be the product of Cicero's rhetorical style, with its constant lists of historical examples (e.g., *Ac.* 2.13), or his desire to inform his Roman audience of the wider framework of Greek philosophy (*Ac.* 1.3–12). But it would be a mistake to dismiss them as merely the irrelevant quirks of ancient argumentation or of Cicero's presentation, since they also have interesting philosophical motivations.

The text presents three stages in the deployment of claims about the history of philosophy. The first, dating back to Arcesilaus' initial turn to scepticism, was the Academic appeal to the Presocratics, Socrates, and Plato as sceptical forebears (*Ac.* 2.72–76 and 1.44–46, replying to Antiochus' criticism in *Ac.* 2.13–15 and 1.15–17).[68] We should note three basic points about this appeal. First, despite appearances, it is actually a history of the *development* of scepticism in reaction to the failures of reason (or dogmatic philosophy): the Presocratics despaired of their efforts to attain knowledge, the methods of Socrates and Plato gave them a more reflective understanding of this failure, but full-fledged scepticism—i.e., a method leading to the suspension of all assent—did not arise prior to Arcesilaus. So Arcesilaus was not relying on the authority of, e.g., Socrates—in fact, he criticized him for asserting dogmatically that he knew that nothing can be known, which presupposes that he knows what would constitute knowledge (*Ac.* 1.45). Second, if we look at the more determinate Academic uses of the Presocratics, it becomes clear that one motive for appealing to them is to offer a second, nondogmatic defence of the Academic thesis of universal inapprehensibility, in addition to the core anti-Stoic argument. So Arcesilaus cites Democritus at *Ac.* 2.32 as someone with a dogmatic theory explaining why it might be that nothing can be known: he thinks that perception does not reveal the atomic structure of the world. This is not a theory Arcesilaus himself believes; but it strikes him as at least as plausible as the Stoic theory—and they must show why it is not. Third, another use of this appeal to precedent is to point out to the Stoics the implausible consequences of dogmatic the-

---

68. See J. Annas, 'Plato the Sceptic', *Oxford Studies in Ancient Philosophy,* suppl. vol. (Oxford 1992), pp. 43–72, and C. Brittain and J. Palmer, 'The New Academy's Appeals to the Presocratics', *Phronesis* 46.1 (2001), pp. 38–72. Arcesilaus' interest in the history of scepticism is also attested in Plutarch *Against Colotes* ch. 26 1121e–22a.

orizing about the real nature of things—as shown by the example of Anaxagoras, who ends up denying that snow even appears white on the basis of his theory that it is solidified water, which is not naturally white (*Ac.* 2.72, 2.100). These preliminary points suggest that the Academic uses of the history of philosophy were considerably more subtle than mere appeals to authority.[69]

The second stage was Antiochus' attempt to reclaim the Platonic heritage from the sceptical Academics in the 90s BCE (discussed above). Since Antiochus did want to rest his claim to philosophical truth partly on the authority and consensus of a tradition, it was vital for him to rescue Socrates and Plato from the Academics' more sceptical interpretations of their work. A notable feature of Cicero's presentation of Antiochus' views is that the Antiochian interlocutors in the two editions of the *Academica* offer quite distinct versions of Socrates and Plato. Lucullus offers an 'ironic' interpretation of Socrates' supposedly sceptical claims—i.e., one that discounts his confessions of ignorance as merely a methodological device—and a picture of Plato as the author of a 'complete philosophical system' (*Ac.* 2.15). Varro, however, thinks of Socrates as genuinely sceptical about knowledge and allows that Plato's work was complex, and hence did not automatically lead to the 'Platonic system' his successors devised (*Ac.* 1.15–17). These conflicting interpretations of Socrates and Plato, along with their Academic counterparts, form part of a tradition of hermeneutic debate about Plato's dialogues that is still very much alive.[70]

The final stage was Philo's assertion of the unity of the Academy in the Roman Books (*Ac.* 1.13; cf. *Ac.* 2.11–12, 2.18). While it seems clear that he claimed that all the Academics from Plato to himself had held the same epistemological views—i.e., the ones he advocated in the Roman Books—the precise nature of his thesis is as controversial as his epistemological innovations. On the interpretation given above, we can infer that it made three claims about the Academic tradition as a whole. They agreed, first, that epistemic certainty—both perceptual

69. There is some evidence that later Academics developed Arcesilaus' original lines on the history of scepticism to suit their own, e.g., mitigatedly sceptical, views; see the anonymous *Prolegomena to Plato's Philosophy,* chapters 7 and 10, and Brittain 2001, chapter 4.

70. The ancient debates on Plato within the Platonic tradition are examined in J. Opsomer, *In Search of the Truth: Academic Tendencies in Middle Platonism* (Brussels 1998), and M. Bonazzi, *Academici e Platonici. Il dibattito antico sullo scetticismo di Platone* (Milan 2003); see also D. Sedley, 'Three Platonist Interpretations of the *Theaetetus'*, in C. Gill and M. McCabe (eds.), *Form and Argument in Late Plato* (Oxford 1996), pp. 79–103.

and rational—is unattainable; second, that the Stoic attempt to secure certainty from perception was bound to fail; and, third, that there is experiential knowledge of a defeasible kind, but that its fallible nature means that the cautious Academic method of investigation on either side is necessary for philosophical questions.[71] These claims were roundly rejected at the time as a historical fabrication (*Ac.* 2.12, 2.18)— by the sceptical Academics because they denied that Arcesilaus and Carneades were sceptical, and by Antiochus also because they gave a too fallibilist epistemology to Plato and the Old Academics. But the idea of the unity of the Academy, if under different interpretations of its unifying features, continued to haunt the Platonist tradition.[72]

A significant difference between Antiochus' appeal to the history of philosophy and the Academics' is that the former presupposes a notion of 'authority' that the sceptics did not accept. Cicero stresses that one of the principal motivations for the Academic method of argument 'on either side' was precisely to prevent the speaker's authority from determining the students' evaluation of philosophical theses (see *Ac.* 2.7–10).[73] In the light of the Academic appeals to history in the text, it may be tempting to agree with Lucullus that this is merely a device for criticizing disfavoured theses (*Ac.* 2.60); but it is notable that even Cicero, with his Roman taste for authoritarian hierarchies, observes this principle by always presenting the Academics in argument with dogmatic opponents. If Philo appealed to the Academic tradition, it was for rational confirmation of his own understanding of the truth. In Antiochus, however, we find the early signs of a conception of Platonic authority that led later interpreters to make interpreting Plato's dialogues their principal means of discovering the truth.

Influence

The influence of the *Academica* on pagan Roman philosophy and Latin literary culture is difficult to measure. The number of direct references

---

71. See Brittain 2001, chapter 4.
72. Platonists disagreed about the role of the Academic sceptics in their tradition. Plutarch, the anonymous commentator on the *Theaetetus,* and Augustine each construed the Academics as fellow-Platonists of some kind; Numenius regarded them as anti-Platonic heretics; see Brittain 2001, chapter 5, and the works listed in note 70 above.
73. This is the Academic position criticized by Aenesidemus in Sextus *M.* 8.51–54 and by Galen in his treatise *The Best Teaching-Method.* The topic was expanded in later Pyrrhonist arguments; see Sextus *PH* 2.37–46 on the criterion 'of the agent'.

to either edition surviving outside of the grammatical tradition (where Cicero's style and vocabulary remained a constant reference point) is small.[74] But this criterion ignores the work's probable role in the more widespread acquaintance with Academic scepticism betrayed by educated writers such as Varro, Seneca, Tacitus, and Aulus Gellius. The influence of Cicero's work on early Christian philosophy in Latin, however, was demonstrably significant and widespread.[75] The most prominent case is that of Augustine, whose epistemology was formed in response to Cicero's arguments.[76] Augustine's authority ensured the survival of interest in the Academics until the Renaissance.[77] Thereafter, Academic scepticism (and Cicero's work on it) was largely overshadowed by its better-known descendants, Pyrrhonism and 'Cartesian' scepticism, until the revival of interest in it in the late twentieth century.[78]

III: The Translation
Greek–Latin–English

The aim of this translation is to render Cicero's work into readable contemporary English for a philosophical audience. To this end, I have tried to preserve consistency in the principal technical terms, where

---

74. Direct references to the *Academica* are found in Pliny *Natural History* 1.31.6, Quintilian *Rhetorical Instruction* 3.6.64, Ammianus Marcellinus *History* 27.4.8, and Caelius Aurelianus *Acute Affections* 3.13. See T. Hunt, *A Textual History of Cicero's Academici Libri* (Leiden 1998), pp. 18–25.

75. The second edition is referred to in Minucius Felix *Octavian* 13.2, Lactantius *Divine Institutes* Book 6, Jerome, e.g., in *Letter* 84.4.1, Augustine (see below), and Martianus Capella *The Marriage of Philology and Mercury* 5.510; see Hunt 1998, pp. 18–25.

76. Augustine's debt to Cicero is set out in detail by H. Hagendahl, *Augustine and the Latin Classics* (Göteborg 1967), and M. Testard, *Saint Augustin et Cicéron* (Paris 1958). His principal anti-sceptical work is *Against the Academics,* a critical reflection on the themes of Cicero's *Academica.* It is translated in P. King, *Augustine* Against the Academicians *and* The Teacher (Indianapolis 1995).

77. The uses to which the *Academica* was put in the Renaissance are studied in C. Schmitt *Cicero Scepticus* (The Hague 1972); cf. Hunt 1998, pp. 26–40, on knowledge of the second edition in the Middle Ages and Renaissance.

78. On the early modern history of scepticism, see, e.g., R. Popkin, *The High Road to Pyrrhonism* (San Diego 1980). The similarities between radical Academic and Pyrrhonist scepticism are examined in G. Striker, 'On the Difference Between the Pyrrhonists and the Academics', in her *Essays on Hellenistic Epistemology and Ethics* (Cambridge 1996), pp. 135–49, and M. Frede, 'The Skeptic's Two Kinds of Assent', in his *Essays in Ancient Philosophy* (Oxford 1987), pp. 201–22.

contemporary English usage allowed it.[79] A basic difficulty for the translator and reader, however, is that Cicero's text is itself to a large degree a work of translation—at least of arguments and terminology—from Greek into Latin, and thus inevitably contains some authorial compromises between readability and philosophical accuracy.

The scope of this problem can be seen by comparing the terms for the core debates about the possibility of knowledge and of action without assent in the original Greek with those used by Cicero.[80] The Academic 'core argument' relies on the Stoic theory that knowledge depends on the subject's *apprehension* or grasp of something through an *impression* of the right sort, i.e., his or her *assent* to a *cataleptic* impression. The Academic 'corollary argument' led to a distinction between assenting to an impression as true and following or *approving* an impression as *persuasive*.[81] The chart on page xli gives a rough idea of the relation between the original Greek technical terms, Cicero's Latin translations, and the English adopted in this translation.

These translations into Latin and English are not neutral with respect to the philosophical controversies in the *Academica*. The wary reader should note three points in particular about the English translation. The first two concern simplifications of Cicero's Latin in the translation, designed to improve its fluency and philosophical precision.

- Where possible, the translation uses only the terms 'apprehend' and 'apprehension' to translate the variety of verbs and nouns Cicero employed to represent the Greek terms *katalambanein* and *katalêpsis*.

Cicero makes it explicit in *Ac.* 2.17 that the three terms he uses are supposed to translate the Greek technical term. His normal usage in this text is to reinforce the technical meaning of these terms by using two

79. The English–Latin–Greek Glossary lists some of the more important terms, with the relevant Greek original (and in bold when Cicero made his translation of it explicit in this text).

80. Cicero's translations for some of the key epistemological terms in the *Academica* are examined in J. Glucker, 'Probabile, Verisimile, and Related Terms', in Powell, *Cicero the Philosopher,* pp. 115–43. For more general treatments of his methods of translations, see note 6 above.

81. The Stoic theory is set out most clearly in *Ac.* 2.145 and 1.41–42; the core Academic argument against it is given in *Ac.* 2.40–42 and 2.83; cf. *Ac.* 2.104 on assent. The closest Greek parallels are in Sextus *M.* 7.150–89, esp. 150–65.

Greek	Latin	English
APPREHENSION:		
katalambanein	percipere, comprehendere, cognoscere	apprehend
katalêpsis	perceptio, comprehensio, cognitio	apprehension
IMPRESSIONS:		
phantasia	visum, visio, impressio, quod videri	impression
katalêptikê phantasia	visum comprehendible, quod percipi posse	*apprehensible impression*
katalêpton (of objects)	quod percipi posse	apprehensible
ASSENT:		
sunkatathesis (Stoic)	adsentiri, approbare	assent, approve
peithein (Academic)	probare, approbare	approve
pithanê phantasia	probabile	persuasive impression

simultaneously. But idiomatic English does not permit the constant use of phrases such as 'grasp or apprehend'.

- Where possible, the translation uses only 'impression' to represent Cicero's usual periphrasis—*quod videri*, literally, 'what is seen' or 'what seems'—for the Greek technical term *phantasia*.

This allows the translation to avoid the mismatch in English between the noun 'impression' and the verb 'seem'. But it comes at the cost of losing an ambiguity that plagues readers of Cicero's Latin, and may be of philosophical interest: unlike the Greek nominalization, Cicero's phrase can refer *either* to someone's impression about an object or state of affairs *or* to the object or state of affairs itself. But the risk of misidentifying the intended sense is not severe, since Cicero explicitly applies the same arguments for and against the indiscernibility (in fact) or indiscriminability (to us) of things to *both* impressions *and* the objects or states of affairs they represent.

The third point is a more vital one for a philosophical understanding of Cicero's text.

- The translation follows Cicero in obscuring the distinction in the original Greek arguments between the active adjective 'cataleptic' (*katalêptikê*) and the passive 'apprehens*ible*' (*katalêptos*). Like Cicero, the translation thus ignores the distinction between a 'cataleptic' impression—i.e., one that provides apprehension of something—and an 'apprehensible' object or state of affairs—i.e., the thing we have an apprehension of. Objects and impressions are both either *'apprehensible'* or *'inapprehensible'*.

Cicero does not recognize this distinction: he systematically applies the periphrasis *quod percipi posse,* literally, 'what can be apprehended', to impressions, in contravention of the Greek usage, even in the technical passages explaining the Stoic definition in *Ac.* 2 (*Ac.* 2.18, 2.77, 2.112–13). And when he gives a formal gloss or translation for 'cataleptic impression' without using a Latin periphrasis in *Ac.* 1.41, he reads the passive Greek term *katalêptos* and renders it with the passive Latin *comprehendibile* (*Ac.* 1.41)—i.e., *'apprehensible'* in both languages.[82] So it seems not to be the result of a difficulty in finding the right translation, but rather a pervasive choice or mistake.

Cicero's reasons for this decision are unclear. It may be a mistake (something even the most careful translator of a difficult set of philosophical texts cannot always avoid). Or he may have thought that it was a negligible terminological simplification: his readers would understand that the question under debate is not whether we have reliable access to our own thoughts or impressions, but rather whether our impressions provide us with reliable access to the world.[83] Or he may have thought that the Stoic view was that we apprehend our impressions as well as their objects—there may be some evidence in other texts to support this interpretation, provided it is not construed

---

82. The contexts in which this rare adjective is used by later writers such as Tertullian, Lactantius, Marius Victorinus, and Augustine—all of whom relied on Cicero's philosophical vocabulary—shows that the adjectival suffix *–ibilis* in Cicero's gloss has its normal, though not necessary, passive sense in this case (i.e., 'can be [verb]-ed', viz. 'apprehensible').

83. If so, Cicero was mistaken, since some of the most philosophically rewarding work of later students of the *Academica* (including Augustine) seems to be the result of misunderstanding his versions of the Stoic definition of apprehension.

as the view that we infer the existence or nature of objects from our impressions.[84] But readers should still be advised that this is an idiosyncratic feature of Cicero's text that does not reflect the original Greek terminology of the Hellenistic Stoics.

These cases show some of the inevitable tension in a translator between the desires for an accurate rendition of Cicero's Latin, an accurate transmission of the (originally Greek) arguments, and a readable English text.

The text

The Latin text of the *Academica*, like most Classical texts, is preserved in a range of medieval manuscripts of various quality.[85] The two principal editions to date have been *M. Tulli Ciceronis Academica* (London 1885) by J. Reid, and *M. Tullius Cicero Fasc. 42 Academicorum Reliquiae cum Lucullo* (Leipzig 1922) by O. Plasberg. Neither edition is fully satisfactory, though Reid provides an excellent commentary, and Plasberg established a plausible text on the basis of a 'stemma' sorting out the 'families' or interrelationships of manuscripts.[86] In this translation I have followed Plasberg's text except where noted in the Textual Appendix. The translation diverges from Plasberg most frequently at textual cruxes, where the manuscript traditions fail to make sense. At these points I have usually found Reid's emendations more helpful, though on one or two occasions I have suggested new readings in an optimistic spirit.

Editorial symbols

[I 1]   The medieval chapter and section numbers in the text (in roman and arabic numerals) are provided for ease of

---

84. Chrysippus defined an impression as "an affection in the soul that showed itself *and* what made it" (Aetius *Doctrines* 4.12.1–2 [*SVF* 2.54]; cf. Sextus *M.* 7.162); and Hierocles seems to spell this out as two coordinate apprehensions in *Elements of Ethics*, 6.1–6.

85. The extant portions of the two editions survived in different manuscript traditions. For a brief summary of the textual traditions in English, see the entries by R. Rouse for 'Academica posteriora' and 'Academica priora' in L. Reynolds (ed.), *Texts and Transmissions: A Survey of the Latin Classics* (Oxford 1983), pp. 112–15 and 124–25. The history of the second edition is thoroughly examined in Hunt 1998.

86. Some more recent work on the text has been done by C. Schäublin for his Latin–German edition *Marcus Tullius Cicero Akademische Abhandlungen Lucullus* (Hamburg 1995). A new edition for the Oxford Classical Texts series is currently under preparation by Tobias Reinhardt.

reference; cross-references in the notes are always to the section numbers. (The occasional round brackets around section numbers indicate divergent section-divisions in Reid's edition; the numbers in square brackets follow Plasberg's divisions.)

* A superscript asterisk at the end of a sentence indicates a textual problem or, more frequently, a minor disagreement with Plasberg about the correct Latin reading; these textual variants are listed in the Textual Appendix.

[ ] Square brackets around words or phrases indicate that they are interpolations by scribes or editors. Square brackets around numbers (e.g., numbered premises of arguments) indicate that they are supplements added by the translator.

< > Angle brackets around words or phrases indicate supplements to the sense suggested by the translator.

‡ ‡ Daggers around words or phrases indicate that the Latin manuscripts fail at these points by preserving meaningless 'words' or ill-formed phrases. The English phrases between daggers are indications or guesses of what Cicero perhaps wrote.

The notes

- The titles of the most commonly cited works by Cicero are abbreviated as follows:

Ac.	*Academica*	*Academica*
ad Att.	*Epistulae ad Atticum*	*Letters to Atticus*
ad Fam.	*Epistualae ad familiares*	*Letters to His Friends*
Div.	*De divinatione*	*On Divination*
DND	*De natura deorum*	*On the Nature of the Gods*
Fat.	*De fato*	*On Fate*
Fin.	*De finibus*	*On Ethical Ends ('On Moral Ends')*
Inv.	*De inventione*	*On Invention*
Leg.	*De legibus*	*On Laws*
Off.	*De officiis*	*On Appropriate Actions ('On Duties')*
Or.	*De oratore*	*On the Orator*
Rep.	*De republica*	*On the Republic*

| Tusc. | *Disputationes Tusculanae* | *Tusculan Disputations* |
| Paradoxa | *Paradoxa Stoicorum* | *The Stoic Paradoxes* |

Two further abbreviations are to standard collections of fragments of the Presocratics and of the Stoics. These collections give the Greek and Latin fragments without English translations; but most translations still cite the fragment numbers from these standard editions.

| DK | *Die Fragmente der Vorsokratiker* vols. 1–3 (Berlin 1952), edited by H. Diels and W. Kranz. |
| SVF | *Stoicorum Veterum Fragmenta* (Leipzig 1903–24), edited by H. von Arnim. |

- The editions of the other fragment collections are listed under their editors' names in Section ix of the Select Topical Bibliography. (The editors' names are given in brackets in the notes.)

- Immediate reference to a fragment at the start of notes (without 'See' or other comment)—e.g., 'Epicurus fr. 234 (Usener)'— indicates that the passage in Cicero is itself listed as a fragment of the relevant author in the collection referred to by its editor's name.

- Page numbers in roman numerals refer to the Introduction.

- Square brackets around an author's name indicate that the work or passage that follows is wrongly ascribed to that author.

- The Glossary of Names provides information on historical and literary characters cited in the text when a note is not supplied.

- Most of the passages from ancient philosophical authors referred to in the notes are translated in standard introductory collections, such as *Hellenistic Philosophy: Introductory Readings* (Indianapolis 1997), edited by Brad Inwood and Lloyd Gerson, or *The Hellenistic Philosophers* (Cambridge 1987), edited by A. A. Long and D. N. S. Sedley.

Select Topical Bibliography

i) Texts, Commentaries, and Translations

Inwood, B., and L. Gerson, *Hellenistic Philosophy: Introductory Readings* (Hackett Publishing Co., Indianapolis rev. 1997).

Long, A., and D. Sedley, *The Hellenistic Philosophers* (Cambridge University Press, Cambridge 1987).

Plasberg, O., *M Tullius Cicero Fasc. 42 Academicorum Reliquiae Cum Lucullo* (Teubner, Stuttgart 1922).

Rackham, H., *Cicero XIX De Natura Deorum, Academica* (W. Heinemann, London 1933).

Reid, J., *The Academics of Cicero* (Macmillan, London 1880).

Reid, J., *M Tulli Ciceronis Academica* (Macmillan, London 1885).

Ruch, M., *Cicero, Academica Posteriora, Liber Primus* (Presses Universitaires de France, Paris 1970).

Schäublin, C., A. Graeser, and A. Bächli, *Marcus Tullius Cicero Akademische Abhandlungen Lucullus* (F. Meiner Verlag, Hamburg 1995).

Straume-Zimmermann, L., F. Broemser, and O. Gigon, *Marcus Tullius Cicero: Hortensius Lucullus Academici Libri* (Artemis, Munich 1990).

ii) Textual History

Hunt, T., *A Textual History of Cicero's* Academici Libri (Brill, Boston 1998).

Reynolds, L., *Texts and Transmissions: A Survey of the Latin Classics* (Clarendon Press, Oxford 1983).

Schäublin, C., 'Kritisches und Exegetisches zu Ciceros 'Lucullus' I', *Museum Helveticum* 49 (1992), pp. 41–52.

Schäublin, C., 'Kritisches und Exegetisches zu Ciceros 'Lucullus' II', *Museum Helveticum* 50 (1993), pp. 158–169.

iii) Cicero

Bringmann, K., *Untersuchungen zum späten Cicero* (Vandenhoeck und Ruprecht, Göttingen 1971).

Glucker, J., 'Cicero's Philosophical Affiliations', in J. Dillon and A. Long (eds.), *The Question of "Eclecticism": Studies in Later Greek Philosophy* (University of California Press, Berkeley 1988), pp. 34–69.

Görler, W., 'Silencing the Troublemaker: De Legibus I. 39 and the Continuity of Cicero's Scepticism', in J. Powell (ed.), *Cicero the Philosopher: Twelve Papers* (Clarendon Press, Oxford 1995), pp. 85–113.

Görler, W., 'Cicero's Philosophical Stance in the *Lucullus*', in B. Inwood and J. Mansfeld (eds.), *Assent and Argument* (Brill, New York/Leiden 1997), pp. 36–57.

Habicht, C., *Cicero the Politician* (Johns Hopkins University Press, Baltimore 1990).

May, J. (ed.), *Brill's Companion to Cicero: Oratory and Rhetoric* (Brill, Boston/Leiden 2002).

Powell, J. (ed.), *Cicero the Philosopher: Twelve Papers* (Clarendon Press, Oxford 1995).

Powell, J., 'Introduction: Cicero's Philosophical Works and Their Background', in J. Powell (ed.), *Cicero the Philosopher: Twelve Papers* (Clarendon Press, Oxford 1995), pp. 1–35.

Powell, J., and J. Paterson (eds.), *Cicero the Advocate* (Oxford University Press, Oxford 2004).

Rawson, E., *Intellectual Life in the Late Roman Republic* (Duckworth, London 1985).

iv) Dialogues

Griffin, M., 'The Composition of the *Academica*: Motives and Versions', in B. Inwood and J. Mansfeld (eds.), *Assent and Argument* (Brill, New York/Leiden 1997), pp. 1–27.

Hartung, H.-J., *Ciceros Methode bei der Übersetzung Griechischer philosophischer Termini* (Hamburg 1970).

Keaveney, A., *Lucullus: A Life* (Routledge, London 1992).

Powell, J., 'Cicero's Translations from Greek', in J. Powell (ed.), *Cicero the Philosopher: Twelve Papers* (Clarendon Press, Oxford 1995), pp. 273–300.

Schofield, M., 'Cicero For and Against Divination', *Journal of Roman Studies* 76 (1986), pp. 47–65.

Shackleton Bailey, D., *Onomasticon to Cicero's Treatises* (Teubner, Stuttgart 1996).

v) Academics

Algra, K., 'Chrysippus, Carneades, Cicero: The Ethical *Divisiones* in Cicero's *Lucullus*', in B. Inwood and J. Mansfeld (eds.), *Assent and Argument* (Brill, New York/Leiden 1997), pp. 107–39.

Allen, J., 'Academic Probabilism and Stoic Epistemology', *Classical Quarterly* 44 (1994), pp. 85–113.

Allen, J., 'Carneadean Argument in Cicero's *Academic Books*', in B. Inwood and J. Mansfeld (eds.), *Assent and Argument* (Brill, New York/Leiden 1997), pp. 217–56.

Allen, J., 'Carneades', in the *Stanford Encyclopedia of Philosophy*, plato.stanford.edu.

Annas, J., 'Plato the Sceptic', in *Oxford Studies in Ancient Philosophy*, suppl. vol. (Clarendon Press, Oxford 1992), pp. 43–72.

Annas, J., *The Morality of Happiness* (Oxford University Press, Oxford 1993).

Annas, J., and J. Barnes, *The Modes of Scepticism: Ancient Texts and Modern Interpretations* (Cambridge University Press, Cambridge 1985).

Barnes, J., 'Antiochus of Ascalon', in M. Griffin and J. Barnes (eds.), *Philosophia Togata: Essays on Philosophy and Roman Society* (Oxford University Press, Oxford 1989), pp. 51–96.

Barnes, J., 'Logic in *Academica* 1 and the *Lucullus*', in B. Inwood and J. Mansfeld (eds.), *Assent and Argument* (Brill, New York/Leiden 1997), pp. 140–60.

Bett, R., 'Carneades' Pithanon: A Reappraisal of Its Role and Status', in *Oxford Studies in Ancient Philosophy* 7 (1989), pp. 59–94.

Bett, R., 'Carneades' Distinction Between Assent and Approval', *Monist* 73 (1990), pp. 3–20.

Brittain, C., *Philo of Larissa: The Last of the Academic Sceptics* (Oxford University Press, Oxford 2001).

Brittain, C., 'Arcesilaus', in the *Stanford Encyclopedia of Philosophy*, plato.stanford .edu.

Brittain, C., and J. Palmer, 'The New Academy's Appeals to the Presocratics', *Phronesis* 46.1 (2001), pp. 38–72.

Brunschwig, J., 'Le fragment DK 70B1 de Métrodore de Chio', in K. Algra, P. van der Horst, and D. Runia (eds.), *Polyhistor: Studies in the History and Historiography of Ancient Philosophy* (Brill, New York/Leiden 1996), pp. 21–38.

Burnyeat, M., 'Can the Sceptic Live His Scepticism?', in M. Schofield, M. Burnyeat, and J. Barnes (eds.), *Doubt and Dogmatism: Studies in Hellenistic Epistemology* (Clarendon Press, Oxford 1980), pp. 20–53.

Burnyeat, M., 'Gods and Heaps', in M. Schofield and M. Nussbaum (eds.), *Language and Logos: Studies in Ancient Greek Philosophy* (Cambridge University Press, Cambridge 1982), pp. 315–38.

Burnyeat, M., 'Antipater and Self-refutation: Elusive Arguments in Cicero's *Academica*', in B. Inwood and J. Mansfeld (eds.), *Assent and Argument* (Brill, New York/Leiden 1997), pp. 277–310.

Burnyeat, M., 'Carneades Was No Probabilist' (unpublished).

Burnyeat, M., and M. Frede (eds.), *The Original Sceptics: A Controversy* (Hackett Publishing Co., Indianapolis 1997).

Cooper, J., 'Arcesilaus: Socratic and Sceptic', in J. Cooper, *Knowledge, Nature, and the Good: Essays on Ancient Philosophy* (Princeton University Press, Princeton 2004), pp. 81–103.

Couissin, P., 'Le Stoicisme de la Nouvelle Académie', *Revue d'histoire de la philosophie* 3 (1929), pp. 241–76 [= 'The Stoicism of the New Academy', trans. J. Barnes and M. Burnyeat, in M. Burnyeat (ed.), *The Skeptical Tradition* (University of California Press, Berkeley 1983), pp. 31–63].

Decleva Caizzi, F., 'Aenesidemus and the Academy', *Classical Quarterly* 42 (1992), pp. 176–89.

Frede, M., 'Des Skeptikers Meinungen', *Neue Hefte für Philosophie, Aktualität der Antike* 15/16 (1979), pp. 102–29 [= 'The Sceptic's Beliefs', in M. Frede, *Essays in Ancient Philosophy* (Clarendon Press, Oxford 1987), pp. 179–200].

Frede, M., 'Stoics and Skeptics on Clear and Distinct Impressions', in M. Burnyeat (ed.), *The Skeptical Tradition* (London 1983), pp. 65–93 [= M. Frede, *Essays in Ancient Philosophy* (Clarendon Press, Oxford 1987), pp. 151–76].

Frede, M., 'The Skeptic's Two Kinds of Assent', in *Essays in Ancient Philosophy* (Clarendon Press, Oxford 1987), pp. 201–22.

Glucker, J., *Antiochus and the Late Academy* (Vandenhoeck und Ruprecht, Göttingen 1978), Hypomnemata Heft 56.

Glucker, J., 'Probabile, Verisimile, and Related Terms', in J. Powell (ed.), *Cicero the Philosopher: Twelve Papers* (Clarendon Press, Oxford 1995), pp. 115–43.

Glucker, J., 'Socrates in the *Academic Books* and Other Ciceronian Works', in B. Inwood and J. Mansfeld (eds.), *Assent and Argument* (Brill, New York/Leiden 1997), pp. 58–88.

Glucker, J., 'The Philonian/Metrodorians: Problems of Method in Ancient Philosophy', *Elenchos* 25.1 (2004), pp. 99–153.

Görler, W., 'Älterer Pyrrhonismus, Jüngere Akademie, Antiochos aus Askalon, § 47 Arkesilaos', in H. Flashar (ed.), *Die Philosophie der Antike 4: Die Hellenistische Philosophie* (Schwabe, Basel 1994), pp. 786–828.

Hankinson, R., *The Sceptics* (Routledge, London 1995).

Heath, T., *Aristarchus of Samos, the Ancient Copernicus* (Clarendon Press, Oxford 1913).

Inwood, B., and J. Mansfeld (eds.), *Assent and Argument: Studies in Cicero's Academic Books* (Brill, New York/Leiden 1997).

Ioppolo, A.-M., *Opinione e Scienza* (Bibliopolis, Naples 1986).

Ioppolo, A.-M., 'Su alcune recenti interpretazioni dello scetticismo dell'Academia', *Elenchos* (2000), pp. 334–60.

Lévy, C., *Cicero Academicus: Recherches sur les Académiques et sur la Philosophie Cicéronienne*, Collection de l'École française de Rome 162 (École française de Rome, Palais farnèse, Rome 1992).

Maconi, H., 'Nova Non Philosophandi Philosophia', *Oxford Studies in Ancient Philosophy* 6 (1988), pp. 231–53.

Mansfeld, J., 'Gibt es Spuren von Theophrasts Phys. Op. bei Cicero?', in W. Fortenbaugh and P. Steinmetz (eds.), *Cicero's Knowledge of the Peripatos*, Rutgers Studies in Classical Humanities 4 (Transaction Publishers, New Brunswick 1989), pp. 133–58.

Mansfeld, J., 'Aenesidemus and the Academics', in L. Ayres (ed.), *The Passionate Intellect: Essays on the Transformation of Classical Traditions* (Transaction Publishers, New Brunswick 1995), pp. 235–48.

Mette, H.-J., 'Zwei Akademiker heute: Krantor von Soloi und Arkesilaos von Pitane', *Lustrum* 26 (1984), pp. 7–94.

Mette, H.-J., 'Weitere Akademiker heute: von Lakydes bis zu Kleitomachos', *Lustrum* 27 (1985), pp. 39–148.

Mette, H.-J., 'Philon von Larisa und Antiochos von Askalon', *Lustrum* 28–29 (1986–87), pp. 9–63.

Schofield, M., 'Academic Epistemology', in K. Algra, J. Barnes, J. Mansfeld, and M. Schofield (eds.), *The Cambridge History of Hellenistic Philosophy* (Cambridge University Press, Cambridge 1999), pp. 323–51.

Sedley, D., 'Diodorus Cronus and Hellenistic Philosophy', *Proceedings of the Cambridge Philological Society* ns 23 (1977), pp. 74–120.

Sedley, D., 'The End of the Academy', *Phronesis* 26 (1981), pp. 67–75.

Sedley, D., 'The Motivation of Greek Scepticism', in M. Burnyeat (ed.), *The Skeptical Tradition* (University of California Press, Berkeley 1983), pp. 9–29.

Striker, G., 'Sceptical Strategies', in M. Schofield, M. Burnyeat, and J. Barnes (eds.), *Doubt and Dogmatism* (Oxford University Press, Oxford 1980), pp. 54–83. [= G. Striker, *Essays on Hellenistic Epistemology and Ethics* (Cambridge University Press, Cambridge 1996), pp. 92–115.]

Striker, G., 'Über den Unterschied zwischen den Pyrrhoneern und den Akademikern', *Phronesis* 26 (1981), pp. 153–71 [= 'On the Difference Between the Pyrrhonists and the Academics', in G. Striker, *Essays on Hellenistic Epistemology and Ethics* (Cambridge University Press, Cambridge 1996), pp. 135–49].

Striker, G., 'Academics Fighting Academics', in B. Inwood and J. Mansfeld (eds.), *Assent and Argument* (Brill, New York/Leiden 1997), pp. 257–76.

Tarrant, H., *Scepticism or Platonism? The Philosophy of the Fourth Academy* (Cambridge University Press, Cambridge 1985).

von Staden, H., 'The Stoic Theory of Perception and Its "Platonic" Critics', in P. Machamer and R. Turnbull (eds.), *Studies in Perception* (Ohio State University Press, Columbus 1978), pp. 96–136.

vi) Influence

Bonazzi, M., *Academici e Platonici. Il dibattito antico sullo scetticismo di Platone* (LED, Milan 2003).

Brittain, C., 'Middle Platonists on Academic Scepticism' in R. W. Sharples and R. Sorabji (eds.), *Greek and Roman Philosophy, 100 BC to 200 AD* (forthcoming 2006).

Frede, M., 'The Skeptic's Two Kinds of Assent', in M. Frede, *Essays in Ancient Philosophy* (Clarendon Press, Oxford 1987), pp. 201–22.

Hagendahl, H., *Augustine and the Latin Classics* (Acta Universitatis Gothoburgensis, Göteborg 1967).

King, P., *Augustine* Against the Academicians *and* The Teacher (Hackett Publishing Co., Indianapolis 1995).

Opsomer, J., *In Search of the Truth: Academic Tendencies in Middle Platonism* (Paleis der Academiën, Brussels 1998).

Popkin, R., *The History of Scepticism from Erasmus to Spinoza* (University of California Press, Berkeley 1979).

Popkin, R., *The High Road to Pyrrhonism* (Austin Hill Press, San Diego 1980).

Schmitt, C., *Cicero Scepticus* (Martinus Nijhoff, The Hague 1972).

Sedley, D., 'Three Platonist Interpretations of the *Theaetetus*', in C. Gill and M. McCabe (eds.), *Form and Argument in Late Plato* (Clarendon Press, Oxford 1996), pp. 79–103.

Tarrant, H., *Scepticism or Platonism? The Philosophy of the Fourth Academy* (Cambridge University Press, Cambridge 1985).

Testard, M., *Saint Augustin et Cicéron* (Etudes augustiniennes, Paris 1958).

vii) Antiochus

Barnes, J., 'Antiochus of Ascalon', in M. Griffin and J. Barnes (eds.), *Philosophia Togata* (Clarendon Press, Oxford 1989), pp. 51–96.

Dillon, J., *The Middle Platonists* (Duckworth, London 1977), pp. 52–113.

Dillon, J., *The Heirs of Plato: A Study of the Old Academy, 347–274 BC* (Clarendon Press, Oxford 2003).

Glucker, J., *Antiochus and the Late Academy*, Hypomnemata 56 (Vandenhoeck und Ruprecht, Göttingen 1978).

Görler, W., 'Antiochos von Askalon über die "Alten" und über die Stoa. Beobachtungen zu Cicero, Academici posteriores 1.24–43', in P. Steinmetz (ed.), *Beiträge zur Hellenistischen Literatur und ihrer Rezeption in Rom*, Palingenesia 28 (F. Steiner, Stuttgart 1990), pp. 123–39.

Görler, W., 'Älterer Pyrrhonismus, Jüngere Akademie, Antiochos aus Askalon', § 52 'Antiochus aus Askalon und seine schule', in H. Flashar (ed.), *Die Philosophie der Antike 4: Die Hellenistische Philosophie* (Schwabe, Basel 1994), pp. 938–80.

Mette, H.-J., 'Philon von Larisa und Antiochus von Askalon', *Lustrum* 28–29 (1986–87), pp. 9–63.

Polito, R., 'The Sceptical Sect: Reception, Self-definition, Internal Conflicts' (forthcoming).

Reydams-Schils, G., *Demiurge and Providence: Stoic and Platonist Readings of Plato's Timaeus* (Brepols, Turnhout 1999).

Sedley, D., 'The Origins of Stoic God', in D. Frede and A. Laks (eds.), *Traditions of Theology* (Brill, Boston/Leiden 2002), pp. 41–83.

Striker, G., 'Academics Fighting Academics', in B. Inwood and J. Mansfeld (eds.), *Assent and Argument* (Brill, New York/Leiden 1997), pp. 257–76.

Tarrant, H., 'The Stoicizing Epistemology of Antiochus of Ascalon', *Dialectic* 25 (1985), pp. 34–49.

viii) Stoics

Annas, J., 'Stoic Epistemology', in S. Everson (ed.), *Epistemology* (Cambridge University Press, Cambridge 1990), pp. 184–303.

Arthur, E., 'The Stoic Analysis of the Mind's Reactions to Presentations', *Hermes* 111 (1983), pp. 69–78.

Barnes, J., 'Language 1.2', in K. Algra, J. Barnes, J. Mansfeld, and M. Schofield (eds.), *The Cambridge History of Hellenistic Philosophy* (Cambridge University Press, Cambridge 1999), pp. 193–213.

Bobzien, S., 'Logic 2–3.1–7', in K. Algra, J. Barnes, J. Mansfeld, and M. Schofield (eds.), *The Cambridge History of Hellenistic Philosophy* (Cambridge University Press, Cambridge 1999), pp. 83–157.

Bobzien, S., 'Chrysippus and the Epistemic Theory of Vagueness', *Proceedings of the Aristotelian Society* 102 (2002), pp. 17–238.

Bobzien, S., 'The Stoics on the Fallacies of Equivocation', in B. Inwood and D. Frede (eds.), *Language and Learning* (Cambridge University Press, Cambridge 2005), pp. 239–73.

Brennan, T., 'Reasonable Impressions in Stoicism', *Phronesis* 41 (1996), pp. 318–34.

Brennan, T., 'The Old Stoic Theory of Emotions', in J. Sihvola and T. Engberg-Pedersen (eds.), *The Emotions in Hellenistic Philosophy* (Kluwer Academic Press, Boston/Dordrecht 1998), pp. 21–70.

Brennan, T., 'Stoic Moral Psychology', in B. Inwood (ed.), *The Cambridge Companion to the Stoics* (Cambridge University Press, Cambridge 2003), pp. 257–94.

Brittain, C., 'Common Sense: Concepts, Definition, and Meaning In and Out of the Stoa', in B. Inwood and D. Frede (eds.), *Language and Learning* (Cambridge University Press, Cambridge 2005), pp. 164–209.

Frede, M., 'The Stoic Doctrine of the Affections of the Soul', in M. Schofield and G. Striker (eds.), *The Norms of Nature* (Cambridge University Press, Cambridge 1986), pp. 93–110.

Frede, M., 'The Stoic Conception of Reason', in K. Boudouris (ed.), *Hellenistic Philosophy* II (International Center for Greek Philosophy and Culture, Athens 1994), pp. 50–63.

Frede, M., 'Stoic Epistemology', in K. Algra, J. Barnes, J. Mansfeld, and M. Schofield (eds.), *The Cambridge History of Hellenistic Philosophy* (Cambridge University Press, Cambridge 1999), pp. 295–322.

Görler, W., '*Asthenes sunkatathesis* zur stoischen Erkenntnistheorie', *Würzburger Jahrbücher für die Altertumswissenschaft* NF 3 (1977), pp. 83–92.

Inwood, B., *Ethics and Human Action in Early Stoicism* (Clarendon Press, Oxford 1985).

Ioppolo, A.-M., 'Presentation and Assent: A Physical and Cognitive Problem in Early Stoicism', *Classical Quarterly* 40 (1990), pp. 433–49.

Menn, S., 'The Stoic Theory of Categories', *Oxford Studies in Ancient Philosophy* 27 (1999), pp. 215–47.

Mignucci, M., 'The Liar Paradox and the Stoics', in K. Ierodiakonou (ed.), *Topics in Stoic Philosophy* (Clarendon Press, Oxford 1999), pp. 54–70.

Mignucci, M., 'Logic III. The Stoics. §8 Paradoxes', in K. Algra, J. Barnes, J. Mansfeld, and M. Schofield (eds.), *The Cambridge History of Hellenistic Philosophy* (Cambridge University Press, Cambridge 1999), pp. 157–76.

Sandbach, F., '*Phantasia katalêptikê*', in A. Long (ed.), *Problems in Stoicism* (Athlone Press, London 1996, second edition), pp. 9–22.

Sandbach, F., '*Ennoia* and *Prolepsis*', in A. Long. (ed.), *Problems in Stoicism* (Athlone Press, London 1996, second edition), pp. 22–37.

Sedley, D., 'The Stoic Criterion of Identity', *Phronesis* 27 (1982), pp. 255–75.

Sedley, D., 'Zeno's Definition of *Phantasia Kataleptikê*', in T. Scaltsas and A. Mason (eds.), *Zeno of Citium and His Legacy: The Philosophy of Zeno* (Pierides Foundation, Larnaka 2002), pp. 137–54.

Striker, G., 'The Problem of the Criterion', in S. Everson (ed.), *Epistemology* (Cambridge University Press, Cambridge 1990), pp. 143–60 [= G. Striker, *Essays on Hellenistic Epistemology and Ethics* (Cambridge University Press, Cambridge 1996), pp. 150–65.]

ix) Editions of Fragments Cited in the Notes

Cramer, J. (ed.), *Anecdota Graeca*, vols. 1–2 (Oxford University Press, Oxford 1835).

Decleva Caizzi, F. (ed.), *Pirrone, testimonianze* (Bibliopolis, Naples 1981).

Des Places, E., *Numenius: Fragments* (Les Belles lettres, Paris 1973).

Diels, H., and W. Kranz (eds.), *Die Fragmente der Vorsokratiker*, vols. 1–3 (Weidmann, Berlin 1952).

Döring, K. (ed.), *Die Megariker: Kommentierte Sammlung der Testimonien* (Grüner, Amsterdam 1972).

Fortenbaugh, W. (ed.), *Theophrastus of Eresus: Sources for His Life, Writings, Thought, and Influence* (Brill, New York/Leiden 1992).

Giannantoni, G. (ed.), *Socratis et Socraticorum reliquiae*, vols. 1–3 (Bibliopolis, Naples 1990).

Isnardi Parente, M. (ed.), *Senocrate – Ermodoro Frammenti* (Bibliopolis, Naples 1982).

Jocelyn, H. D. (ed.), *The Tragedies of Ennius: The Fragments* (Cambridge University Press, Cambridge 1969).

Mette, H.-J., 'Zwei Akademiker heute: Krantor von Soloi und Arkesilaos von Pitane', *Lustrum* 26 (1984), pp. 7–94.

Mette, H.-J., 'Weitere Akademiker heute: von Lakydes bis zu Kleitomachos', *Lustrum* 27 (1985), pp. 39–148.

Mette, H.-J., 'Philon von Larisa und Antiochos von Askalon', *Lustrum* 28–29 (1986–87), pp. 9–63.

Skutsch, O. (ed.), *The Annals of Q. Ennius* (Clarendon Press, Oxford 1986).

Usener, H. (ed.), *Epicurea* (Teubner, Leipzig 1887).

Vahlen, J. (ed.), *Ennianae Poesis Reliquiae* (Teubner, Leipzig 1854).

van Straaten, M. (ed.), *Panaetii Rhodii Fragmenta* (Brill, Leiden 1962).

von Arnim, H. (ed.), *Stoicorum Veterum Fragmenta*, vols. 1–4 (Teubner, Leipzig 1903–24).

Warmington, E. H. (ed.), *Remains of Old Latin*, vols. 1–4 (Harvard University Press, Cambridge 1936–56).

Wehrli, F. (ed.), *Die Schule des Aristoteles: Texte und Kommentar*, vols. 1–10 (Schwabe, Basel 1967–69).

Analytical
Table of Contents

Academici Libri Book 1:

ON ACADEMIC
SCEPTICISM

Lucullus
(*Academica* Book 2)

Introduction

[I 1] Lucius Lucullus was quite cut off from the life of the City at the time when his remarkable intellect and remarkable interest in the most valuable systematic arts—and the learning he had acquired in every liberal study worthy of a well-born man—could best have flourished in the forum.[1] While he was still just a young man, he prosecuted his father's enemies, with the help of his brother (his equal in energy and devotion to their family), to his great credit. But then he went out to Asia as a quaestor, where he governed the province for a number of years to rather extraordinary praise. Next he was made an aedile magistrate in his absence, and then immediately a praetor (he was allowed this office earlier than usual by special legislation). After that he was sent to Africa, and thereafter attained the consulship, an office he performed in a way that led everyone to admire his diligence without recognizing his intellect. After that he was sent by the senate to the Mithridatic War, in which he outdid not just the general estimation of his military virtue, but the renown of his predecessors as well.

[2] This was particularly surprising because praise for his generalship was not something generally anticipated in someone who had spent his youth in legal work and the lengthy period of his quaestorship at peace in Asia while Murena was waging war in Pontus. But the extraordinary breadth of his intellect didn't require the unschooled training provided by experience. As a result, by spending the whole journey sailing out to Asia in questioning experienced men and reading military history by turns, he arrived there already a general, although he had set out from Rome a novice in military affairs. But then he had an almost divine memory for facts, though Hortensius had a better one for words; still, to the extent that facts are more useful than

---

1. See the Glossary of Names for the dates and details of Lucullus' career (described in *Ac.* 2.1–4), and for further information on all the people named in the text.

3

words in practical pursuits, his memory was the more impressive. It was this sort of memory, they say, that Themistocles—a man I rank without hesitation as the chief of the Greeks—had to an extraordinary degree; in fact, he is said to have replied to someone promising to pass on to him a systematic art of memory (which was just developing at that time) that he would rather learn how to forget—presumably because whatever he had heard or seen stuck in his memory.[2] Yet, for all his natural intellect, Lucullus acquired the system Themistocles had spurned as well. As a result, he kept facts engraved in his mind in the way we put in writing what we want to record.

[3] Lucullus was such a good general in every aspect of war—in battles, assaults, naval engagements, and in managing the equipment and supplies needed throughout a war—that his opponent, the greatest king since Alexander, used to say that he recognized him as a greater leader than any he had read about.[3] And he displayed such foresight in reestablishing and ordering the cities of Asia, and was so fair, that even today the province continues to maintain the institutions Lucullus set up by following in his footsteps (so to speak). Yet, though it was to the great advantage of the republic, his foreign service meant that his powerful virtue and intellect were absent from the eyes of the forum and senate-house longer than I would have wished. Worse still, once he had returned victorious from the Mithridatic War, he gained his triumph three years later than he should have, owing to the machinations of his enemies. In fact, because I was consul at the time, I practically led this distinguished man's chariot into the city; and I would relate how useful his advice and influence were for me then, in the midst of the gravest events, if doing so didn't require talking about myself, which isn't called for at this point. So I will deny him the testimonial he deserved rather than express it to my own credit.

[II 4] Still, the actions of Lucullus deserving the accolade of popular renown have been celebrated in both Greek and Latin writings: I share the knowledge of these public matters with many people. But there are some more private details that I and a few others learned from him personally on many occasions. Lucullus was interested in both literature of all kinds and philosophy much more seriously than those who didn't know him thought—and not just as a young man, but also in his

---

2. The offer to teach Themistocles the art of memory came from the poet Simonides; see Cicero *Fin.* 2.104.
3. Lucullus' opponent was Mithridates VI of Pontus; see the Glossary of Names.

several years as proquaestor and even during the war (when a general's preoccupation with military affairs is usually so great that very little leisure is left to him even in his tent). In fact, both as a quaestor and as a general, Lucullus kept Antiochus (the student of Philo) with him, because he considered him the best of the philosophers in intellect and knowledge. And his memory was so good (as I have already said) that, by listening to arguments repeatedly, he easily learned things he could have memorized even at the first hearing. He also took extraordinary delight in reading the books he had heard about from Antiochus.

[5] But I sometimes worry that though I wish to enhance the renown of such public characters, I may actually diminish it. A lot of people thoroughly dislike Greek literature, and more dislike philosophy; and if the rest don't disapprove of these subjects, they still find discussion of them by the leaders of the state not quite fitting. For my part, however, when I hear that Marcus Cato learned Greek in his old age, and when history reports that Panaetius was the only companion Publius Africanus took with him in the famous embassy he undertook before his censorship, I no longer need any further authority for studying Greek literature or philosophy. [6] That leaves my response to those who would rather that such serious characters were not involved in conversations of this kind. I suppose they think the meetings of famous men should be silent, their conversations banal, or their discussions about trivial subjects! Moreover, if philosophy was rightly praised in one of my books, engaging with it is obviously something highly appropriate for any important or eminent man—with the single proviso that people like myself, whom the Roman people have placed in this position, should make sure that nothing is detracted from our public work through our private interests.[4] But I never let my work stray from the public arena while it was incumbent on me to serve—I didn't even let myself write anything unconnected with the law. So why should anyone criticize my leisure now when I'm not just trying to avoid idleness or losing my touch, but also striving to benefit as many people as possible? Thus, when I add these less known or less publicized praises to the celebrated and familiar attainments of my characters, I believe that their renown isn't just undiminished, but actually augmented. [7] There are also people who deny that the disputants in my books had real knowledge of the subjects they debated—but they seem to me to envy the dead as well as the living.

---

4. Cicero's praise of philosophy was in his (lost) protreptic dialogue *Hortensius* (completed in 46 BCE), to which the *Lucullus* and *Catulus* are sequels; see page xi.

[III]   That leaves a class of critic that disapproves of the philosophical position of the Academy.[5] We would take this more seriously if anyone approved of any philosophical system other than the one he followed himself. As for us, we can't demur when others disagree with us, since it is our practice to say what we think against every position.*[6] But our case is straightforward, because we want to discover truth without any contention, and we search for it conscientiously and enthusiastically. To be sure, knowledge is always surrounded with difficulties, and the obscurity of the things themselves and weakness of our judgments is such that one can see why the earliest and most learned philosophers lost confidence in their ability to discover what they desired. Still, they didn't give up, and we won't abandon our enthusiasm for investigation owing to exhaustion. Nor do our arguments have any purpose other than to draw out or 'formulate' the truth or its closest possible approximation by means of arguing on either side.*

[8]   The only difference between us and philosophers who think that they have knowledge is that they have no doubt that the views they defend are true, whereas we hold many views to be persuasive, i.e., ones that we can readily follow but scarcely affirm. But we are freer and less constrained because our power of judgment is intact and we aren't compelled by any obligation to defend a set of views prescribed and practically imposed on us by someone else.* Other philosophers, after all, labour under two constraints. First, they are chained to one spot by bonds formed before they were able to judge what was best. Second, they make their judgments about subjects they don't know at the weakest point in their lives under pressure from a friend or captivated by a single speech from someone they heard for the first time; and they hang on to the philosophical system they happened to adopt as their salvation from the storm that drove them into it. [9]   They claim, of course, to be entrusting themselves entirely to someone they judge to have been wise. This is a procedure I would approve if

---

5. *Ac.* 2.7–9 gives a general defence of Academic scepticism; see page xii and *DND* 1.10–12. The Academics' philosophical method is criticized by Lucullus in *Ac.* 2.32–36 and 2.60 and defended by Cicero in *Ac.* 2.98–111. Their critique of the dogmatic reliance on authority (*Ac.* 2.8–9) is expanded in *Ac.* 2.114–15.

6. A superscript asterisk in the translation indicates that part of the sentence relies on a reading of the Latin text that deviates from Plasberg's Teubner edition. The Latin readings adopted here are listed in the Textual Appendix. In most cases, the difference in meaning is very slight; when it is of philosophical interest, a note is supplied.

untaught novices had the capacity to make such judgments—though deciding who is wise seems to be a particular function of people who are already wise. Still, assuming they did have this capacity, they could only judge after they had heard all the issues and knew the views of the other philosophers as well.* But they have made their judgments at a single hearing and submitted themselves to one person's authority.* I don't know how it is that most people would rather go wrong by defending to the hilt a view they have grown to love than work out without intransigence which view is most consistent.

I have often investigated or debated these subjects at length, both at other times and, on one occasion, at Hortensius' villa (which is near Bauli), when Catulus, Lucullus, and I had arrived there the day after our stay with Catulus.[7] We had in fact arrived there rather early, because it had been decided that, if there were wind, Lucullus would sail to Naples and I to Pompeii. So, when we had talked a bit in the colonnade, we sat down in that space. **[IV 10]** Then Catulus said: "Since the subject of our investigation was pretty much unraveled yesterday, the whole question seems just about dealt with. But I am still waiting, Lucullus, for the arguments you heard from Antiochus, which you promised you would give." Hortensius added: "Indeed, I did more than I wanted—the whole thing should have been reserved intact for Lucullus.* But perhaps it has, since I just said what came readily to hand, whereas I am looking for something a bit deeper from Lucullus." Then Lucullus replied: "Your expectation doesn't really disturb me, Hortensius, although nothing is worse for someone who hopes to gratify his audience. It doesn't disturb me very much because I'm not worked up about how well I'm going to prove the points I make: the arguments I'm going to make aren't mine or ones that, if they weren't true, I wouldn't rather that I lost than won. (Though, as the case now stands, although it was shaken by yesterday's discussion, I can assure you that it still seems absolutely true to me.) So I shall proceed as Antiochus did. I know the material, because I listened to him with my mind free and with considerable interest, and heard him quite often on the same subject—but I am making your expectations of me even greater than Hortensius just did!" When he had given this preamble, we turned our minds to listen.

7. Allusions to the discussion at Catulus' villa 'yesterday' are implicit references to the (lost) *Catulus,* the first book of the two-part first edition of the *Academica;* see pages xx–xviii.

Lucullus' Speech

[11] Lucullus said: "When I was proquaestor in Alexandria, Antiochus was with me, and Antiochus' friend, Heraclitus of Tyre, was already there in Alexandria.[8] Heraclitus had been a pupil of Clitomachus for many years, and also of Philo; he was a man with a good, even prominent reputation in the philosophical school that is now being called back to life from virtual extinction.[9] I often listened to Antiochus' debates with him, and both of them argued mildly.* But then those two books by Philo, which Catulus spoke about yesterday, were brought to Alexandria and came into the hands of Antiochus for the first time. And, although he was by nature a very mild man—no one could be more gentle than him—he began to get angry. I was surprised: I had never seen him do so before. But Antiochus appealed to Heraclitus' memory, asking him whether these views seemed to be Philo's, or whether he had ever heard such views from Philo or any other Academic. He said no. But he recognized Philo's writing; and indeed, this couldn't be doubted, since my friends Publius and Gaius Selius and Tetrilius Rogus (all learned men) were present, and they said that they had heard these views in Rome from Philo, and transcribed the two books from Philo himself. [12] That was when Antiochus made the criticisms that yesterday Catulus reminded us had been made by his father against Philo, and many others as well—in fact, he couldn't restrain himself from publishing a book called the 'Sosus' against his teacher.* And, though I listened carefully to Heraclitus arguing against Antiochus, and likewise to Antiochus against the Academics, I paid more attention at the time to Antiochus in order to learn the whole case from him. We spent a lot of time like this on just that one debate, arguing for several days, with Heraclitus there, and many other scholars (among them Aristus, Antiochus'

---

8. Lucullus' speech reports Antiochus' objections to Academic scepticism, partly in response to its presentation in the lost *Catulus*. It is divided into three main sections: an introduction concerned with various historical controversies raised in the *Catulus* (*Ac.* 2.11–18); a wide-ranging defence of the possibility of attaining apprehension as defined by the Stoics (*Ac.* 2.19–39); and a critical review of the sceptical counterarguments (*Ac.* 2.40–60).

9. The Academy ran out of steam, and probably ceased to exist as an organized institution in Athens, after Philo's death in 84/3 BCE, four years after 'the Sosus affair' described in this paragraph. Cicero defends his decision to revive its scepticism through his books in *DND* 1.11–12. (Heraclitus and the other philosophers mentioned below had fled from Athens to Alexandria or Rome to avoid the Mithridatic War.)

brother, as well as Aristo and Dio, the people he most valued after his brother). But let's pass over the part against Philo: he is a less serious adversary because he absolutely denies that the views defended yesterday were held by the Academics. Despite his lying, he is an easier adversary. So let's turn to Arcesilaus and Carneades."[10]

[V 13] When he had said that, Lucullus started again like this: "First, in citing the early physicists, what you are doing"—here he addressed me by name—"seems to me to be exactly what seditious citizens do when they list a selection of famous men from the past, trying to represent them as populists, in order to make themselves look like them.[11] They start with Publius Valerius, who was consul in the first year after the expulsion of the kings; and they list all the other consuls who proposed populist laws during their year of office granting rights to appeal. Then they turn to better-known cases: to Gaius Flaminius, who proposed an agrarian law against the will of the senate a few years after the Second Punic War, when he was a tribune of the people, and who was subsequently twice made consul; to Lucius Cassius; and to Quintus Pompeius. They usually count even Publius Africanus in this number. Next, they assert that those two very wise and distinguished brothers, Publius Crassus and Publius Scaevola, were the sources of Tiberius Gracchus' laws (the former openly, as we can still see, the latter more obscurely, as they suspect). They also count Gaius Marius in—and they are certainly not wrong about him. Once they have set out this long list of names of remarkable people, they claim that they are pursuing what these men began.

10. This paragraph presents our main evidence for the controversy caused by Philo's Roman Books (written in 88/7 BCE); see pages xxx–xxxi and xxxvii–xxxviii. The Roman Books offered an epistemological innovation (see *Ac.* 2.18) supported by a historical thesis of the philosophical unity of the Academic tradition (see *Ac.* 1.13). Antiochus' lost 'Sosus' objected to the former claim as self-defeating and to the latter as a patent fabrication (the 'lie' of *Ac.* 2.12 and 2.18). The reactions of Heraclitus and Catulus' father—both faithful Academic sceptics (cf. *Ac.* 2.148)—and Cicero's failure to defend Philo suggest that Antiochus was right to reject the Roman Books' interpretation of the earlier Academics.

11. Lucullus' criticism of the Academics' interpretation of the history of philosophy in *Ac.* 2.13–15 picks up on a theme alluded to in *Ac.* 2.7 and no doubt explained in detail in the lost *Catulus;* see pages xxxv–xxxvii and C. Brittain and J. Palmer, 'The New Academy's Appeals to the Presocratics', *Phronesis* 46.1 (2001), pp. 38–72. Cicero defends the Academic history in *Ac.* 2.72–76 and 1.44–45. (Lucullus explains the political analogy by reference to the demagogy of Saturninus, a populist tribune in 100 BCE; Cicero might add the more recent example of Clodius; see the note to *Ac.* 2.144.)

[14] "This is just what you do, when you want to subvert philosophy, as they did the republic, despite its current well-established state: you cite Empedocles, Anaxagoras, Democritus, Parmenides, Xenophanes, and even Plato and Socrates. But Saturninus—to name my family's worst enemy—had nothing in common with those early leaders; nor are Arcesilaus' misrepresentations comparable with the modesty of Democritus. No doubt those physicists did very occasionally cry out like mentally disturbed people, when they were at a loss on some topic—in fact Empedocles does so to such an extent that I sometimes think he is raving—declaring that everything is hidden, that we sense nothing, discern nothing, and that we can't discover what anything at all is like. But for the most part they—all of them, in my view—seem rather to affirm some views too strongly, and to profess to know more than they do. **[15]** But so what if they did hesitate then, like newborn children in unfamiliar territory? Are we to think that nothing has been explained through so many centuries by the supreme efforts of the greatest intellects? Isn't this rather what happened? Just as Tiberius Gracchus rose up to subvert the peace of an excellent republic, so once stable philosophical systems had been established, Arcesilaus arose to overturn philosophy, hiding behind the authority of those who had denied—he claimed—that anything could be known or apprehended.

"We must anyhow remove both Plato and Socrates from that group: the former, because he left a complete philosophical system inherited by the Peripatetics and Academics, who differ in name but concur in fact (and even the Stoics disagree with them more in their terminology than in their views).[12] As for Socrates, he used to ascribe the larger part in arguments to the people he was trying to refute by deprecating his own contribution. So, since he said one thing and thought another, it was his practice to use the kind of dissimulation the Greeks call *eirôneia* ['irony'] (an attribute Fannius says Africanus had, and one Fannius explained shouldn't be considered a fault in him because Socrates had had it, too).[13]

---

12. The essential agreement of the Peripatetics and Old Academics is a central tenet of Antiochus' syncretism; see *Ac.* 1.16–42, esp. 1.17, and pages xxxi–xxxvii. (For Antiochus' understanding of the Stoics, see *Ac.* 2.16.)
13. Lucullus' characterization of Socrates' philosophical method as marked by rhetorical *dissimulatio* or 'irony' (see Cicero *Or.* 2.269–70 and *Brutus* 202) stands in marked contrast to Varro's portrait in *Ac.* 1.16–17. Lucullus deploys the rhetorical conception of irony in order to discount Socrates' protestations of ignorance; hence Cicero's objections in *Ac.* 2.74 (cf. *Ac.* 1.44–45). See J. Glucker, 'Socrates in the

[**VI 16**] "But let's assume, if you like, that those old doctrines didn't amount to knowledge. Has nothing changed now that these subjects have been investigated since the time Arcesilaus objected to Zeno (as it's thought), and, in his desire to overturn Zeno's definitions, tried to cloak the clearest things with darkness? (Though on our view, Zeno made no new discoveries, but revised his predecessors by altering their terminology.)[14] Arcesilaus' position wasn't widely held at first, despite the prominence he achieved by the sharpness of his intellect and his curiously attractive manner of argument. After him, it was retained by Lacydes alone. Later, however, it was strengthened by Carneades, who was four generations from Arcesilaus (since he was a student of Hegesinus, who was a student of Evandrus, the pupil of Lacydes, who had studied with Arcesilaus). But Carneades maintained the Academic position for a long time—he lived for ninety years—and his students did rather well. Clitomachus was his most industrious student, as the number of his books reveals, but Hagnon was equally remarkable for his intellect, Charmadas for his eloquence, and Melanthius of Rhodes for his charm.[15] (Metrodorus of Stratonicea was also thought to have known Carneades well.) [**17**] More recently, your teacher Philo worked with Clitomachus for many years; and while Philo lived the Academy didn't lack an advocate.

"But what I am now trying to do, namely, argue against the Academics, is something that some philosophers—and those no mean ones—didn't think should be done at all. They thought that there is no reason to argue with people who approve nothing; and they criticized Antipater the Stoic for being keen on doing so. In their view, there was no need to define knowledge, i.e., the 'apprehension' (or, to translate literally, the 'grasp') they call *katalêpsis*, and it was unscientific to try to persuade anyone that some things are apprehensible, because nothing is clearer than *enargeia*, as the Greeks put it. (I'll call this 'perspicuity' or 'plain evidence', if that's all right. I will coin words,

---

Academic Books and Other Ciceronian Works', in B. Inwood and J. Mansfeld (eds.), *Assent and Argument* (New York/Leiden 1997), pp. 58–88.

14. Lucullus means that Arcesilaus' arguments with Zeno were, in effect, an attack on the 'Platonic system' mentioned in *Ac.* 2.15, since Zeno's Stoicism was for the most part merely a restatement of that position. This was Antiochus' view; see *Ac.* 1.33–42 and 1.43, *DND* 1.16, and *Fin.* 5.74, with pages xxxi–xxxv.

15. 'Hagnon' is an editorial correction for the manuscripts' incoherent Latin. Reid suggested reading the name 'Aeschines' instead. Both are obscure Academics. See the Glossary of Names on these and the other Academics listed in this paragraph.

too, if need be, so that Cicero"—he named me with a smile—"doesn't think he is the only one allowed to do this.) So they didn't think that one could find a linguistic formulation more manifest than the 'plain evidence' itself or believe that things so clear should be defined. Another group of philosophers averred that they wouldn't have said anything on behalf of the 'plain evidence' first; but they thought that it was right to respond to arguments against it, to prevent people from being deceived. [18] But most philosophers don't disapprove of definitions even of evident things: they think that the subject is a suitable one for investigation and that their opponents are people worth arguing with.[16]

"Philo, however, introduced certain novelties <into the debate about apprehension>, because he found it difficult to resist the criticisms of the Academics' intransigence. But he openly lied, for which he was criticized by Catulus senior, and also led himself into precisely the position he was afraid of, as Antiochus explained. When he claimed that nothing was apprehensible (this is how I translate *akatalêpton*) if the latter was as Zeno defined it—i.e., as an impression (by now we are sufficiently used to this word for *phantasia* from yesterday's discussion) stamped and molded from its source in a way that it couldn't be from what wasn't its source.[17] (In our view, Zeno's definition was absolutely correct: how can you apprehend anything, in such a way that you are quite confident that it is apprehended or known, if something false could be just like it?)—Well, when Philo weakens and does away with this, he does away with the criterion of known and unknown.

---

16. The first two views about defining and defending a conception of apprehension are difficult to assign to specific philosophers. But Cicero notes a parallel division amongst Epicurean philosophers with regard to defining the good in *Fin.* 1.30–31, and since the Stoics unanimously accepted the use of definition, it is likely that Antipater's critics (the first group) were Epicurean. Antiochus' conception of 'perspicuity'—the manifest clarity warranting the truth of at least some of our perceptual impressions—is further explained in *Ac.* 2.45–46.

17. The Stoic definition of an 'apprehensible' impression—i.e., one that provides an apprehension of an object or state of affairs when its subject assents to it—is set out in more detail in *Ac.* 2.77; cf. *Ac.* 2.112–13, 2.145, and 1.40–42, with Sextus *M.* 7.248, Diogenes Laertius *Lives* 7.46 (*SVF* 2.65, 2.53). See pages xix–xxii and M. Frede, 'Stoic Epistemology', in K. Algra, J. Barnes, J. Mansfeld, and M. Schofield (eds.), *The Cambridge History of Hellenistic Philosophy* (Cambridge 1999), pp. 300–316. (The phrase 'from its source' translates *ex eo unde esset*, literally 'from the thing it was from'.) Cicero's use of the term 'apprehensible' to apply to cataleptic impressions, rather than to their objects, may be misleading; see pages xxxix–xliii.

The result is that nothing is apprehensible—so he ends up unintentionally back in the position he was trying to avoid.[18] For this reason, the purpose of my entire speech against the Academy is to retain the definition Philo wanted to overturn. And if I fail to attain that, I will concede that nothing is apprehensible.[19]

[VII 19] "Let's start with the senses.[20] Their judgments are so clear and certain that if human nature were given the choice—if a god demanded of it whether it is satisfied with its senses when they are sound and undamaged or whether it requires something better—I can't see what more it could ask for. But don't expect me to give counterarguments here dealing with the bent oar or the pigeon's neck: I'm not someone who claims that everything is exactly as our impressions represent it. Epicurus can see to that (and a lot more as well)! Still, in my judgment, there is a great deal of truth in the senses, providing they are healthy and properly functioning and all obstacles and impediments are removed. That's why we often want the light changed or the positions of the things we're looking at, and we reduce or increase their distance from us and alter many conditions until our vision itself provides the warrant for its own judgment.[21] The same goes

18. *Ac.* 2.18, along with a parallel passage in Sextus *PH* 1.235, provides our only information on the epistemological thesis of Philo's Roman Books (for which see *Ac.* 2.11–12 and 1.13). It appears from Antiochus' criticism that Philo effectively proposed dropping the clause from Zeno's definition that guaranteed that 'apprehensible' impressions could not be false (the third clause in the standard Greek versions)—presumably to allow for a fallible form of knowledge the Academic sceptics might accept. Antiochus objected that without that clause we can never be sure that we have apprehended anything, which he took to be incompatible with our conception of knowledge. See pages xxx–xxxi.

19. The arguments that follow (*Ac.* 219–60) presuppose the truth of the Stoic definition of apprehension. The remainder of Lucullus' speech is thus directed at Academic sceptics who accept Zeno's definition and deny only that it is ever satisfied—i.e., all the Academics prior to Philo's controversial Roman Books (cf. *Ac.* 2.12 fin.). See *Ac.* 2.78.

20. The arguments for the existence of apprehension in *Ac.* 2.19–27 rely on the Stoic definitions of the cognitive states of perception, technical perception, conception, memory, art, scientific knowledge, etc. Lucullus does not define 'perception', the first case, since it is the paradigmatic case covered directly by Zeno's definition in *Ac.* 2.18.

21. Antiochus' claim here that our senses are criterial of truth when their proper functioning is unimpeded finds a very close parallel in a passage from the Younger Stoics in Sextus *M.* 7.258.

for sounds, smells, and flavours. So none of us would demand keener judgment in any of the various senses.

[20] "But if you add the practice and skill that allow one's eyes to dwell on paintings or one's ears on songs, can anyone fail to see the power of the senses? There's so much detail painters see in shadow and relief that we don't see! And so much detail in music escapes us that practitioners in this field pick up on: at the first notes of the flute, before we even have an inkling of it, they say that it's the *Antiopa* or *Andromacha*![22] (It's unnecessary to talk about taste or smell, though they still have some sort of critical ability, even if it is imperfect.) What about touch, and especially the kind philosophers call the 'inner touch' of pleasure or pain? The Cyrenaics think that this is the only criterion of truth because it is what we experience.[23] [21] Can anyone really say that there's no difference between someone in pain and someone experiencing pleasure? Isn't a person who thinks that manifestly insane?

(21)[24] "Such are the things we claim are apprehended by the senses. The next set are just like them, though we don't claim that these are apprehended by the senses themselves, but by the senses in a certain respect—e.g., 'That is white', 'This is sweet', 'That is melodious', 'This is fine-scented', 'This is rough'. Our apprehension of this set now comes from the mind rather than the senses. Next comes: 'That is a horse', 'That is a dog'. Then we get the rest of the series, which connects more significant things and encapsulates what we might call a filled-out apprehension of things—e.g., 'If something is human it is a mortal animal partaking in reason.' It's from this set <of impressions> that our conceptions of things are stamped on our minds, and without them there can be no understanding, investigation, or argument.[25]

22. The Stoic notion of a technical (or expert's) impression is attested in Diogenes Laertius *Lives* 7.51 (*SVF* 2.61), with the additional remark that "a statue is seen in different ways by an expert and by the layman". (Sextus *M.* 7.248, however, notes that ordinary 'apprehensible' impressions are always formed with 'expertise'.) Cicero replies to this argument in *Ac.* 2.86.

23. Elsewhere the Cyrenaic criterion is said to be the subject's internal experience or affection (*pathos*), which covers perceptual and other sensations in addition to pleasure and pain; see *Ac.* 2.76 and 2.142, Sextus *M.* 7.191, Diogenes Laertius *Lives* 2.92, and Plutarch *Against Colotes* ch. 24 1120c.

24. Section numbers in round brackets mark the section divisions in older editions, including Reid's, where they diverge significantly from Plasberg's divisions.

25. This paragraph describes the Stoic view of the process of cognitive development leading to rationality, which is grounded in the possession of a set of

[22] "But suppose there were false conceptions (since you seemed to use the term 'conception' for *ennoia*). Well, if our conceptions were false or stamped on our minds from <true> impressions that couldn't be discriminated from false impressions, then how would we put them to use? How would we see what was compatible with something or incompatible with it?[26] In that case there's no room left at all for memory, which is our only storehouse not just of philosophy but also of the experience we derive from life and of all the arts. What sort of memory can there be of false contents? Can anyone remember anything he hasn't apprehended and doesn't retain in his mind?[27]

"Again, how can there be a systematic art that isn't constituted by not one or two but a set of apprehensions?[28] If you take that away, how will you distinguish the expert from the layman? It's no accident that we call one person an expert and not another: we say this when we see that one of them has a set of apprehensions and the other doesn't. Now there are two kinds of art: those that only discern their object by

conceptions obtained in this way; see *Ac.* 2.30, Aetius *Doctrines* 4.11 (*SVF* 2.83), and Diogenes Laertius *Lives* 7.49. If the first stage refers to nonconceptualized sensory input grasped by the senses alone—as opposed to just the sensory contribution to rational impressions—it should mark the prerational perception of infants. (The Stoics held that all *adult* human impressions are rational, and that rational impressions are all at least partly conceptualized; see Diogenes Laertius *Lives* 7.51 [*SVF* 2.61] and 7.63.) See M. Frede, 'The Stoic Conception of Reason', in K. Boudouris (ed.), *Hellenistic Philosophy* II (Athens 1994), pp. 50–63, and C. Brittain, 'Common Sense: Concepts, Definition, and Meaning In and Out of the Stoa', in B. Inwood and D. Frede (eds.), *Language and Learning* (Cambridge University Press, Cambridge 2005), part I.

26. "If something is human, it is a mortal animal partaking in reason" (*Ac.* 2.21 above) is a plausible example of a Stoic conception. Its logical form is supposed to illuminate the connection between concept-possession and rationality, since the Stoics took the ability to discern relationships of consequence (*akolouthia*, 'compatibility') to be an immediate result of achieving rationality (see Sextus *M.* 8.275–76 [*SVF* 2.223]) and this conception already shows the relation between being human and e.g., being rational. See Frede 1994.

27. Sextus *M.* 7.373 (*SVF* 2.56) indicates that Zeno had called memory "the storehouse of our impressions". A later Stoic source defined an individual memory as "the apprehension of a past assertible [i.e., roughly, a tensed proposition] which was apprehended through perception when it was present"; see Plutarch *The Cleverness of Animals* 961c. Cicero replies to these arguments in *Ac.* 2.106.

28. The Stoics defined an art or expertise as "a system of coordinately employed apprehensions aimed at something useful in life"; see Sextus *PH* 3.188 (and *SVF* 1.73, 2.93–97). Cicero replies to this argument in *Ac.* 2.107 and 2.144–46.

the mind and active or productive arts. So, in the former case, how can a geometer discern things that either don't exist or can't be discriminated from something false? Or, in the latter case, how can a musician compose rhythms and produce his verse? The same goes for the related arts whose activity consists entirely in performance and action. What could any art bring about if the person taking it up doesn't have a set of apprehensions?

[**VIII 23**] "The study of the virtues also provides very strong confirmation that many things are apprehensible. We define scientific knowledge as not just an apprehension of something, but one that is secure and immutable; so we claim that it, too, like the virtues, depends entirely on such apprehensions.[29] Likewise for wisdom, the art of life, which gives rise to the constancy of the wise. But suppose their constancy didn't depend on any apprehension or knowledge. Then I'd like to know where it does come from, and how; and why the good man resolves to endure every torture or be wracked by intolerable pain rather than give up on an appropriate action or his word. Why would he impose such heavy constraints as these on himself if he didn't rely on anything apprehended, known, or determined that would explain why this was fitting? It's impossible for anyone to value impartiality and fidelity so highly that there's no punishment he would refuse in order to maintain them, unless he has given his assent to <impressions> that can't be false.

[24] "As for wisdom itself, first, how will it deserve the name of wisdom if it does not know whether or not it *is* wisdom?[30] Second, how will wisdom have the courage to take on an action or to see it through to the end when there's nothing certain for it to follow? Indeed, when

29. The term 'scientific knowledge' translates the Greek *epistêmê*, which the Stoics used to describe both the epistemic status of individual apprehensions in the wise person and his knowledge of the sciences; see *Ac.* 2.145 and 1.41–42. The Stoics defined the major virtues as sciences or arts constituted by a set of theorems apprehended by the wise person (cf. *Ac.* 2.27), although they also recognized psychic health and strength as nontheoretical virtues; see Diogenes Laertius *Lives* 7.90 and Stobaeus *Eclogues* 2.7.5b p. 62 (*SVF* 3.278).

30. The Stoics defined wisdom as "the knowledge of divine and human things" and philosophy as the art that puts it into practice; see Sextus *M.* 9.13 and Aetius *Doctrines* 1 proem 2 (*SVF* 2.35–36). Its content includes the theorems of (Stoic) physics, ethics, and logic, as well as those of the particular moral virtues; see *Ac.* 2.114–17.

it doubts what the final good is and so doesn't know the end to which all actions are referred, how can it be *wisdom?* Here's another obvious point: something must be determined as the initial thing for wisdom to follow when it begins to act, and that initial thing must be suited to our nature. Otherwise our impulse (I mean this to translate *hormê*)— which stirs us to action, i.e., to have an impulse towards the object of our impression—can't be moved.[31] **[25]** But we must first have an impression of what moves our impulse, and believe it, and that can't happen if the object of our impression can't be discriminated from something false. So how can the mind be moved to have an impulse if it doesn't apprehend whether the object of the impression is suited to our nature or alien to it? Similarly, if no action strikes our mind as appropriate, it will never act at all, never be stirred to do anything, never be moved. But if we're ever going to perform any action the impression we have must strike us as true.[32]

[26] "Here's another point: if these Academic views are true, reason—the light and illumination of life, as we might call it—is entirely done away with. Will you persist in your perversity all the same? Reason provides the starting point for investigation and reason achieves virtue when it has strengthened itself by investigation; and investigation is the impulse for apprehension, ending in discovery. But no one discovers what is false, nor can something that remains unclear be a discovery—rather it is when something that had been veiled (so to speak) has been revealed that it is called a discovery. Thus <reason> contains both the starting point for investigation and its result, i.e., apprehension. That's why proof (*apodeixis* in Greek) is defined as

---

31. *Ac.* 2.24–25 relies on the Stoic theory of rational action. Action in general is caused by 'impulse' towards something striking the agent as "appropriate per se"; but in the case of rational agents it is caused by their *assent* to an "impulsive impression" of this sort; see Stobaeus *Eclogues* 2.7.9 p. 86 with Seneca *Letter* 113.18 (*SVF* 2.169), and T. Brennan, 'Stoic Moral Psychology', in B. Inwood (ed.), *The Cambridge Companion to the Stoics* (Cambridge 2003), pp. 257–94. (The Stoic notion of appropriate action, and its relation to what is 'suited to our nature', is set out in *Ac.* 1.36–37.)

32. This is the first example of the Stoic 'inactivity' (*apraxia*) argument; see page xxiii. But Lucullus seems to conflate two versions here. The Stoic theory of action he is drawing on only requires that the agent assent to an impulsive impression, not that the impression is 'apprehensible'; see *Ac.* 2.37 and Plutarch *Against Colotes* ch. 26 1122a–c. Their theory of happiness, however, also requires that the agent's actions are correct and selected wisely, which presupposes that they are guided by apprehension; see *Ac.* 2.39.

'an argument from apprehended premises leading to something that wasn't apprehended before.'[33]

[IX 27] "But if all impressions were the way the Academics say they are, so that they could just as well be false and no examination could discriminate them, how could we say that anyone had proved anything or discovered anything? What confidence could we have in proofs? And since philosophy ought to progress by arguments, how will it get results? Indeed, what will become of wisdom? Wisdom shouldn't doubt itself or its principles (what philosophers call its *dogmata*). None of its principles can be betrayed without a crime, because betraying a principle means betraying the law of truth and rectitude, which in turn gives rise to betrayals of friendships and of public duties.[34] So it's impossible to doubt our view that none of the wise person's principles can be false—or rather, that it's not enough for them not to be false, but they must also be secure, fixed, established, and immovable by any argument. But they can't be like that (or even give us the impression they're like that) on the Academic view, since the Academics claim that the impressions from which all principles arise don't differ at all from false impressions.

[28] "This gave rise to the demand Hortensius made, that you should at least admit that the wise person apprehends the claim that nothing is apprehensible. Antipater used to make the same demand: it is still consistent, he maintained, for someone affirming that nothing is apprehensible to say that this one claim is apprehensible though nothing else is.[35] But Carneades resisted him more forcefully, saying that, far from being consistent, it was actually grossly inconsistent: *someone*

---

33. This paragraph relies on the Stoic definitions of 'investigation', 'discovery', and 'proof' (it is cited by von Arnim as *SVF* 2.103 and 2.111). The first two definitions are paralleled in Clement *Miscellanies* 6.14 (*SVF* 2.102). The Stoics defined proof or demonstration as the subclass of true valid arguments meeting two further requirements: their premises are evident and are "revelatory of something <previously> unclear" in virtue of their intrinsic content; see Sextus *PH* 2.140–43 and *M.* 8.422 (*SVF* 2.239) and *Ac.* 2.44. The connection with reason is spelled out in *Ac.* 2.30–31.

34. See *Fin.* 3.48. Cicero responds to this claim in *Ac.* 2.133.

35. Antipater's argument for excepting the claim 'nothing is apprehensible' from its own scope is difficult to reconstruct from the dismissive remarks here and in Cicero's response at *Ac.* 2.109. But see M. Burnyeat, 'Antipater and Self-refutation: Elusive Arguments in Cicero's *Academica*', in B. Inwood and J. Mansfeld (eds.), *Assent and Argument* (New York/Leiden 1997), pp. 280–90.

claiming that nothing is apprehensible makes no exceptions; it follows nec-
essarily that, since it hasn't been excepted, the claim itself can't be apprehen-
sible, either.[36] **[29]** Antiochus seemed to press this point more cogently.
Given that the Academics take it to be a principle (you understand by
now that I mean by this a *dogma*) that nothing is apprehensible, he argued that they shouldn't vacillate over this principle as they do over
other things, particularly since it constitutes the essence of their view.
The determination of truth and falsity and what is known and unknown is, after all, the governing rule of any philosophy. So given that
they have taken up this view and want to teach which impressions
should be accepted or rejected, they clearly ought to apprehend the
principle itself, which is the source of every judgment of truth or falsity. The criterion of truth and the ethical end are, he argued, the two
principal issues in philosophy: no one can be wise while they're ig-
norant of either the origin of knowledge or the goal of appetition and
so don't know where one sets out from or needs to arrive. To hold
these in doubt, and not to have a confidence in them that can't be dislodged, is utterly foreign to wisdom. Antiochus' was thus a better approach for demanding from the Academics that they should at least
admit that they apprehend the claim that nothing is apprehensible.[37]
But I've said enough, I think, about the inconsistency of their entire
view—if someone who approves nothing can have a view at all.

[X 30] "The next topic is wide-ranging, but since it is a little more rec-
ondite (it includes a bit of physics), I'm afraid I may be granting my
opponent greater opportunity for licence. What else can I expect on a
hidden or obscure subject from someone who's trying to rob us of the
light? Still, it could be argued in detail that nature employed great
artistry in constructing first every animal and then humans in particular; and one could thus show the power the senses have: how first
impressions strike us, then impulse follows under their stimulus, with
the result that we then direct our senses towards the things we want
to apprehend.[38] For the mind, which is the source of the senses and is

36. Here and throughout the translation, the quoted claims or objections of the
speaker's principal opponents—Cicero or sceptical Academics in *Ac.* 2.11–62, Lucullus or Antiochus (or the Stoics) in *Ac.* 2.64–147—are italicized when they are not
reported in indirect speech.
37. Antiochus' revision of Antipater's argument relies on the view that philosophical 'schools' are individuated by a set of specific doctrines, attested in Diogenes
Laertius *Lives* 1.18–20; see page xxxiv. Cicero replies to this argument in *Ac.* 2.109–10.
38. A detailed account of the providential artistry displayed in the construction of

even itself identical to the senses, has a natural power it directs at the things by which it is moved.[39] Thus it seizes on some impressions for its immediate use, while storing away others as the source of memory; but it organizes the rest of our impressions by their similarities—and these give rise to our conceptions of things (which the Greeks sometimes call *ennoiai* and sometimes *prolêpseis* ['pre-conceptions']). After the addition of reason, proof, and a wealth of countless facts, one's apprehension of all those facts becomes apparent, and reason itself, now perfected in these stages, achieves wisdom.[40]

[31] "So since the human mind is wholly adapted for scientific knowledge of the world and for constancy of life, it welcomes knowledge beyond all else; and it loves *katalêpsis* ['apprehension'] (which, as I said, translates literally as a 'grasp') both on its own account—nothing is dearer to the mind than the light of truth—and for its use. Hence it uses the senses, produces the systematic arts as almost second senses, and strengthens philosophy to such a pitch that it creates virtue, the one thing that makes our whole lives coherent.[41] So people who deny that anything is apprehensible rob us of the very instruments or tools of life, or rather they completely overturn all of life and deprive animals of their minds. As a result it's difficult for me to criticize their rashness to the degree my case demands.

[32] "Though, as a matter of fact, I can't really determine what their intention or idea is.[42] When we press Academics with a point like 'If

---

human beings along these lines is given by the Stoic Balbus in Cicero's *DND* 2.133–53, especially 2.145–47.

39. On the Stoic view, the five perceptual faculties are parts of the soul emanating from the mind (*hêgemonikon*), but perception as such is a function of the latter; see Aetius *Doctrines* 4.4 and 4.21 (*SVF* 2.826, 2.836). Lucullus' qualified identification of the mind and senses is paralleled by the unnamed dogmatists in Sextus *M*. 7.307 (*SVF* 2.849) who claim that "the same faculty is in one respect that of thought and another that of perception."

40. This paragraph summarizes the development of reason through the stages Lucullus has identified in *Ac*. 2.21–23 and 2.26. Reason is perfected as the set of preliminary or pre-conceptions it started out as (*Ac*. 2.21–22) are 'articulated' into technical conceptions by investigation (*Ac*. 2.26); see *Ac*. 1.42, Plutarch fr. 215f (ed. Sandbach = *SVF* 2.104), and Brittain, 'Common Sense', 2005, part I.

41. The Stoic process leading from our natural love for apprehension to the development of the sciences and eventually to a coherent life—i.e., wisdom—is explained in *Fin*. 3.17–21. A rather different Antiochian model is given in *Fin*. 5.41–45.

42. In *Ac*. 2.32–36, Lucullus defends the role of the Stoic 'apprehensible' impression

your conclusions were true, everything would be unclear', sometimes they reply: *What's that to us? Is that our fault? Blame nature for con-
cealing truth 'in the abyss', as Democritus says.*[43] But some of them are
more sophisticated and demur at our charge that on their view everything is unclear. They try to show that something's being 'unclear' is
quite different from its being 'inapprehensible', and they distinguish
these two terms. So let's deal with the second group, the ones who
make this distinction. (We can forget about the ones who claim that
everything is as unclear as whether the number of stars is even or odd.
They're hopeless cases.) Their idea is—and I noticed that you were
particularly moved by this—that there are 'persuasive' or, as it were,
'truth-like' impressions, and this is what they use as their guiding rule
both for conducting their lives and in investigation and argument.[44]

[XI 33] "But how can this be a rule for truth and falsity if their indiscriminability means that we can't have a conception of truth or falsity?
If we do have one, after all, true and false should be as different as
right and wrong. But if there's no difference between them, there's no
rule: someone whose impressions <aren't distinctive of what's true>
but are shared by what's true and false alike can't have any criterion
or mark of truth at all. The Academics, of course, say that they're only
doing away with one point—that an impression can be true in such a
way that there couldn't be a false one just like it—while conceding
everything else. But it is childish for them to deny that they're doing
away with 'everything else', when the thing they've done away with
is the means by which everything is judged. It's as if someone were
to say that he hadn't deprived a person of perceptible objects when
he's had their eyesight removed! Just as in that case the objects are

---

as the criterion of truth by arguing that the Academics cannot find an alternative
'practical criterion' for action or debate.

43. Democritus fr. B117 (DK); a fuller version in Diogenes Laertius *Lives* 9.72 reads,
"In reality we know nothing, since truth is in the abyss." See *Ac.* 2.73 and page xxxvi.

44. The first group of Academics are identified in *Ac.* 2.59 as followers of Arcesilaus; cf. Eusebius *Preparation for the Gospel* 14.7.15 (= [Numenius] fr. 26.107–10 Des
Places). The second group of Academics relies on Carneades' distinction between
'persuasive' (though still 'inapprehensible') and 'unclear' impressions to provide
a range of 'practical criteria'. Cicero replies to the arguments of *Ac.* 2.32–36 in
2.98–111. See J. Allen, 'Academic Probabilism and Stoic Epistemology', *Classical
Quarterly* 44 (1994), pp. 85–113, and 'Carneadean Argument in Cicero's *Academic
Books*', in B. Inwood and J. Mansfeld (eds.), *Assent and Argument* (New York/Lei-
den 1997), pp. 217–56.

recognized by means of our eyes, so 'everything else' is recognized by means of impressions—but through a mark distinctive of true impressions, not one shared by true and false alike.[45] Hence, whether it's 'persuasive impressions' or 'unimpeded persuasive impressions', which was Carneades' idea, or something else again that you're proposing to follow, you're going to have to come back to the sort of impression at issue between us.[46] **[34]** However, if the properties of that impression are shared by false impressions, there won't be any criterion, because a distinctive property can't be marked by a shared sign.[47] But if the properties aren't shared, I have got what I want— since I am looking for a true impression such that there couldn't be a corresponding false impression.

"They make the same mistake when, under pressure from the truth itself, they try to distinguish 'perspicuous' from 'apprehensible' impressions. Their idea now is to show that there are perspicuous impressions that are true and stamped on the mind or intelligence but still aren't apprehensible. But how could you say that something is perspicuously white when it's possible that something black is giving rise to the impression that it's white? And how are we going to say that such impressions are perspicuous or accurately stamped when it's unclear whether the mind is moved in response to something true or vacuously?[48] That leaves you with no colour, body, truth, argument, senses, or anything perspicuous at all.

45. This objection is identical to one given by the Younger Stoics in Sextus *M.* 7.260. Galen also deployed it against the neo-Academic Favorinus in the second century CE; see Galen *The Best Teaching-Method* ch. 5.

46. The distinction between 'persuasive' and 'unimpeded and persuasive' impressions is explained in Sextus' more detailed presentation of Carneades' 'practical criterion' in *PH* 1.227–29 and *M.* 7.166–89. The distinction is criticized again in *Ac.* 2.44 and 2.59, and defended by Cicero in *Ac.* 2.104–9. See Allen 1994.

47. If it is not a mistake, Lucullus' suggestion that the distinctive mark of truth possessed by 'apprehensible' impressions is a 'sign' (repeated at *Ac.* 2.36) implies that Antiochus adopted or slipped into an Academic misinterpretation of the Stoic view (see Carneades' argument at Sextus *M.* 7.160–64). On the Stoic view, the 'apprehensible' impression is a natural and automatic criterion of truth; we do not *infer* the truth of its content from a 'sign'. See page xxxv and G. Striker, 'Academics Fighting Academics', in B. Inwood and J. Mansfeld (eds.), *Assent and Argument* (New York/Leiden 1997), pp. 257–76.

48. The Stoics distinguished perceptual impressions—i.e., perceptual thoughts caused by external objects in the appropriate way—from cases of illusion or

[**35**] "This has put them in the nasty position that there's always someone to ask them, no matter what they say, 'So that, at least, is something you apprehend?' But they laugh off such questions, because it's not their purpose to argue that people can't assert or contend for anything without some certain and distinctive mark of the thing they are advocating. But, in that case, what do you mean by your 'persuasive impressions'? If you mean that you rely on what strikes you and seems persuasive at, in effect, first glance, what could be sillier than that? (**36**) But if they say that they follow impressions that arise from some examination or detailed consideration, they still won't find any way out.[49] [**36**] First, because our trust in impressions that don't differ at all is removed from all of them equally. Second, because they allow that after the wise person has played his part thoroughly by subjecting everything to a meticulous examination, it's still possible for his impression to be truth-like and yet very far from being true. So even if they do approach the truth for the most part or its closest approximation, as they say they do, they still won't be able to be confident in their claims. If they're to have confidence, their impressions will have to have a distinct mark of truth. Since they have suppressed or obscured that, what truths will they think they have attained? Indeed, is there anything more absurd than their saying, '*I follow this because it is in fact a sign or evidence for that; but it may turn out that what it signifies is false or entirely nonexistent*'? But that's enough about apprehension. If anyone should have it in mind to undermine what I have said, the truth will have no difficulty defending itself even without my support.

[**XII 37**] "Now that we have a satisfactory understanding of the issues I have been explaining, I will make a couple of points about approval or assent (which the Greeks call *sunkatathesis*).[50] This is a big

---

imagination caused by 'vacuous motions of the mind'; see Diogenes Laertius *Lives* 7.50 and Aetius *Doctrines* 4.12.1–5 (*SVF* 2.54, 2.55), and *Ac.* 2.47–54 below.
49. These objections are also found in Sextus *M.* 7.435–38. Cicero's dismissive response to them in *Ac.* 2.98–101 suggests that they were aimed at the mitigated sceptics' increasing reliance on certain types of 'persuasive' impression as evidence for the truth; see page xxix and C. Brittain, *Philo of Larissa: The Last of the Academic Sceptics* (Oxford 2001), chapter 2.
50. Lucullus' discussion of assent in *Ac.* 2.37–39 draws on the Stoic theory introduced by Zeno; see *Ac.* 1.40–42. The first argument—*Ac.* 2.37, reprised at *Ac.* 2.38 fin.—depends on the Stoic view that 'perception', i.e., veridical perceptual thought,

topic, of course, but we did the groundwork a bit earlier. First, when I was explaining the power of the senses, it also became clear that many things are apprehended by them, which can't happen without assent. Second, since the principal difference between an animal and something inanimate is that an animal acts in some way (it's impossible even to imagine what an animal that did nothing would be like), we must either deprive the animal of its senses or allow it the faculty in our control, i.e., assent. [**38**] In fact, by not allowing people to perceive or assent, there's a sense in which the Academics actually rob them of their minds. For just as the balance of a scale must sink down when weights are placed on it, so the mind must yield to perspicuous <impressions>; just as an animal can't fail to have an impulse towards something that appears suited to its nature (what the Greeks call *oikeion*), it can't fail to approve a perspicuous thing it is presented with.[51]

"Although, if the views I have argued for are true, there's no point in talking about assent at all, since when someone apprehends anything, they automatically assent. But there are other consequences, too: neither memory, nor conceptions, nor the arts can exist without assent. Nor, more importantly, will the property of having anything in our power belong to someone who doesn't assent to anything. [**39**] But what place is there for virtue if nothing depends on ourselves? It is particularly absurd for the Academics to think that the vices are in their control and that no one errs except through assent, but that the same should not be true for virtue, when the constancy and strength of virtue are entirely constituted by the impressions it has assented to and approved.[52] At any rate, we must have an impression and assent

---

is a kind of apprehension (as Lucullus has argued in *Ac.* 2.19–21) and therefore involves assent; see *Ac.* 1.40 and 2.108. The second argument in this section (reprised at *Ac.* 2.39 fin.) is a version of the 'inactivity argument' set out in *Ac.* 2.24–25; but Antiochus departs from the Stoic theory by ascribing assent and voluntary action to animals here and in *Fin.* 5.38. Cicero replies to this argument in *Ac.* 2.108.

51. This argument appears to credit Antiochus with the view that 'apprehensible' impressions are necessarily met with assent. This is a view some scholars ascribe to Chrysippus and, with a qualification, to the Younger Stoics at Sextus *M.* 7.257; but *Ac.* 2.53, 2.94, and 2.107 imply that this was not the Stoic view. If so, the argument should perhaps be taken as a claim about our natural propensity to assent in such cases, rather than a strict necessity. Cicero replies to this argument in *Ac.* 2.108.

52. The Stoics held that voluntary action and moral responsibility depend on assent (i.e., our ability to make judgments about the world); see *Ac.* 1.40. But since suspending assent is as voluntary as giving it under the Stoic theory, Lucullus'

to it before we act; so anyone who does away with impressions or assent does away with action from life altogether.

[**XIII 40**] "Now let's look at the arguments our Academic opponents usually employ against us.[53] But before I do that, I should let you see the basic 'building blocks' their position depends on. First, then, they devise a classificatory system for 'impressions' (as we are calling them), defining their nature and kinds, including the sort that is apprehensible—and they do so in as much detail as the Stoics. Second, they set out two points that constitute practically the whole subject of our debate:

- when an impression is such that there can be another impression just like it, not differing from it at all, it is not possible that one of them is apprehensible, while the other isn't.

- they <count as> 'not differing at all', not only when they are just like each other in every respect, but also when they can't be discriminated.

Once this basis is in place, they bring their whole case together in a single proof as follows:

[1] some impressions are true, others false; and,

[2] a false impression isn't apprehensible; but,

[3] every true impression is such that one could also have a false impression just like it. And,

[4] when two impressions are such that they don't differ at all, it isn't possible that one of them is apprehensible, while the other isn't. Therefore,

---

formal argument seems ineffective against the Academics. They agreed that (epistemic) virtue and vice depend on our use of the faculty of assent, since they argued that assent leads to opinion and error (*Ac.* 2.66–67), while the suspension of assent is wise (*Ac.* 2.108).

53. In *Ac.* 2.40–58, Lucullus counters the Academics' indiscriminability (*aparallaxia*) arguments designed to show the nonexistence of 'apprehensible' impressions. *Ac.* 2.40–44 sets out the Academic 'core argument' and Antiochus' general objections to it; *Ac.* 2.45–58 examines the two main types of Academic argument for indiscriminability.

[5] no impression is apprehensible.[54]

[41] "They take it that two of the premises they need for the conclusion they're driving at are conceded, since no one denies them. They are:

[2¹] false impressions aren't apprehensible; and,

[4¹] when two impressions don't differ at all, it's not possible that one is such that it is apprehensible, while the other such that it isn't.

But they defend the remaining two premises at length and with various arguments, namely, the premises:

[1¹] some impressions are true, others are false; and,

[3¹] every impression from something true is such that there could also be an impression from something false just like it.[55]

[42] "They don't skim over these two claims—in fact, they elaborate them in a way that demonstrates a good deal of attention and diligence. They divide the subject into three major parts. The first deals with the senses, and the second with the products of the senses and of ordinary experience (which it is their intention to render obscure). Then they come to the third part, arguing that nothing is apprehensible by reason or inductive inference, either.[56] They also chop up these

---

54. The Academic 'core argument' set out in this paragraph is recapitulated by Cicero in *Ac.* 2.83; cf. Sextus *M.* 7.154 and 7.160–64. See pages xx–xxii and M. Frede, 'Stoics and Skeptics on Clear and Distinct Impressions', in M. Burnyeat (ed.), *The Skeptical Tradition* (London 1983), pp. 65–93. Cicero's use of 'apprehensible' to describe cataleptic impressions—i.e., ones providing apprehension of an object or state of affairs—rather than their objects may be particularly misleading here; see pages xxxix–xliii. (The two points preceding the argument are glosses on premise [4], the crucial move for the argument; the second point, about the irrelevance to this argument of the distinction between metaphysical indiscernibility and phenomenal indiscriminability, is elaborated in *Ac.* 2.52, 2.58, and 2.84.)

55. The superscripts added to the premise numbers here and in *Ac.* 2.44 indicate minor variations in the phrasing of the premise. The premises are also rephrased in *Ac.* 2.83.

56. The three parts of the Academics' argument structure Lucullus' defence of apprehension in *Ac.* 2.19–27 (*Ac.* 2.19–20 covers the senses, *Ac.* 2.21–22 their products,

general parts into even smaller sections, doing the same for the other parts as you saw them do with the senses in yesterday's discussion. And their idea in each single case, dissected into its smallest parts, is to make out that all true impressions have corresponding false impressions that don't differ at all from the true ones—and since that's what impressions are like, they aren't apprehensible.

[**XIV 43**] "While I acknowledge that this precision is absolutely appropriate for philosophy, it is quite inapposite for the cause of the Academics deploying it. Using definitions, partitions, and other technical figures—as well as similarities and dissimilarities and their detailed or fine distinction—is the method of people who are confident that the views they defend are true, stable, and certain, not of people proclaiming that they are no more true than false. What would they do, after all, if anyone were to ask them whether one of their definitions could be applied to absolutely anything else? If they said it could, what grounds would they have to claim that their definition is true? If they said it couldn't, they would have to admit that the thing articulated in their definition was apprehensible, given that even their true definition couldn't be applied to anything false.* But that's the last thing they want to do!

"The same points can be made at every stage of their argument. [**44**] If they say that they clearly discern the things they're arguing about, without being impeded by any overlap between their <true and false> impressions, they will be admitting that they apprehend them. But if they deny that true impressions can be distinguished from false, what basis can they have for further progress?[57] We will block them in the same way we have already. An argument just can't be probative unless you take the premises you're going to use to be such that there can't be any false ones just like them. Hence, if an argument that has advanced by relying on apprehended premises has the result that

---

and *Ac.* 2.22–27 reason). They also structure Cicero's attack in *Ac.* 2.79–98 (*Ac.* 2.79–87 deals with the senses, *Ac.* 2.88–90 with their products, and *Ac.* 2.91–98 with reason). Chrysippus' use of this division is attested in *Ac.* 2.87. (The term 'inductive inference' translates *coniectura*, which often has the weaker sense of 'guesswork'. But the context demands a method or faculty the Stoics take to be capable of yielding apprehension.)

57. This argument reapplies the practical objections of *Ac.* 2.33–36 to the Academics' philosophical methods; a similar argument is ascribed to Aenesidemus in Photius *Library* 212 170a.31–38.

nothing is apprehensible—how could we find anything more inconsistent than that? The very nature of a formal argument promises to disclose something nonapparent, and, to that end, to apply truths from perception and perspicuous premises.[58] So what sort of argument can the Academics make, when they make out that their claims are about their impressions rather than what is the case?

"Their worst mistake, however, is to take these two radically inconsistent premises to be consistent: first,

[1²] there are some false impressions (and in accepting this they own that some are true); and then again,

[3²] there is no difference at all between true and false impressions.

But you assumed the first premise as if there were a difference—hence the former is undermined by the latter, and the latter by the former.[59]

[45] "Still, let's press on a bit and do so without seeming partial to our own views: let's go through what they say in detail so we don't leave anything out. The first thing to note is that the perspicuity I mentioned is sufficiently forceful to disclose to us what is, just as it is.[60] But to make our grip on perspicuous things more stable and constant, we still need a better method or greater diligence—otherwise we may be driven away from things that are clear in their own right by sleights of hand, i.e., by sophisms. (Epicurus wanted to repair the errors that seem to disturb our apprehension of the truth by just saying that it is proper to the wise person to divorce opinion from perspicuity. But he got nowhere because he didn't do anything to remove the error of opinion itself.)[61] [XV 46] Hence, since there are two factors working against perspicuous or evident things, two remedies are required. One problem is that people don't cast their minds or concentrate enough on perspicuous things to be able to recognize the remarkable clarity they manifest. The other is that some people give up on the

---

58. See the definition of 'proof' in *Ac.* 2.26.
59. A similar objection is ascribed to Aenesidemus in Photius *Library* 212 170a.26–31. Cicero responds to this argument in *Ac.* 2.111.
60. See *Ac.* 2.17. As Lucullus indicates at the end of *Ac.* 2.46, his arguments in *Ac.* 2.19–27 were direct defences of 'perspicuity'.
61. Epicurus fr. 223 (Usener). See Epicurus' *Letter to Herodotus* 49–52 (Diogenes Laertius *Lives* 10.49–52) and *Ac.* 2.79–80.

truth when they have been outmaneuvered and deceived by sophistic arguments they can't resolve. So we need to have at hand both responses that can be made in defence of perspicuity—which I have already given—and the weapons required to block their arguments and dispel their sophisms—which I have decided to do next.

[47] "Since the Academics have a methodical approach, I will set out their arguments systematically. The first type tries to show that there are often <persuasive> impressions of things that don't exist at all, since our minds are moved vacuously by what is not the case in exactly the same way as by what is the case.[62] *After all,* they say, *you claim that some impressions are sent by god, for instance in dreams and revelations from oracles, auspices, or entrails.* (They report that these are accepted by their Stoic opponents.) *Well,* they ask, *how is it that god can make persuasive impressions that are false, but can't make persuasive impressions that approximate the truth very closely? Or, if he can also do that, why not persuasive impressions that can only just be discriminated <from true impressions>, though with considerable difficulty? And if that, why <not false but persuasive impressions> that don't differ at all <from true impressions>?*

[48] "Next, they point out that *the mind can be moved just by itself, as the pictures we produce in our imagination and the occasional impressions of sleepers or madmen reveal.* So it's plausible that the mind can also be moved in such a way that it can't discriminate whether such impressions are true or false—and even in such a way that there's no difference between such impressions <and true impressions>. If so, when people tremble or grow pale, there would be no way to distinguish whether their trembling and pallor was brought about by a mental motion induced by themselves or because something terrible was presented from without: there would be no difference between the internally and externally induced cases.* To sum up, *if no false impressions are persuasive, that's another argument. But if they exist, why not also <false> impressions that can't easily be discriminated <from true impressions>? Why not <false> impressions that really don't differ at all <from true impressions>? Especially when you yourselves say that the wise person in a state of madness restrains himself from all assent because there's no apparent distinction between his <true and false> impressions.*

---

62. The first type of Academic argument, from abnormal states of mind, is examined in *Ac.* 27–53; see Sextus *M.* 7.402–8 and pages xxi–xxii. The supplement of 'persuasive' is necessary here because the Stoics (and Antiochus) accept the existence of 'vacuous impressions'; see the note on *Ac.* 2.34 (and *Ac.* 2.49 below). Cicero responds to Lucullus' objections in *Ac.* 2.88–90.

[**XVI 49**] "Antiochus had a great deal to say against all these 'vacuous impressions'—there was a whole day's discussion about this one matter—but I suppose I shouldn't do the same, but just give the main points. And the first thing to criticize is their use of an extremely sophistic form of argument—one that usually meets with very little approval in philosophy—in which something is added or subtracted little by little and progressively. (They call this the 'sorites' ['heap'], because they produce a heap by the addition of single grains.) This is clearly a fallacious and sophistic form of argument.[63] You build it up like this: if god has presented a sleeper with an impression that's persuasive, why not also one that's extremely truth-like? Next, why not one that's difficult to discriminate from a true impression? Next, one that can't even be discriminated? And finally, one that doesn't differ from a true impression at all?

"If you reach this far because I have conceded each successive point to you, it will be my fault; but if you proceed on your own authority, it's yours. [**50**] Who will grant you the assumptions that god can do everything or that he would act like this if he could?[64] Again, how is it that you assume that if one thing can be similar to another, it follows that it can also be difficult to discriminate from it and then that they can't even be discriminated and finally that they are identical? In that case, if wolves are similar to dogs, you'll end up saying that they are identical.* No doubt some actions that aren't honourable are similar to those that are, and some things that aren't good to goods, and some quite inartistic products to artistic ones: so why do we hesitate to affirm that there is no difference between them in *these* cases? Can we really not see incompatibilities? In fact, nothing can be transferred from its own kind into another kind.* But if you could bring it about that impressions of distinct kinds didn't differ at all, we would

63. Cicero sketches a formal or logical sorites puzzle in *Ac.* 2.90–92. Carneades was notorious for his use of the nonformal epistemological analogue employed above; see, e.g., his theological arguments in Cicero *DND* 3.43–52 and Sextus *M.* 9.182–84.
64. Chrysippus allowed that god sometimes presents us with false impressions through dreams or prophecies, although he denied that this amounted to deception, since god's intention is not that we should assent to them, but just to influence us to pursue a certain action in response to them; see Plutarch *Stoic Contradictions* ch. 47 1055f and 1057a–b (*SVF* 3.177). (The Academics in Cicero's works often assume that the Stoic god can do anything; see *DND* 3.92 and *Div.* 2.86. But the Stoics denied that god can do wrong; see Seneca *Letter* 95.47 [*SVF* 2.1117].)

discover things that could belong both to their own and to another kind. How can that happen?[65]

[51] "Next, there is one riposte for all 'vacuous' impressions, whether they are fashioned by the imagination (which we concede does often happen), or in repose or through wine or insanity. We will just say that perspicuity—which is the thing we must keep a very tight grip on—is missing from all impressions of this sort. Is anyone representing something to himself or picturing it by imagination unaware of the difference between perspicuous and 'vacuous' impressions, once he has roused and recollected himself?

"The same argument applies to dreams. Or do you think that when Ennius had been walking in the garden with his neighbour Servius Galba, he said, 'It seemed to me I walked with Galba'? Yet when he had a dream, he related it thus:

'The poet Homer seemed to be present.'[66]

Likewise in the *Epicharmus:*

'I seemed to dream that I was dead.'[67]

We make light of such impressions as soon as we have woken up, since we don't consider them on a par with what we have done in the forum.

[XVII 52] "*But while we are having them, their 'look' during sleep is the same as that of the things we see when we are awake.*[68] First, there is a difference—but let us leave that aside. What we *do* say is that there isn't the same force or soundness in the mind or senses of people who are

---

65. Lucullus' argument relies on the Stoic doctrine of the identity of indiscernibles, i.e., of the uniqueness of individuals and of individual kinds or species; see *Ac.* 2.56. True and false impressions cannot be completely identical, since the identity of two 'kinds' would rule out the grounds for the existence of either (and our ability to single them out); see *Ac.* 2.54, 2.56, and 2.58.

66. Ennius *Annales* Bk. 1 fr. 3 (Skutsch). See the Glossary of Names for explanations of the context of the literary citations by Lucullus.

67. Ennius *Epicharmus* fr. 1 [*Varia* 45] (Vahlen).

68. Here and in *Ac.* 2.58, Lucullus' term *species* is translated as 'look', with the implication that the Academic argument he objects to is a new one, concerned with the psychological or phenomenological content of impressions as they are experienced. But the term can also be construed as a variant for the 'kinds' mentioned in *Ac.* 2.50 and 2.55; see Striker 1997, pp. 270–72 with her n. 6.

asleep as there is in people who are awake. Not even intoxicated people do what they do with the same approval as the sober: they doubt, they hesitate, they sometimes recollect themselves, and they assent more weakly to their impressions—and when they have slept it off, they understand how light those impressions were. The same thing happens to the insane, so that when they are beginning to go mad, they feel it and they say that they have impressions of things that are not the case; and when they're recovering, they realize it, and repeat that line of Alcmaeon's:

'but my heart agrees with the vision of my eyes not at all . . .'[69]

[53] *"But the wise person restrains himself in madness so as not to approve falsehoods in the place of truths.*[70] And he often does at other times, too, if his senses happen to be slow or heavy in some way, or if his impressions are too obscure, or if he is prevented from discerning by lack of time. Nevertheless, this point—that the wise person sometimes restrains his assent—tells entirely against you: for if there were no difference between impressions, he would either always restrain his assent, or never.*

"But you can see from this type of argument as a whole what a silly approach the Academics have in their desire to confound everything. *We are looking for the criterion of someone serious, constant, strong-minded, and wise: we are using the examples of dreamers, madmen, and drunkards. Do we realize how inconsistent all the arguments of this type are? If we did, we would not be so ridiculous as to cite people burdened by sleep or bereft of their minds and hence to assert both that there is a difference between the impressions of the sober and sane and those of people otherwise affected, and that there is no difference.* [54] Don't they even notice that they are rendering everything unclear—which is not their idea at all? (I call 'unclear' what the Greeks call '*adêla*'.)[71] If things are such that it makes no

---

69. Ennius *Alcmaeon* fr. 15a (Jocelyn). See *Ac.* 2.89–90.

70. Although this Academic argument (first alluded to in *Ac.* 2.48) is not elaborated or defended by Cicero, it may imply that the Stoic sage is supposed to suspend assent even from 'apprehensible' impressions under certain conditions, as Cicero argues in *Ac.* 2.94 and 2.107. See the note on *Ac.* 2.38 above.

71. Lucullus' objection is that the first type of Academic argument is inconsistent with the Carneadian Academics' advocacy of 'persuasive impressions' as the criterion for their own action. If the Academics' impressions are no more vivid or coherent than those of a madman, they should accept Arcesilaus' view that everything is completely 'unclear', rather than attempting to discriminate an intermediate category between the 'unclear' and the 'apprehensible'; see *Ac.* 2.32 and 2.59.

difference whether one's impressions are those of an insane or sane person, who can be sure of his own sanity? Trying to achieve this result is itself a sign of no slight insanity!

"<The second type of Academic argument> involves the childish pursuit of the similarities of twins or of seals stamped from signet rings.[72] Who on our side denies that similarities exist, given that they are apparent in many things? Yet if it is enough to do away with apprehension that many things are similar to many others, why aren't you satisfied with that, especially when we concede it? Why do you go on to maintain something the nature of things does not permit, by denying that each thing is in its own kind and just as it is, i.e., that there aren't any shared features that don't differ at all between two or more things?[73] Take it as granted that eggs are very similar to eggs, and bees to bees: what are you fighting for?* What are you driving at with your twins? That they are similar—the point with which you could have been satisfied—is conceded; but your idea is that they aren't similar but absolutely identical, which simply cannot happen.

[55] "Next you fly off to the physicists, the very people who are particularly ridiculed in the Academy (and even you, Cicero, will not be able to keep yourself away from them shortly). *Democritus claims that there are innumerable worlds,* you say, *and indeed worlds such that some of them are not only similar to each other, but so altogether perfectly and absolutely matched that there is simply no difference between them at all. And the same goes for people.*[*74] Then you demand that, if one world is so

72. The second type of Academic argument, from the similarities of objects, is examined in *Ac.* 2.54–58; see Sextus *M.* 7.408–10 and pages xxi–xxii. Cicero responds to Lucullus' objections in *Ac.* 2.84–87.
73. Lucullus appears to overstate this objection: the problem is not 'shared features', which provide the grounds for the similarities he acknowledged, but the idea that they might completely overlap. See the analogous arguments about impressions in *Ac.* 2.33–34 and 2.44.
74. Democritus fr. A81 (DK); see *Ac.* 2.125 and Brittain and Palmer 2001, pp. 66–67. Elsewhere Democritus is ascribed the views that there are innumerable coexistent, though perishable, worlds and that a type-identical world might recur; see Diogenes Laertius *Lives* 9.44 (fr. A1 DK) and Hippolytus *Refutation of All Heresies* 1.13 (fr. A40 DK), and Simplicius *Commentary on Aristotle's* On the Heavens p. 310 (fr. A 82), respectively. But only Cicero—and perhaps [Hippocrates] *Letter* 10 (Littré 9.322)—suggests that he argued for the existence of innumerable simultaneous and identical worlds. (The text of the rather abrupt final sentence is corrupt, perhaps because several phrases have been lost. But the sense required seems clear from the end of *Ac.* 2.56.)

matched with another world that there is not even the slightest difference between them, it should be conceded to you that in this world
of ours, too, something is so matched with something else that it does
not differ at all, that there is no difference between them. *Why,* you will
ask, *is it not only possible but actually the case that in other worlds (indeed,
in innumerable other worlds) there are innumerable Quinti Lutatii Catuli
made out of those atoms from which Democritus avers that everything comes
to be, but in all of this world another Catulus cannot be brought about?*

[**XVIII 56**] "Well, in the first place, you summon me to Democritus,
with whom I do not agree. In fact, I refute him on the grounds—clearly
explained by more refined physicists—that individual things have individual properties.*[75] Imagine that those ancient Servilii (the ones
who were twins) were as similar as they are said to have been; do you
suppose that they were actually identical? They were not recognized
apart in public, but they were at home; nor by other families, but they
were by their own. Or don't we see that it comes about as a matter of
course that, once we have had practice, we discriminate easily people
who we thought we could never tell apart—so easily that they do not
seem in the slightest degree similar?

[**57**] "You can put up a fight on this point, if you like: I won't fight back.
I will even concede that the wise person himself—the subject of our
whole discussion—will suspend his assent when confronted by similar things that he does not have marked off; and that he will never assent to any impression except one such that it could not be false. But
he has a particular skill by which he can distinguish true from false impressions in <normal> cases and he must bring experience to bear on
those similarities.[76] Just as a mother discriminates her twins as her eyes
become accustomed to them, so you, too, will discriminate them, if you
practise. You see how the similarity of eggs to each other is proverbial?
Nevertheless, we have heard that there were quite a few people on

75. Lucullus means the Stoics, as Cicero makes explicit in *Ac.* 2.85; see Plutarch
Common Conceptions ch. 36 1077c (*SVF* 2.112) and the texts collected in *SVF* 2.376–98
with D. Sedley, 'The Stoic Criterion of Identity', *Phronesis* 27 (1982), pp. 255–75, and
S. Menn, 'The Stoic Theory of Categories', *Oxford Studies in Ancient Philosophy* 27
(1999), pp. 215–47.
76. The skill of the wise consists in their highly developed recognitional ability,
grounded in the set of apprehensions that constitutes their minds and their complete avoidance of opinion, i.e., of assent to nonapprehensible impressions; see *Ac.*
2.107. But, as Lucullus points out here, their recognitional ability is limited to some
extent by their particular experience.

Delos, when things were going well for them there, who used to rear a great number of hens for their living; well, when these men had inspected an egg, they could usually tell which hen had laid it.

[58] "Nor does this work against us, since it is all right for us *not* to be able to discriminate those eggs: that doesn't make it any more reasonable to assent that this egg is that one, as if there were absolutely no difference between them.** I have my rule—to judge such impressions true as cannot be false—from which I may not depart by a hair's breadth (as they say), lest I confound everything. If there is no difference between <true and false impressions>, that's the end not only of our apprehension of true and false, but also of their nature. Hence another view you sometimes express is also absurd—that, when impressions are stamped on our minds, you don't assert that there is no difference between the stampings themselves, but only between their 'looks' or, as it were, 'forms'.[77] As if impressions were not judged by their 'looks'! And they won't have any credibility once the mark of true and false has been removed.

[59] "It's particularly absurd, however, for you to say that you follow persuasive impressions if you are not impeded in any way.[78] First, how can you *not* be impeded when true and false impressions are not distinct? Second, how can something be the criterion of truth when it is shared by falsehood? These views necessarily spawned the Academics' *epokhê*, i.e., suspension of assent. Though Arcesilaus was rather more consistent in this, if what some people think about Carneades is true, since if nothing is apprehensible—a view both held—we must do away with assent. (What is more pointless than approving something that isn't known?) But we heard yesterday that Carneades was occasionally liable to sink so low as to say that the wise person would have opinions, i.e., that he would err.[79] In my view, at any rate, it is not as certain that some things are apprehensible—about which I have now been arguing for too long—as that the wise person will have no opinions, i.e., that he will never assent to anything false or unknown.

---

77. See the note to *Ac.* 2.52.
78. See *Ac.* 2.33–36 and 2.104.
79. An allusion to Catulus' discussion of his father's mitigated scepticism in the lost *Catulus;* see *Ac.* 2.12, 2.18, and 2.148. This is the Academic position ascribed by Philo and Metrodorus to Carneades in *Ac.* 2.78 and rejected by Cicero in *Ac.* 2.66–67. See pages xxviii–xxx.

[60] "That leaves their claim that one should argue on either side of every question in order to discover the truth.[80] Well, I'd like to see what they have discovered. *It is not our practice,* he says, *to display our view.* What actually are these mysteries? Why do you hide your views as if they were something shameful? *So that our students,* he says, *are guided by reason rather than authority.* What if they were guided by both? Is that really worse? Still, there is one thing they don't hide: that nothing is apprehensible. Is their authority in no way prejudicial on that matter? It seems to me to be extremely prejudicial. Who would have followed such perspicuously false and manifestly preposterous views without Arcesilaus' mastery of arguments and force of eloquence and Carneades' even greater powers?

[XIX 61] "That is pretty much what Antiochus said in Alexandria then. (He repeated it still more insistently, many years later when he was with me in Syria, shortly before he died.)[81] But now I have established my case, and since you are a great friend as well as a few years younger than me," he said to me, "I won't hesitate to give you a warning. You have extolled philosophy vigorously enough to stir our friend Hortensius despite his earlier disagreement.[82] So how can you follow a philosophy that confounds true and false, cheats us of a criterion, robs us of approval, and makes us bereft of our senses? The Cimmerians were deprived of the sight of the sun by a god or nature, or perhaps by the location of the place they lived in; yet even they had fires they could use for light. But the people you approve have shrouded everything in so much darkness that they have left us without even a spark to make things out with. In fact, if we followed them, we would be constrained by bonds that would prevent us from moving at all. [62] For by doing away with assent, they have done away

---

80. The Academics always claimed that their method of argument 'on either side' was a positive search for truth. Some later Academics also considered it the best way to teach philosophy; see *Ac.* 2.7–9, Galen *The Best Teaching-Method* 1, and pages xi–xii and xxviii. (The Academic criticism of 'authority' is dramatized in *Ac.* 2.62–63.) Augustine used this passage to argue that the Academics had an esoteric doctrine of dogmatic Platonism; see his *Against the Academics* 3.37–43 and fr. 35 below (cf. Sextus *PH* 1.234). But the objection Lucullus actually makes is that Academic teaching amounts to nothing more than an endorsement of scepticism.

81. Lucullus and Antiochus were companions in Alexandria in the mid 80s BCE during the First Mithridatic War and in Syria in the late 70s during the Second Mithridatic War; see *Ac.* 2.4.

82. Lucullus alludes to the fictional success of Cicero in the *Hortensius,* the (lost) companion dialogue to the first edition of the *Academica.*

with every mental motion and practical action—something that not only can't be done rightly, but can't be done at all! You should also consider whether this isn't a view that you should be the last person to defend. Weren't you the person who revealed a deeply hidden affair, who brought it into the light, and said on oath that you had 'ascertained' it (as I could also have said, since I knew it from you)?[83] And now you're going to say that there is nothing that can be known or apprehended? Please, please, take care, or the authority you have from that excellent affair will be diminished by your own words." When he had said that, he came to a stop.

Interlude

[63] Hortensius was extremely impressed, as he had been throughout Lucullus' speech, even to the point of raising his hands in admiration several times—quite understandably, since I don't think that the case against the Academy has ever been made more precisely. So he started encouraging me to give up my view as well, whether as a joke or because he really thought so, I wasn't quite sure. Then Catulus said to me: "If Lucullus' speech shifted you—and it was clearly a feat of memory, precision, and elegance—I have nothing to say: I don't think that you should be deterred from changing your view if you think you ought to. But I would advise you not to let yourself be moved by his authority. He came pretty close to warning you just now," he said with a smile, "to watch out for a dastardly tribune (and as you can see, there will always be a good supply of them!).* So one of them may march you off to the assembly and ask how it is consistent for you to say that nothing can be discovered for certain when you said before that you had 'ascertained' something! Please don't let that frighten you! As for the case itself, I for one would rather you disagreed with Lucullus; but if you yield to him, I won't be particularly surprised. After all, I recall that Antiochus also abandoned his view as soon as he saw fit, although he had thought otherwise for many years!"[84] When Catulus had said that, everyone looked to me.

---

83. Lucullus alludes to Cicero's role in uncovering and suppressing the Catilinarian conspiracy during his consulship in 63 BCE; see page ix. Cicero's robust self-congratulation for his achievement irritated his peers, who soon began to make jokes about things he was alleged to have 'ascertained'; see Cicero *ad Att.* 1.14.5, *ad Fam.* 5.5.2, and, e.g., [Sallust] *Invective* 3.
84. See *Ac.* 2.71.

Cicero's Speech

[**XX 64**] At this point I was no less worked up than I tend to be in my more important legal cases, so I started my speech with something along these lines.[85] "The part of Lucullus' speech on the subject at hand, Catulus, moved me as one by someone learned, eloquent, and well prepared, who passed over nothing that could be said for his case—but not so much that I have lost faith in my ability to reply to him. His authority, however, is so great that it clearly would have moved me, if you hadn't opposed it with your own no lesser authority. So I will get to it—though, if I may, I will first say a few words about my own reputation.

[**65**] "If I have applied myself to this philosophical view in particular from a desire for contention or ostentation, I take it that my character and nature should be condemned, not just my stupidity. Even in unimportant matters intransigence is criticized and misrepresentation is punished by law as well. So when it's a question of the condition and plan of my entire life, would I really want to contend aggressively with other people or waste their time and my own as well? So if I didn't think it inept in an argument of this sort to do something that is occasionally done in debates about the republic, I would swear an oath by Jupiter and my ancestral gods: I am burning with the desire to discover the truth and my arguments express what I really think. [**66**] How could I not desire to find the truth when I rejoice if I find something truth-like?[86] But just as I judge this, seeing truths, to be the best thing, so approving falsehoods in the place of truths is the worst. Not that I am someone who never approves anything false, never assents, and never holds an opinion; but we are investigating the wise person. I am actually a great opinion-holder: I'm not wise. I don't guide my thoughts by that little star, the Cynosure,

---

85. Cicero's speech responds to the criticisms of Academic scepticism given by Lucullus in *Ac.* 2.11–60 and in the lost *Catulus* ('yesterday'). It is divided into three main sections: a complicated introduction discussing various historical controversies (*Ac.* 2.64–78); a restatement and defence of the Academic arguments against Stoic apprehension and in favour of the Academic 'practical criterion' (*Ac.* 2.79–111); and a critical review of the dissensions of dogmatic philosophers designed to show their failure to achieve apprehension, while also undermining Antiochus' pretensions to represent the Old Academy rather than the Stoa (*Ac.* 2.112–46).

86. Cicero defends his position as an Academic sceptic in the general terms set out in *Ac.* 2.7–9. Charges of contention or intransigence and misrepresentation were also made against Arcesilaus; see *Ac.* 1.44 and 2.14.

'in whose guidance the Phoenicians trust at night in the deep,' as Aratus says, and thus sail on a more direct course, because they watch the star that 'revolves on an inner course with a short circuit'.[87] Rather, I guide my thoughts by the bright Septentriones (*Helikê* in Greek),[88] i.e., by more easily accessible principles, not ones refined almost to the vanishing point. As a result, I err or wander farther afield. But it's not me, as I said, but the wise person we are investigating. When these <less precise> impressions strike my mind or senses sharply, I accept them, and sometimes even assent to them (although I don't apprehend them, since I think that nothing is apprehensible). I'm not wise, so I yield to these impressions and can't resist them.[89]

"As for the wise person, however, Arcesilaus agrees with Zeno that his greatest strength is precisely to make sure that he isn't tricked and see to it that he isn't deceived.[90] Nothing is farther from the picture we have of the seriousness of the wise person than error, levity, or rashness. So what shall I say about the strength of resistance in the wise person? In fact, Lucullus, you, too, agree that he doesn't hold any opinions. And since that's something you approve—I'm sorry to deal with things back to front: I will get myself back in order shortly—tell me how strong you think this argument is first: [**XXI 67**]

[1] If the wise person ever assents to anything, he will sometimes hold an opinion;

[2] but he will never hold an opinion;

[3] so he won't ever assent to anything.

---

87. The quotations are from Cicero's own translation of Aratus' *Phaenomena* 1.37–44. The two lines come from a connected passage cited more extensively in Cicero's *DND* 2.106 (*Aratea* fr. 7 Soubiran). The Cynosure is the constellation of the Little Bear.
88. *Helikê* or the Septentriones is the constellation of the Great Bear.
89. The elaborate navigation metaphor in this paragraph is supposed to explain Cicero's position as a (weak) follower of Clitomachus' radical scepticism; see page xvi. Here and in *Ac.* 2.112–13 he accepts the views that nothing can be known and that it is irrational to hold opinions, and hence that it is rational to suspend all assent. But he acknowledges that he is sometimes so struck by 'persuasive impressions' that he cannot restrain himself from assenting to them, and thus that he holds opinions even though he takes this to be irrational (unlike the mitigated sceptic of *Ac.* 2.59).
90. See *Ac.* 2.77. Zeno's view is explained in *Ac.* 1.41–42; one explanation for Arcesilaus' agreement is given in *Ac.* 1.45.

Arcesilaus approved this argument, since he supported the first and second premises. Carneades sometimes gave as his second premise the concession that the wise person would sometimes assent; and from this it followed that the wise person would hold opinions (a conclusion you won't accept, and rightly, in my view).[91] But the Stoics, with Antiochus in agreement, thought that the first premise—if the wise person were to assent, he would hold opinions—was false: they thought that he could distinguish false from true and inapprehensible from apprehensible <impressions>.

[68] "Our view, however, is, first, that even if anything is apprehensible, the very habit of assent is slippery and dangerous.[92] Hence, since it's agreed that it is extremely vicious to assent to anything false or unknown, it's better to restrain all assent so the wise person doesn't go awry by advancing rashly. False and true, and inapprehensible and apprehensible <impressions> are so close to each other—if indeed there are any of the latter: we will see about that shortly—that the wise person shouldn't commit himself to such a precarious position. If, on the other hand, I take from our side the premise that

[4] nothing is apprehensible,
and accept from you your concession that

[2] the wise person holds no opinions,
the result will be that

[3] the wise person will withhold all assent.

So you must see whether you prefer this or the conclusion that the wise person will hold an opinion. *Neither*, you say. Therefore, I will try to show that nothing is apprehensible, since the whole controversy turns on this.[93]

91. This is the first explicit statement of the Academics' 'corollary argument'; see pages xxii–xxiii and xxviii–xxx and G. Striker, 'Sceptical Strategies', in M. Schofield, M. Burnyeat, and J. Barnes (eds.), *Doubt and Dogmatism* (Oxford 1980), pp. 54–83. Arcesilaus' version is also attested in Sextus *M.* 7.155–57. The motivation behind Carneades' occasional revision of it is disputed by radically and mitigatedly sceptical Academics in *Ac.* 2.59, 2.78, and 2.148.
92. Cicero threatens assent here with a sorites argument of the sort set out in *Ac.* 2.92–94. A fuller version of this epistemological sorites argument is given in Sextus *M.* 7.415–22.
93. See *Ac.* 2.78.

[**XXII 69**] "But first a few words on Antiochus. Antiochus studied with Philo the very views I am defending for so long that it was acknowledged that no one had studied them longer; he also wrote about them very acutely—and attacked them in his old age no less acutely than he had previously defended them. So, although he was clever— and he was—his lack of consistency weakens his authority. When did the day dawn, I wonder, that showed him the thing whose existence he had denied for many years, the mark distinguishing true from false <impressions>? Did he think something up? What he says is the same as the Stoics.[94] Perhaps he was ashamed to have had such thoughts. Why didn't he transfer his allegiance to others, and particularly to the Stoics, since this was their disagreement with the Academics? Was he really dissatisfied with Mnesarchus or with Dardanus, the leaders of the Stoics in Athens at that time? He never left Philo until after he started to have his own students.[95] [**70**] And then how was it that the 'Old Academy' was suddenly called back to life? He seems to have wanted to retain the honour of this name while defecting from the school itself. At least, there were some who said that he did it for renown, and even that he hoped that his followers would be called 'Antiochians'. My view, however, is that he couldn't withstand the combined onslaught of all the philosophers. There are some shared views amongst them on other subjects, of course; but this is the one view of the Academics that none of the other philosophers approves.[96] So he yielded. Just as people who can't bear the sun beneath the New Shops seek the shade of the Maenian balconies, so, when things got hot, Antiochus sought the shade of the Old Academics.[97]

94. Antiochus' explicit agreement with the Stoics is restricted to his acknowledgment of the existence of 'apprehensible' impressions here; but Cicero intimates below that his debt to them is more substantial. Sextus criticizes Antiochus for "transferring the Stoa into the Academy" through his attempts to show that "Stoic doctrines are already present in Plato" (*PH* 1.235).
95. Since Antiochus already had his own students when he arrived in Alexandria in late 87 BCE (see *Ac.* 2.11–12), we can infer from this passage that his split with Philo predated the latter's Roman Books and the Sosus affair of *Ac.* 2.11–12. He probably defected in the late 90s BCE.
96. The controversial Academic view is their rejection of the criterion for truth, i.e., of the existence of the distinguishing mark of 'apprehensible' impressions mentioned above and in *Ac.* 2.71.
97. The New Shops and Maenian balconies were both in the Roman forum; the latter were ancient buildings associated with Maenius, who was a consul in 338 BCE. (In *Ac.* 1.46 Cicero denies that the term 'New Academy' correctly describes the sceptical Academics on the grounds that Plato and Socrates are 'old' but sceptical.)

[71] "There's an argument Antiochus used to use when he held that nothing was apprehensible. Which view did Dionysius of Heraclea apprehend with that certain mark by which one ought to assent to claims: the one he held for many years when he believed his teacher Zeno, that only what is honourable is good? Or the one he defended later, that 'honourable' is an empty name and pleasure the highest good? The point Antiochus wanted to make from Dionysius' change of view was this: nothing can be imprinted on our mind from something true that can't be similarly imprinted from something false.[98] Well, he has ensured that the argument he based on Dionysius is one that other people based on him! But more on Antiochus another time; now let's turn to what you said, Lucullus.

[XXIII 72] "And first let's see if there's anything in what you said at the beginning—that we make mention of philosophers from the past in the way that seditious people cite famous citizens who are also populists.[99] Such people want to look like good men, though they're up to no good. But we say that the views we have are ones that you yourselves allow were held by the most eminent philosophers. Anaxagoras said that snow was black; could you bear it if I said the same?[100] No! You couldn't bear it if I even considered it a matter for doubt! Yet who was Anaxagoras? Are we to consider *him* a 'sophist'? (This was what people who practised philosophy for show or for money were called by the Greeks.) No: he was highly praised for his earnestness as well as his intellect. [73] What should I say about Democritus? Who could we compare, not just for the greatness of his mind, but also of his spirit, with someone who dared to start his book with 'This is what I have to say about the totality of things'?[101] He excludes nothing from the scope of his assertions, since nothing could exist beyond the totality of things! Who doesn't rank this philosopher above Cleanthes or Chrysippus or the other philosophers of later times? In comparison with him, such people seem to me to be fifth-rate. And yet he doesn't say what we do, because we don't deny that

---

98. Conversions from one philosophical school to another by established philosophers were rare. Another famous case is that of Polyaenus, deployed by Cicero in *Ac.* 2.106.

99. In *Ac.* 2.72–76, Cicero replies to Lucullus' criticisms of the Academic appeals to the Presocratics and Plato and Socrates in *Ac.* 2.13–15; see pages xxxv–xxviii and Brittain and Palmer 2001.

100. See *Ac.* 2.100 and Sextus *PH* 1.33 (Anaxagoras fr. A97 DK).

101. See Sextus *M.* 7.265 (Democritus fr. B165 DK).

something is true, though we do deny that anything is apprehensible. No! He flatly denies that there is any truth; and rather than saying that the senses are obscure, he calls them 'dark'.[102] Indeed, Metrodorus of Chios, his greatest admirer, claimed at the beginning of his book *On Nature:* 'I declare that we don't know whether we know anything or nothing, not even whether we know that or not, or altogether whether anything is the case or not.'[103]

[74] "You think that Empedocles is raving; but I think that the note he strikes is absolutely right for the subjects he discusses. Are we to suppose that *he* blinds us or deprives us of our senses, if he takes the view that their power is too limited to judge the objects they are set over?[104] As for Parmenides and Xenophanes, they criticize almost angrily—admittedly in less good verse, but still in verse—the arrogance of people who dare to say that they have knowledge, when nothing can be known.[105] *Socrates and Plato should be removed from this group,* you said. Why? I can't speak more certainly about anyone. Indeed, I seem to have lived with them—so many of their conversations have been recorded, from which it can't be doubted that Socrates thought that nothing could be known. He made just one exception, that he knew that he knew nothing, and excluded nothing else. What should I say about Plato? He certainly wouldn't have set out Socrates'

102. See Sextus *M.* 7.138–39 (Democritus fr. B11 DK), which contrasts the 'dark' or obscure cognition of sense-perception with the 'genuine' cognition of reason. Democritus' denial of the existence of truth here is probably equivalent to his claim in *Ac.* 2.32 that truth is hidden 'in the abyss', i.e., that truth is inaccessible. The Academics' view about their access to truth is restated in *Ac.* 2.111.

103. Metrodorus fr. B1 (DK). Cicero probably cites Metrodorus' view to confirm his sceptical interpretation of Democritus, rather than as an independent authority in his own right, since he is missing from the lists of Presocratics in *Ac.* 2.14 and 1.44–45. (The text of the Metrodorus fragment is corrupt and the precise form of the Greek original is unclear; see J. Brunschwig, 'Le fragment DK 70B1 de Métrodore de Chio', in K. Algra, P. van der Horst, and D. Runia (eds.), *Polyhistor: Studies in the History and Historiography of Ancient Philosophy* (New York/Leiden 1996), pp. 21–38.)

104. A sceptical interpretation of Empedocles' theory of the senses is given in Sextus *M.* 7.122–25, citing fr. B1 (DK); see also Diogenes Laertius *Lives* 9.73, which cites lines 7–8 and 5 of B1.

105. Cicero is no doubt thinking of Xenophanes' famous denial of knowledge in fr. B34 (DK), which is cited with a sceptical interpretation by Sextus in *M.* 7.49–52. The sceptical case is harder to establish from the extant fragments of Parmenides; but he is critical of the senses in fr. B7 (cited by Sextus in *M.* 7.114) and of the cognitive powers of embodied minds in fr. B16 (cited by Aristotle in *Metaphysics* 4.5 1009b).

views in so many books if he hadn't approved them. He had no reason to portray someone else's 'dissimulation', especially when it was so consistent.[106]

[**XXIV 75**]   "You can see, I think, that I am not just citing celebrated people, as Saturninus did, but following no one who isn't famous or eminent. And yet I could have used your antagonists Stilpo, Diodorus, and Alexinus, though they are petty philosophers, adducing tangled and barbed 'sophisms' (this is the Greek term for silly, fallacious arguments).[107] But why compile material from them when I have it from Chrysippus, the person who is supposed to keep the Stoics' portico standing?[108] Look how much he wrote against the senses and against the approved results of ordinary experience! *But he also resolved his objections.* I don't think so; but let's assume he did. He clearly wouldn't have compiled so many arguments that were liable to deceive us by their persuasive power unless he saw that they were hard to resist.   [**76**] What do you think of the Cyrenaics, who are far from contemptible philosophers?* They say that nothing external is apprehensible: they apprehend only things they experience with internal touch, like pain, or pleasure; and they don't know what has which colour or sound—their experience is just that they are affected in some way.[109]

"That's enough about authorities—although you also wanted to know whether I agreed that the truth could have been discovered in the many centuries since those early philosophers, given the great number of intellects seeking it with such perseverance. I will deal with what has been discovered a bit later, and make you the judge of it. But to see that Arcesilaus didn't fight with Zeno in the spirit of criticism,

---

106. Cicero rejects Lucullus' ironic interpretation of Socrates' confessions of ignorance (in *Ac.* 2.15) here and in *Ac.* 1.44–45. But his explanation here seems to depend on an aporetic interpretation of Plato's Socratic dialogues, rather than the apparently dogmatic scepticism of *Ac.* 1.44–45; see Cooper 2004.

107. Stilpo, Diodorus, and Alexinus represent the range of 'dialecticians' of the late fourth and early third centuries BCE (see 'Megarians' in the Glossary of Names). The logical work of the various dialecticians often had paradoxical implications for perception and the perceptible world, and hence may have been used for their sceptical effect by Arcesilaus; see Diogenes Laertius *Lives* 4.33 and D. Sedley, 'Diodorus Cronus and Hellenistic Philosophy', *Proceedings of the Cambridge Philological Society* ns 23 (1977), pp. 74–120.

108. See *Ac.* 2.87. Diogenes Laertius *Lives* 7.183 cites the line, "Without Chrysippus, there would be no Stoa."

109. See *Ac.* 2.20 and 2.142.

but because he wanted to discover the truth, consider this.[110] **[77]**
None of Zeno's predecessors had ever explicitly formulated, or even
suggested, the view that a person could hold no opinions—and not
just that they could, but that doing so was necessary for the wise person. Arcesilaus thought that this view was both true and honourable,
as well as right for the wise person. So he asked Zeno, we may suppose, what would happen if the wise person couldn't apprehend anything, but it was a mark of wisdom not to hold opinions. Zeno replied,
no doubt, that the wise person wouldn't hold any opinions because
there was something apprehensible. So what was that? An impression, I suppose. Well, what kind of impression? Then Zeno defined it
thus: an impression from what is, stamped, impressed, and molded
just as it is.[111] After that, Arcesilaus went on to ask what would happen if a true impression was just like a false one. At this point, Zeno
was sharp enough to see that no impression would be apprehensible
if one that came from what is was such that there could be one just like
it from what is not.* Arcesilaus agreed that this was a good addition to
the definition, since neither a false impression, nor a true impression
just like a false one, was apprehensible. So then he set to work with
his arguments, to show that there is no impression from something
true such that there could not be one just like it from something false.

[78] "This is the one disagreement still outstanding. The view that the
wise person won't assent to anything has no part in this controversy:
he could fail to apprehend anything and yet still have opinions. In
fact, this is said to have been the position approved by Carneades—
although, since I trust Clitomachus rather than Philo or Metrodorus, I consider it a position he argued for rather than approved.[112]
But let's put this to one side. It is quite clear that once opinion and

---

110. See *Ac.* 2.66–67 and Sextus *M.* 7.153–57. This passage should probably be read
as a 'philosophical reconstruction' rather than the record of an actual debate, since
our other evidence suggests that the Stoic response to Arcesilaus came from Zeno's
students rather than their leader. The paragraph serves as Cicero's reply to Lucullus' criticisms of Arcesilaus in *Ac.* 2.13–16.

111. See *Ac.* 2.18. The phrase 'from what is' in this version of Zeno's definition is
replaced by 'from something true' in *Ac.* 2.112. These glosses show that Cicero construes the 'source' of 'apprehensible' impressions—mentioned in *Ac.* 2.18—as a
state of affairs or 'assertible' rather than a physical object; cf. Sextus *M.* 8.85–86. (The
passage may also show that the 'third clause' of Zeno's definition was an addition
designed to clarify it in the face of Academic criticism; cf. Sextus *M.* 7.252.) See
Frede 1999, pp. 300–312.

112. See *Ac.* 2.59. The mitigated scepticism advocated there—and by Catulus

apprehension have gone, what follows is the suspension of all assent. Hence, if I show that nothing is apprehensible, you must allow that the wise person will never assent.[113]

[**XXV 79**] "So what *is* apprehensible, if not even the senses give true reports?[114] You defend them, Lucullus, with a stock argument— though it was precisely to stop you doing that that I exceeded my brief yesterday and said so much against the senses. But you say that you weren't moved by the bent oar or the pigeon's neck. First, why not? I recognize, after all, that my impressions misrepresent the oar and show several colours on the pigeon's neck, though there isn't more than one. Second, were these the only examples I gave? While the rest stand, your case falls.*[115]

"*My senses are veracious,* he says. In that case, you have a ready authority, though one who makes his case in a very dangerous way. Epicurus rests his case on one point: if a single sense has given false evidence once in a lifetime, we should never believe any sense.[116] [**80**] This is frank—to trust in your witnesses and stand firm in your perversity!* Thus Timagoras the Epicurean denies that he has ever had the impression of doubled flames from a candle when he pressed his eye: the deception derives from opinion, not his eyes.[117] As if the question

---

senior in *Ac.* 2.11–12, 2.18, and 2.148—is ascribed here to an interpretation of Carneades adopted by Philo and Metrodorus. See pages xxviii–xxx.

113. See *Ac.* 2.18 fin. Cicero and Lucullus both think that it is irrational to hold opinions (see *Ac.* 2.66–68), so they agree that the point at issue is just whether Stoic apprehension is possible.

114. In *Ac.* 2.79–90, Cicero recapitulates the Academic arguments against the possibility of apprehension on the basis of perception in response to Lucullus' criticisms. The first section, *Ac.* 2.79–82, argues that the senses as such are fallible and far weaker than Lucullus claimed in *Ac.* 2.19.

115. See *Ac.* 2.81–82. These Academic arguments against the capacity of the senses to yield apprehension—i.e., their arguments from conflicting appearances—are preserved in more detail in Sextus *M.* 7.411–14. (The text of the last sentence is corrupt. Plasberg suggests an unnecessary Epicurean objection here.)

116. Epicurus fr. 251 (Usener), repeated at *Ac.* 2.101. This is a version of the notorious Epicurean doctrine that all perceptions are true; see *Ac.* 2.19 and 2.83. The doctrine is adumbrated in Epicurus' *Principal Doctrine* 24 (Diogenes Laertius *Lives* 10.147), and defended in Diogenes Laertius *Lives* 10.31–32 and Lucretius *The Nature of Things* 4.469–521.

117. Epicurus identifies 'opinion' as a secondary mental motion and the source of error in our perceptually based judgments in his *Letter to Herodotus* 49–52 (Diogenes

were what is the case, not what impression one has! But let's let Timagoras follow his leaders.* What about *you*, Lucullus? You say that some perceptual impressions are true, some false: so how do you distinguish these cases? Stop using stock arguments, please: we grow these at home!*

"If a god were to ask you, you said, *"Provided only that you have sound and undamaged senses, what more do you want?",* what would you reply? I just wish he would ask, so he could hear how badly he has done by us!* Assuming that what we see is true, how far can we see? Looking from this spot straight ahead, I can see Catulus' house in Cumae, but not the one in Pompeii, although there is nothing interposed to hinder my sight—it's just that my vision can't stretch that far.* It's a wonderful view: I can see Puteoli. But I can't see my friend Gaius Avianius, though he may be taking a stroll in Puteoli's Portico of Neptune. [81] Yet there was that person who gets cited in lectures who could see things 1,800 stades away; and some birds can see further than that.[118] So my reply to that god of yours would be impudent: I am not at all happy with the eyes I have. He will tell me that my vision is sharper than that of the fish who can no more be seen by us, although they are now no doubt right under our eyes, than our presence can be detected by them.* Just as the water sheathes them, so the thick air sheathes us.

"But we want nothing more. What? Don't you think that moles want the light? Though I wouldn't complain to god that I can't see far enough as much as I would that I *can* see what isn't true. Do you see that ship there? It seems stationary to us, while to the people on the ship, this villa seems in motion.[119] Of course, you can investigate the explanation for these impressions; but even if you find it—which I am inclined

---

Laertius *Lives* 10.49–52); see Lucretius *The Nature of Things* 4.462–68 and *Ac.* 2.45 above. Timagoras' position is perhaps misstated here: the Epicurean claim that all perceptions are true relies on a narrow sense of perceptual content that does not correspond exactly with the Stoic or Academic notion of a perceptual impression.
118. The first case concerns someone who was supposed to have been able to see ships leaving the harbour in Carthage on the North African coast from a hillside in Lilybaeum on the west coast of Sicily, about 120 miles away; see Pliny *Natural History* 7.85.
119. The moving ship and bent oar are stock examples of conflicting sensory appearances, cited, e.g., by Sextus in *M.* 7.414 and Lucretius in *The Nature of Things* 4.387–90 and 4.438–42. Cases relying on differences depending on position are grouped by Sextus as the fifth sceptical mode in *PH* 1.118–23.

to think you won't be able to do—you won't have shown that you have a truthful witness, but that there is a reason why your witness gives false evidence. **[XXVI 82]** But why go on about the ship when I know that the oar didn't satisfy you? Perhaps you're looking for something a bit bigger. Well, what could be bigger than the sun? The mathematicians prove that it is eighteen times bigger than the earth—but look how tiny it seems to us![120] To me, at any rate, it seems about a foot across. Epicurus, however, thinks that it could be a bit smaller than it seems, but 'not much'—though in fact he thinks that it is either exactly as, or not much bigger than, it seems, so that his eyes aren't deceiving him at all, or 'not much'![*121] What happened to that 'once in a lifetime' pledge, then? But let's leave the gullible Epicurus to think that the senses never deceive. He thinks so even now, although the sun is hurtling around with such a thrust that we can't even imagine how fast it's going, and yet still it seems stationary to us.

[83] "But, to narrow down our debate, please note how small our disagreement is. There are four premises to the conclusion that nothing can be known or apprehended, which is the only subject at question here. They are that

[1] there are some false impressions;

[2] those [scil. false] impressions aren't apprehensible;

[3] when two impressions don't differ at all, it's not possible that one is apprehensible, while the other isn't;

[4] there is no true impression derived from the senses that may not be paired with another impression that doesn't differ from it at all but isn't apprehensible.

120. This figure for the relative size of the sun in relation to the earth is not recorded for any of the major ancient mathematicians or astronomers; see T. Heath, *Aristarchus of Samos, the Ancient Copernicus* (Oxford 1913), pp. 337–50. But it is ascribed to Serapion of Antioch, whose work was known to Cicero (see *ad Att.* 2.4.1 and 2.6.1), in *Anecdota Graeca* 1 p. 373.25–26 (Cramer). It may also be the Stoic view; see *Ac.* 2.128.
121. A paraphrase of Epicurus' *Letter to Pythocles*, given in Diogenes Laertius *Lives* 10.91: "In relation to us, the size of the sun, moon, and other stars is just as it seems; in relation to itself it may be either bigger than we observe, or a bit smaller, or just the same." See Cicero *Fin.* 1.20, which adds that Epicurus also took its apparent size to be "about a foot across".

Everyone concedes the second and third of these four premises. Epicurus doesn't grant the first; but you, our current opponents, concede that one, too. So the battle is entirely over the fourth premise.[122]

[84] "Well, someone looking at Publius Servilius Geminus who thought he was looking at his twin Quintus had an inapprehensible impression, because his true and false impressions weren't distinguished by any mark. But without that means of distinguishing them, what mark that couldn't be false would he have had for recognizing Gaius Cotta, who was consul twice with Publius Geminus?* You deny that there is such similarity between things in nature. (You're certainly putting up a fight, though one with a flexible adversary.) You may well be right; but there could be one between our impressions.[123] If so, that similarity deceives the senses—and if one similarity deceives them, it will render everything doubtful. For without the criterion by which he's supposed to be recognized, even if the person you're looking at actually is the person you think you're looking at, you still won't be judging by the mark you say we're supposed to use to avoid false, but exactly alike, impressions. [85] So, since Quintus Geminus can seem to you to be Publius, what guarantee do you have to rule out the possibility that someone who isn't Cotta seems to you to be Cotta, given that we have impressions that aren't true?

"Everything has its own kind, nothing is identical with something else, you say. It's certainly the Stoic view, and not a particularly credible one, that no strand of hair in the world is just like another, nor any grain of sand.[124] I could refute this view, but I have no desire to put up a fight. It doesn't matter, for our purposes, whether the objects of our impressions don't differ at all or can't be discriminated, even if they do differ. Still, if there can't be such similarity between people, what about between statues? Are you saying that Lysippus couldn't have made a hundred Alexanders just like one another, if he used the same bronze, the same process, the same tool, etc.? Tell me what marking you would have used to differentiate them! [86] How about if I

---

122. See *Ac.* 2.40–42, where the Academic 'core argument' is set out in more detail. The arguments from similarity in *Ac.* 2.84–87 support premise [4] with the second line of argument criticized by Lucullus in *Ac.* 2.54–58; see Sextus *M.* 7.408–10 and pages xxi–xxii.
123. See *Ac.* 2.40, 2.52, and 2.58, and 2.85 below.
124. See the note on *Ac.* 2.56.

stamp a hundred seals into wax of the same type with this ring? Are you really going to be able to find a means of distinguishing them? Or will you need to find a ring-maker like that Delian chicken-farmer you found who could recognize eggs? **[XXVII]** But you appeal to technical skill even in support of the senses.[125] *A painter can see details we can't; an expert recognizes the song at the first notes of the flute.* So what? Doesn't this tell against you, if we can't see or hear without complex skills to which few can aspire (at least in this country)?

Next you bring up that wonderful story telling us about the great artistry nature used in the construction of our senses and mind and in the whole design of human beings. **[87]** Have you given any reason why I shouldn't fear the rashness of holding this opinion? Can you really affirm, Lucullus, that there is a power, and a wise one at that, which created—or, to use your term, constructed—human beings intentionally? What kind of construction was this? Where did it take place? When? Why? How? Your treatment of these issues is clever, and your arguments elegant; so by all means hold these views, as long as you don't affirm them. But I will get to physics shortly, if only to prevent your showing up as a liar when you said I would a little while back.[126]

"Turning to clearer matters, I will now set out the general problems. Books are filled with these, and not just by our side, but by Chrysippus, too. (Indeed, the Stoics often complain that Chrysippus energetically sought out all the arguments against the senses or perspicuity, ordinary experience, and reason, but was rather weaker when it came to his counterarguments, and thus provided Carneades with his weapons.)[127] **[88]** These problems are precisely the ones you dealt with so diligently.[128] *The impressions of people who are asleep or intoxicated or*

---

125. See *Ac.* 2.20. Cicero points out that the Delian chicken-farmer of *Ac.* 2.57 is a special case, since his alleged abilities fit into the Stoic category of 'technical perception'.
126. See *Ac.* 2.30–31. Cicero returns to physics in *Ac.* 2.116, and to the question of divine creation in *Ac.* 2.119–21; his conclusion in *Ac.* 2.127–28 is an expansion of his remarks here.
127. Chrysippus wrote a series of works for and against 'ordinary experience' (*sunêtheia*), which his followers regarded as outdoing Carneades' derivative arguments; see *Ac.* 2.75 and Plutarch *Stoic Contradictions* ch. 10 1036b–c (*SVF* 2.109). His many works on logical paradoxes such as the sorites and liar probably constituted his arguments against 'reason'; see *Ac.* 2.91–98.
128. The arguments from abnormal states of mind in *Ac.* 2.88–90 support premise [4] of the 'core argument' in *Ac.* 2.83 with the first line of argument criticized by Lucullus in *Ac.* 2.47–54; see Sextus *M.* 7.402–8 and pages xxi–xxii.

insane are weaker than those of people who are awake, sober, or sane, you said. How so? *Because when Ennius woke up he didn't say that he had seen Homer, but that he had seemed to, while Alcmaeon said 'but my heart agrees not at all . . .'.*[129] (And much the same for the intoxicated.) As if anyone denies that when a dreamer wakes up he thinks they were dreams, or that someone in remission from a fit of madness thinks that the impressions he had in his fit weren't true!* But that's not the point: the question is what kind of impression they had at the time. Unless, that is, we're going to think that, just because he dreamed it, Ennius didn't hear the whole of that speech starting 'Devotion of my mind . . .' just as if he were hearing it while awake.[130] Of course he could take his impressions to be the dreams they were once he woke up; but, asleep and awake, his impressions were approved on an equal basis.* Again, doesn't Iliona have so much faith that her son spoke to her in her dream (beginning 'Mother, I call to you . . .') that she even believed it when she woke up? Otherwise, why did she say, 'Come, stay, listen: tell me again . . .'?[131] Does she strike you as someone with less trust in her impressions than waking people?

[XXVIII 89] "What should I say about the insane? Well, what about that neighbour of yours, Catulus, called Tuditanus? Does anyone who's entirely in his right mind think that what he can see is as certain as Tuditanus thought his impressions were? What about the Ajax who cried:

'I can see you, I can see you! Live, Ulysses, while you may!'[132]

Didn't he cry out twice over that he could see when he couldn't see anything at all? What about Euripides' Hercules? While he was shooting his children (taking them to be Eurystheus'), murdering his wife, and trying to kill his father as well, wasn't he just as moved by false impressions as he would have been by true ones? What about Alcmaeon, your favourite, who denies that his 'heart agrees with the vision of his eyes'?[133] Doesn't he exclaim, at the onset of a fit, 'Whence arises this flame?' And then:

129. The two quotations from Ennius are repeated from *Ac.* 2.51–52. See the Glossary of Names for explanations of the context of the literary citations by Cicero.
130. Ennius *Annales* Bk. 1 fr. 5 (Skutsch).
131. Pacuvius *Iliona* fr. 210–11 (Warmington). Cicero continues the first quotation in *Tusc.* 1.106 (the speaker is her dead son Polydorus): "Mother, I call to you, though you soothe your cares in deep sleep and do not pity me: rise up and bury your son!"
132. The line is probably from Ennius' *Ajax*. Cicero supplements the line in *Or.* 3.162 with the additional threat: "Take your last look at the sun's radiance!"
133. See *Ac.* 2.52. The remaining quotations in this paragraph are from Ennius'

'Come here, come here! They're here—
they're coming for me!'

What about when he implores the girl:
  'Help me, get this plague away from me,
  this flame-waving power which is torturing me!
  They're coming girt with grey snakes;
  they're surrounding me with burning torches!'

Can you really doubt that he has the impression that he can see the
Furies? Likewise for the next bit:

  'Long-haired Apollo is bending
  his gilded bow, pulling with his left hand;
  Diana is hurling a torch from the moon.'*

[90] If these were real events, would Alcmaeon have believed them
more than he did on account of these impressions? (His heart apparently 'agreed with his eyes'.)

"I set out these cases to secure the conclusion—which is as certain as
anything can be—that there is no difference between true and false
impressions with respect to the mind's assent. But you quite miss the
point when you refute the false impressions of the insane or dreamers by their own subsequent recollection. The question isn't what recollection dreamers or the insane have when they are awake or their
fits subside, but what kind of impression they had at the time. But
that's enough on the senses.

[91] "What is apprehensible by reason?[134] *Dialectic was discovered as the
'arbiter' and judge of truth and falsity*, you say.[135] Which truths and false-

---

Alcmaeon, fr. 15b (Jocelyn). (The text of the final two lines is disputed. The translation follows the suggestion of an anonymous correspondent of Reid's in switching
the positions of 'left hand' and 'moon'.)

134. In *Ac.* 2.91–98, Cicero gives a series of arguments designed to show the weakness of reason by undermining the principles of Stoic logic. The main sections concern the sorites paradox (*Ac.* 2.92–94) and the liar paradox (*Ac.* 2.95–98). The
connections between the arguments are not always clear, but both sections can be construed as attacks on the principle of bivalence (see *Ac.* 2.95) and the validity of basic
Stoic inferences, i.e., of modus ponens, the Stoic 'first indemonstrable' form of argument (see *Ac.* 2.96); see J. Barnes, 'Logic in *Academica* 1 and the *Lucullus*', in B. Inwood
and J. Mansfeld (eds.), *Assent and Argument* (New York/Leiden 1997), pp. 14–60.

135. Stoic dialectic covered a much wider field than the more strictly 'logical' top-

hoods, and in what subjects? Is the dialectician to judge what is true or false in geometry? Or in literature? Or in music? *No. He doesn't know such subjects.* In philosophy, then? But what do questions about the size of the sun have to do with him? What ability does he have to judge what the highest good is? So what *is* he to judge? *Which conjunctions and disjunctions are true; which statements are ambiguous; what follows from something and what is incompatible with it.* But if dialectic judges these cases and ones like them, it makes judgments about itself—and yet it promised more. Being in a position to judge just these cases wouldn't enable it to adjudicate the important questions in the rest of philosophy.[136]

[92] "But since you place such value on this art, you'd better make sure that the whole thing isn't going to end up telling against you. It starts off gaily explaining the parts of speech, the resolution of ambiguities, and the methods of argument; but after a few more steps it comes to a rather slippery and dangerous spot: the sorites, which you were just saying was a fallacious form of argument.[137] [XXIX] So what if it is fallacious? Are we to blame for that fault? Nature didn't give us any knowledge of limits to let us decide how far to go in any case. And this isn't just true for a heap of wheat (the case it took its name from): in any case at all when we are asked little by little when someone is, e.g., rich or poor, or famous or obscure, or things are many or few, big or small, long or short, or wide or narrow, we are unable to reply for certain how much needs to be added or taken away.

[93] "*But sorites arguments are fallacious!* So crack them if you can, so they don't bother you—they certainly will, if you don't take precautions. *But we do take precautions,* you say: *Chrysippus thinks that when*

---

ics Cicero mentions below; see Diogenes Laertius *Lives* 7.41–44, *Ac.* 2.142–46, and the exposition of Old Academic dialectic in *Ac.* 1.19 and 1.30–33.

136. The argument for the restricted scope of logic is derived indirectly from Plato's attack on rhetoric in *Gorgias* 453–54; Carneades uses a similar argument against divination in Cicero *Div.* 2.9–11. (The Stoics claimed that logic is the only capacity able to judge itself as well as other objects; see Epictetus *Discourses* 1.1.4.)

137. See *Ac.* 2.49. Alternative versions of the sorites paradox are given in Galen *On Medical Experience* 16.1–17.3, Sextus *M.* 7.416–21, and Diogenes Laertius *Lives* 7.82. Chrysippus wrote several works on it; see his remarks in *Logical Investigations* 3.9.7–12 (*SVF* 2.298a) and the book titles in Diogenes Laertius *Lives* 7.192 and 7.197. His diagnosis and 'solution' of the paradox remain disputed; see, e.g., M. Mignucci, 'Logic III. The Stoics, §8 Paradoxes', in K. Algra et al. (eds.), *The Cambridge History of Hellenistic Philosophy* (Cambridge University Press, Cambridge 1999) and S. Bobzien, 'Chrysippus and the Epistemic Theory of Vagueness', *Proceedings of the Aristotelian Society* 102 (2002), pp. 17–238.

one is asked to specify gradually whether, e.g., three things are few or many one should come to rest (hêsukhazein, *as they put it) a little bit before one reaches 'many'.*[138] As far as I'm concerned, Carneades replies, you can snore if you like as well. But how does that help you? There's someone coming after you who's going to wake you from your sleep and keep asking you the same questions. Whatever number it was that you stopped at, if I add one to it, will that make 'many'? Carry on further, for as long as you like. What more do I need to say? After all, you admit it: you can't specify the last time it is 'few' and the first time it is 'many'. And this problem seeps so far that I can't see the limit it can't reach. [94] *Well, it does me no harm,* you say: *I will hold back my horses like a skilled charioteer before I come to the limit, especially when the spot the horses are headed to is precipitous. That's how I restrain myself—by not replying for too long when I'm asked captious questions.*[139] But if you have a reply you could make but don't, you're behaving arrogantly; and if you don't have one, you don't apprehend the answer, either. If your reason is that this case is obscure, I allow it. Yet you claim that you don't carry on to the point where it is obscure—which means you're halting at manifest cases.* But if the point is just that you're not *saying* anything, you aren't achieving anything. What does someone trying to catch you out care whether he traps you when you're silent or speaking? If, on the other hand, you specify without any doubt that it is 'few' as far as, let's say, nine, but halt before ten, then you're withholding your assent from cases that are certain and manifest as well. But that's just what you don't let me do in obscure cases![140] So your dialectical art doesn't help you at all against sorites arguments, because it doesn't teach you to specify the first or last case in a process of addition or diminution.

---

138. Chrysippus fr. 2.277 (*SVF*). Chrysippus' 'precaution'—viz., to refuse to continue to answer sorites questions at a certain point in the series—is understood as a recommendation that one should suspend assent by Cicero in *Ac.* 2.94 and by Sextus in *PH* 2.253 and *M.* 7.416 (*SVF* 2.275–76); see S. Bobzien, 'The Stoics on the Fallacies of Equivocation', in B. Inwood and D. Frede (eds.), *Language and Learning* (Cambridge 2005) pp. 239–73.

139. The Stoic answer adapts a line from Lucilius cited by Cicero (*ad Att.* 13.21.3) in connection with Carneades' understanding of *epokhê* (the suspension of assent): "Hold back your chariot and horses as a good charioteer often must!" (fr. 1249 Warmington).

140. See *Ac.* 2.107. Cicero's argument is spelled out in more detail by Sextus in *M.* 7.416–21. If Chrysippus recommends suspending assent while the answers are still 'clear', he allows that we can (and should) suspend assent even to 'apprehensible' impressions under certain conditions; see the note on *Ac.* 2.38 and Bobzien 2002.

[95] "Here's another problem: your dialectical art ends up under-mining its own principles, like Penelope unraveling her weaving. Is that our fault or yours? A basic principle of dialectic is that anything asserted (they call what is 'stated', as it were, an *axiôma* ['assertible']) is either true or false.[141] Well, in that case, are examples like this true or false? If you say that you are lying and what you say is true, you're lying and saying something true.*[142] You claim that arguments of this kind are 'insoluble', but this is more irritating than our claims about 'inapprehensible' impressions. [XXX] But I'll leave that aside. My question now is this: if these arguments are insoluble and no criterion can be discovered to put you in a position to determine whether they are true or false, what's happened to that definition of yours that an assertible is what is either true or false? Given any assumptions, I con-clude ‡ that certain things follow from them and others, ‡ which are their contraries, are to be rejected.*[143] [96] Well, what is your judg-ment on the form of this argument?

[1] If you say that it is light now and what you say is true, it's light.

[2] But you are saying that it is light now and what you are say-ing is true.

[3] Therefore it's light.

141. The Stoics defined a proposition or 'assertible' as what is either true or false; see Diogenes Laertius *Lives* 7.65 (*SVF* 2.193), Sextus *M.* 8.74 (*SVF* 2.187), and Cicero *Tusc.* 1.14 and *Fat.* 38.
142. Chrysippus wrote at least ten books on the liar paradox (listed in the catalogue of his books in Diogenes Laertius *Lives* 7.196–97). The main evidence for his reso-lution of it is this passage (*Ac.* 2.95–98) and Plutarch *Common Conceptions* ch. 2 1059d–e; see Barnes 1997 and Mignucci 1999. (The text of this sentence is corrupt. The reading accepted here is supported in Mignucci, 'The Liar Paradox',1999. The case Cicero gives is probably supposed to contain the plural 'examples' suggested by the previous sentence—viz., 'If you say that you are lying and what you say is true, you are lying' *and* 'If you say that you are lying and what you say is true, you are saying something true'. Both are required to generate the paradox.)
143. Reid's emendation, which is accepted in the translation, gives a general logi-cal rule to the effect that the premises in a valid form of argument have recogniza-ble implications. But Chrysippus refuses to accept the inferences to [6] and to [12], even though they are identical in form to the acceptable inferences to [3] and to [9], respectively (*Ac.* 2.96). Thus, if his solution to the liar paradox is right, this logical form (modus ponens, the Stoic first indemonstrable) is invalid (*Ac.* 2.98).

It's clear that you accept this type and are very keen to say that it is a valid argument—that's why you make it the first valid form of argument in your teaching. So either you accept any argument made in this form or this art of yours doesn't exist.

"In that case, see whether or not you're going to accept this argument:

[4] If you say that you are lying and what you say is true, you're lying.

[5] But you are saying that you are lying and what you are saying is true.

[6] Therefore you're lying.

How can you fail to accept this argument when you have accepted the earlier one of the same form? This comes from Chrysippus, but even he didn't solve it. After all, what would he make of this argument?

[7] If it is light, it's light.

[8] But it is light.

[9] Therefore it's light.

He would allow it, of course, since the nature of a conditional compels you to concede the consequent once you have conceded the antecedent. So what's the difference between this argument and the following one:

[10] If you are lying, you're lying.

[11] But you are lying.

[12] Therefore you're lying.

You say that you can neither accept nor reject this argument. But then why can you in the other case? If there is a valid art, method, or approach in logic, if there really is logical force in the argument, it's the same in both cases.

[97] "But the last straw is their demand that these 'insoluble arguments' should be considered special exceptions. They'd better summon a tribune: they'll never get such an exception from me.[144] After all, they don't get Epicurus—who scorns and mocks the whole art of

---

144. The Stoic demand seems to be that these cases should be taken to be special 'exceptions' of the sort they refuse to grant to Epicurus in the case of future

dialectic—to concede the truth of the assertion 'Either Hermarchus will be alive tomorrow or he will not'. And yet the dialecticians declare that every assertion so disjoined (i.e., in the form 'P or not-P') isn't just true but necessary as well. But notice how alert Epicurus is, though they think he is slow. He says: "If I concede that one or the other of these is necessary, it will be necessary that Hermarchus will either be alive to-morrow or not. But there is no such necessity in nature."[145] So let the dialecticians, that is, Antiochus and the Stoics, fight with him! He's the one who overturns the whole art of dialectic. If a disjunction from con-tradictories (by which I mean one in which one disjunct affirms what the other denies) can be false, no disjunction is true.

[98] "So what's their quarrel with me? I'm just following their own rules. On occasions like this Carneades used to joke: 'If my conclusion is valid, I stick to it; but if it's invalid, Diogenes should pay me back my *mina*.'[146] (He had learned dialectic from Diogenes the Stoic, you see, and this was the fee charged by dialecticians.) So I follow the methods I learned from Antiochus. But when I do that, I can't see how I should judge that 'If it is light, it's light' is true on the ground that I learned that every conditional composed from a single assertion is true, without *also* judging that "If you are lying, you're lying" is com-posed in the same way. So I will either judge that both are alike or that if the latter isn't true the former isn't either.

[XXXI] "But let's abandon all these barbed arguments and the di-alecticians' twisted approach to debate altogether, and show who *we* are. Once Carneades' view has been thoroughly explained, all your Antiochian objections will collapse.[147] Moreover, to make sure that no

---

contingents. This suggests that Chrysippus' solution to the liar paradox involved denying that assertions such as 'I am lying' have a truth-value; see Barnes 1997 and Mignucci, 'The Liar Paradox', 1999. (The term *exceptio*, 'exception', originally re-ferred to a legal maneuver a litigant could try to enforce on a reluctant magistrate by appealing to a tribune.)

145. Epicurus fr. 376 (Usener); see Cicero *DND* 1.70 and *Fat.* 21. The first sentence should probably be emended to read, "If I concede that one or the other of these is *true,* it will be necessary that . . .", since Epicurus' fear—as the parallels in Cicero (above) confirm—is that conceding the preexisting truth of either disjunct means recognizing its necessity.

146. One mina was worth one hundred drachmae, which was something like thirty to fifty days' work for a manual labourer in 150 BCE.

147. In *Ac.* 2.98–111, Cicero defends the consistency of the Academics against Lucullus' criticisms. *Ac.* 2.98–105 argues that Clitomachus' defence of Carneades'

one suspects that I'm making up what I'm going to say, I will use citations from Clitomachus—since he worked with Carneades right up to his old age, and he was a clever man, as you'd expect from a Carthaginian, as well as a serious and diligent scholar. There are four books of his *On Suspending Assent*, but the citations I am about to give are from the first. **[99]** 'Carneades' view is that there are two categories of impressions, the first subdivided on the principle that some impressions are apprehensible, some aren't, the second on the principle that some impressions are persuasive, some aren't. Now the Academic arguments against the senses and against perspicuity pertain to the first category, and shouldn't be directed at the second. So his view', Clitomachus says, 'is that while there are no impressions allowing for apprehension, there are many allowing for approval. It would be contrary to nature were there no persuasive impressions'—and the result would be the complete overturning of life that you remarked on, Lucullus.*[148]

"So many perceptual impressions deserve our approval, too, provided only that one remembers that none of them is such that there couldn't be a false impression not differing from it at all. Thus the wise person will use whatever strikes him as persuasive, if nothing contrary to its persuasiveness presents itself; and the whole structure of his life will be governed in this way. After all, the wise person you promote also follows persuasive <impressions> in many cases—i.e., impressions that aren't apprehended or assented to, but are truth-like.[149]

'practical criterion' is immune to the objections of *Ac.* 2.32–36; *Ac.* 2.106–11 responds to specific criticisms in *Ac.* 2.22–44.

148. Clitomachus' 'positive' views (as opposed to his arguments or reports of Carneades' arguments) are known only from Cicero's citations in *Ac.* 2.99 and 2.103–4 and the remarks in *Ac.* 2.78 and 2.108. His interpretation of Carneades draws on the distinction between the 'unclear' and 'inapprehensible' in *Ac.* 2.32, which allows for the identification of inapprehensible but persuasive impressions as Carneades' 'practical criterion' in *Ac.* 2.33–36; see pages xxv–xxvii. Cicero regards this as a satisfactory response to the 'inactivity' objections of *Ac.* 2.31, 2.37–39, and 2.61–62.

149. Cicero seems to appeal here and in *Ac.* 2.109 to the Stoic doctrine of 'reasonable impressions' (*to eulogon*), in virtue of which the sage can act in conditions of uncertainty. The Stoic view is attested only in the stories in Diogenes Laertius *Lives* 7.177 and Athenaeus *Deipnosophists* 8.354e (*SVF* 1.624–25). But the most plausible interpretation conflicts with Cicero's claim in holding that the Stoic sage does assent in uncertain conditions—but to impressions that it is reasonable to do something, rather than that doing it is straightforwardly the right thing to do; see

Indeed, if he didn't approve them, his whole life would be under-mined. **[100]** Here's one case: when he steps into a boat, does the sage apprehend in his mind that he is definitely going to arrive? How could he? Still, should he set out from here to Puteoli, thirty stades away, in a tested vessel, with a good helmsman, and in calm weather like this, he would have the persuasive impression that he will arrive there safely.

"So he will deliberate about what to do or not to do on the basis of im-pressions of this type. (And he will be quicker to approve <the im-pression that> snow is white than Anaxagoras was! The latter didn't just deny that it was white, but even that he *had* the impression that it was white, because he knew that the water snow comes from is black.)[150] **[101]** And anything that induces in him a persuasive im-pression without any impediment will move him to act. He isn't sculpted from stone or hewn from wood: he has a body and a mind and he's stirred to think and perceive. So he has many true impres-sions; but these impressions don't have that distinctive and peculiar mark of apprehension you require. Thus, in his view, the wise person doesn't assent, because a false <impression> could arise that is exactly the same as the true one.

"In fact, what we say against the senses is no different from what the Stoics say: they allow that many things are false—i.e., that the way such things are is quite different from the perceptual impressions they give rise to. **[XXXII]** Now if it's true that there's even one false perceptual impression, there's someone ready to deny that anything is apprehen-sible by the senses. Hence, without a word from us, one principle from Epicurus and another from you are enough to do away with appre-hension. Which is Epicurus' principle? 'If any perceptual impression is false, nothing is apprehensible.'[151] And yours? *There are false perceptual impressions.* What follows? I don't need to add anything; the conclusion speaks for itself: 'nothing is apprehensible'. *I don't concede the first prem-ise to Epicurus,* you'll say. So fight him: he disagrees with you on all fronts. Don't fight me: there's at least one thing I definitely agree with

---

T. Brennan, 'Reasonable Impressions in Stoicism', *Phronesis* 41 (1996), pp. 318–34. (Cicero's interpretation perhaps derives from Arcesilaus' polemical adaptation of the Stoic view, cited in Sextus *M*. 7.158.)

150. Anaxagoras fr. A97 (DK); cf. fr. B10.8–11. This is an expansion of Cicero's claim in *Ac.* 2.72; see page xxxvii and Brittain and Palmer 2001, pp. 51–53.

151. See *Ac.* 2.83. Epicurus' position is explained in *Ac.* 2.79.

you about—that the senses admit falsity. **[102]** The most surprising thing about these objections is that they should come from Antiochus in particular, to whom our position was perfectly well known, as I said a bit earlier. Anyone can, of course, criticize us off his own bat because we deny that anything is apprehensible—though such criticism is rather thin. But what seems unsatisfactory to you is our claim that there are persuasive <impressions>!* Well, perhaps it is.[152]

"Still, we should certainly try to escape the objections you keep brandishing at us: *So you don't understand anything? You can't hear anything? Nothing is clear to you?* I explained a bit earlier on Clitomachus' authority how Carneades dealt with these objections. Now listen to the way these topics are dealt with by Clitomachus in the book he wrote for the poet Gaius Lucilius (he had already written on the same subjects in a book for Lucius Censorinus, the man who shared the consulship with Manius Manilius). He used pretty much these words—I know them well, because the basic primer, as it were, for the subjects currently at issue is contained in this book. At any rate, the book says: **[103]** 'The Academics hold that there are dissimilarities between things, such that some give rise to persuasive impressions, some don't. Nevertheless, this is not sufficient reason to claim that some <impressions> are apprehensible while others aren't, because many false <impressions> are persuasive, but nothing false can be apprehended or known. So, he says, people who claim that we are robbed of the senses by the Academics are completely mistaken. The Academics never claimed that there is no colour, flavour, or sound; what they did argue was that there was no distinctive mark of truth or certainty in such things that was never found elsewhere.'[153] **[104]** After expounding these points, Clitomachus added: 'The wise person is said to suspend

152. Cicero presumably means that Lucullus rejects the Academics' *use* of persuasive impressions as their 'practical criterion' (cf. *Ac.* 2.105), since the view that some impressions are persuasive was one Carneades borrowed from the Stoics; see Sextus *M.* 7.242–43 (*SVF* 2.65). (The translation follows Reid's punctuation, since Plasberg's construal of the Latin is unidiomatic.)

153. See *Ac.* 2.99. In this citation, Clitomachus allows that the differences in plausibility in our impressions may often reflect objective differences between things, even if there is no reliable method for discerning when this is the case. He takes the Academic recognition of persuasive impressions to be sufficient to deflect the objections that they rob us of our senses (*Ac.* 2.30, 2.33, 2.38, 2.61), and do away with colour and truth altogether (*Ac.* 2.34). Cicero makes the same point in *Ac.* 2.101. The intellectual honesty of this sceptical move is doubted by Numenius in fr. 27.19–32 (Des Places).

assent in two senses: in one sense, when this means that he won't assent to anything at all; in another, when it means that he will restrain himself even from giving responses showing that he approves or disapproves of something, so that he won't say "yes" or "no" to anything. Given this distinction, the wise person accepts the suspension of assent in the first sense, with the result that he never assents; but he holds on to his assent in the second sense, with the result that, by following what is persuasive wherever that is present or deficient, he is able to reply "yes" or "no".[154] ‡ Since ‡ the person who keeps himself from assenting to anything nevertheless wants to move and act,' Clitomachus maintained, 'there are still impressions of the kind that excite us to action; and likewise, there are still responses we can use when questioned on either side, by just following our impressions on the matter, provided we do so without assent.*[155] Yet not all impressions of this kind are approved, but only those that aren't impeded by anything'. [105] Perhaps you don't approve these claims; and they may of course be false; but they certainly aren't vexatious. We don't rob you of the light; rather, we claim to accept the very impressions that you claim to apprehend, as long as they are persuasive.

[XXXIII] "So now that we have introduced and established the persuasive <impression>, and set it free without let, hindrance, or any impediment, you see, of course, Lucullus, that your advocacy of perspicuity falls through. The wise person I am talking about will see the sky, earth, and sea with the same eyes as your sage, and will perceive everything else subject to each sense with the same senses. This stretch of sea, which now looks dark as the west wind gets up, will

---

154. Clitomachus distinguishes between dogmatic 'assent' and the sceptic's 'approval' by identifying two kinds of suspension of assent. The first kind is not explained until the end of *Ac.* 2.104, but it presumably means the refusal to accept that an impression is true (the negative correlative of dogmatic assent). The second kind of suspension of assent is universal: a flat refusal to accept any impression in any way at all. The Clitomachian Academic rejects the second kind of suspension in approving or 'assenting' to persuasive impressions; but he continues to suspend assent in the first sense because he acts on persuasive impressions without thereby taking them to be true; see pages xxv–xxvii and R. Bett, 'Carneades' Pithanon: A Reappraisal of Its Role and Status', *Oxford Studies in Ancient Philosophy* 7 (1989), pp. 59–94, and 'Carneades' Distinction Between Assent and Approval', *Monist* 73 (1990), pp. 3–20. (Sextus *PH* 1.220 and [Numenius] fr. 26.107–10 [Des Places] give historically misleading versions of this distinction.)

155. The Latin manuscripts start this sentence with a negative phrase, which is rightly rejected by all editors. The translation follows Reid's emendation.

look the same to our wise person. Yet he won't assent <to this impression>, because it looked green to us a moment ago, and it will look gray in the morning, and the patch that is glinting and gleaming where it is glittering in the sun is unlike the patch right next to it. So even if you could give an explanation for this, you still couldn't defend the claim that the visual impression you had is true.[156]

[106] "*What happens to memory if we don't apprehend anything?* That was one of your questions. Well, is it true that we can only remember impressions we have apprehended? Is it true in the case of Polyaenus? He is said to have been a great mathematician, who later, in agreement with Epicurus, came to believe that geometry was false.[157] Is it true that he therefore forgot what he used to know? But falsehoods aren't apprehensible, as you think, too. So if memory is only of things apprehended, everything anyone remembers is something he has apprehended. Nothing false is apprehensible, then, and Siron remembers all of Epicurus' doctrines—so they all turn out to be true! That's fine by me; but you must either concede that that's the case—which is far from your intention—or you're going to have to give memory back to me and admit that there's space for it even if there's no apprehension.[158] [107] *What will happen to the systematic arts?* Which arts? The ones that explicitly allow that they use only inductive inferences rather than scientific knowledge? Or the ones that just follow our impressions and don't have that skill enabling you to discriminate true from false <impressions>?[159]

"Then there are the two objections that are the lynchpins of your case. The first is your denial of the possibility that anyone should assent to nothing. *That's obvious.** Yet Panaetius (who is pretty much the best of the Stoics, in my view) says that he has doubts about something that every other Stoic except him thinks is quite certain, namely, that the

---

156. See *Ac.* 2.79 and 2.81.

157. Epicurus fr. 229a (Usener). The Polyaenus story is repeated in Cicero *Fin.* 1.20. Epicurus took the principles of standard Greek geometry to be incompatible with both experience and the truth of atomism; see *Ac.* 1.5–6.

158. The argument relies on Lucullus' use of the Stoic definition of memory as a kind of apprehension in *Ac.* 2.22.

159. See *Ac.* 2.22. Cicero includes philosophy among the arts using only 'inductive inference' (*coniectura;* see note to *Ac.* 2.42) in *Ac.* 2.116–17. Navigation and medicine are more standard cases of 'stochastic' or conjectural arts. An explicit example of the third kind of art is Empiricist medicine, to which Cicero also alludes in *Ac.* 2.122. Cicero expands on this argument in *Ac.* 2.144–46.

responses of entrail-diviners, auspices, oracles, dreams, and prophecies are true. So he restrains his assent about this.[160] But if he can do that even in matters his teachers hold to be certain, why can't the wise person do the same in every other case? Is there really any assertion that the wise person can approve or disapprove but can't doubt? Do you really think that you can do this at any stage you like in a sorites argument, but he can't come to a similar halt in every other case, especially when it's open to him to follow unimpeded truth-like <impressions> without assent?[161]

[108] "The second is your denial of the possibility of action of any kind by someone who fails to approve anything with assent. *One must first have an impression, which itself involves assent.** You see, the Stoics claim that our perceptions are themselves assents and that action follows them (because impulse results from them); hence, everything goes if <apprehensible> impressions go.[162] [XXXIV] A lot has been said and written on either side about this, but we can deal with the whole issue briefly.* For my part, I regard standing firm against one's impressions, fighting off opinions, and restraining one's assent from slipping as great *actions;* and I believe Clitomachus when he writes that Carneades had accomplished an almost Herculean labour in that he had driven assent—i.e., opinion and rashness—from our minds, as one would drive out a wild and savage monster. Still, to abandon that part of my defence, what's going to impede the action of someone who follows unimpeded persuasive <impressions>?[163] [109] *The very fact that he has decreed that even the impressions he approves are inapprehensible,* you say. In that case, that's going to impede you as well

160. Panaetius fr. 70 (Van Straaten); see Cicero *Div.* 1.6. Diogenes Laertius *Lives* 7.149 asserts that Panaetius denied that divination was an art at all; but Cicero is probably right to think that he was agnostic.

161. See *Ac.* 2.94. This is Cicero's response to the objection in *Ac.* 2.38.

162. See *Ac.* 2.24–25 and 2.37–39. The supplement is necessary because the Stoics characterized 'perception' as our assent to an 'apprehensible' impression produced by the senses (see *Ac.* 1.40–41). But—despite Lucullus' treatment of the objection in *Ac.* 2.24–25—they did not deny that we often assent to inapprehensible perceptual impressions or that assent to the latter was sufficient for action (see *Ac.* 2.39 fin.).

163. Cicero accepts Clitomachus' view that the universal suspension of assent is the rational response to our failure to apprehend anything (see *Ac.* 2.66 and 2.78). But he is prepared to concede the Stoic view that suspending assent is not an 'action' as such, but rather a 'mental motion' (*Ac.* 2.62), since he also accepts Clitomachus' and Carneades' 'practical criterion' as a mechanism for action in the requisite Stoic sense (*Ac.* 2.104–5).

when you're sailing, sowing, marrying, and having children, and in many other affairs when you have nothing to follow except persuasive <impressions>.*[164]

"But you dig up that well-tried and often refuted objection, *though not,* you say, *in the way Antipater raised it, but more cogently. Antipater was criticized,* you say, *for saying that it was consistent for someone affirming that nothing was apprehensible to say that just that claim was apprehensible.* That seemed a bit rich even to Antiochus, as well as self-contradictory! *After all, one can't consistently say that nothing is apprehensible if one says that something is apprehensible.** So Antiochus thinks *that Carneades should have been pressed in this way instead. Given that a wise person can't have principles unless they are apprehended or known, Carneades should at least allow that this principle itself is apprehended—i.e., that the wise person holds that nothing is apprehensible.** As if the wise person has no other principles and could live his life without principles! [110] But just as he holds those as persuasive rather than apprehended principles, so with this one, that nothing is apprehensible. If he had a mark of apprehension in this case, he would use the same mark in the other cases. Since he doesn't have any such mark, he makes use of persuasive <impressions>—and that's why he has no fear of giving the impression that he is confounding everything and rendering everything unclear. Thus, when asked about what it is appropriate to do or many other things in which he is practised and experienced, he won't say that he doesn't know, as he does when asked whether the number of the stars is even or odd. There aren't any persuasive <impressions> in such unclear cases; but where there are persuasive <impressions>, the wise person won't lack something appropriate to do or say.[165]

[111] "You didn't overlook a fourth criticism from Antiochus, either—unsurprisingly, since it is quite remarkable, and one that Antiochus used to say greatly disturbed Philo. *In assuming, first, that there are some false impressions, and, second, that those impressions don't differ at all from*

---

164. See *Ac.* 2.99. This is Cicero's response to the objection in *Ac.* 2.59.
165. See *Ac.* 2.27–29. Cicero's response relies on the distinction between the 'unclear' and 'inapprehensible' set out in *Ac.* 2.32 and explained in 2.98–105. (The number of the stars was a standard example of something 'unclear'; see Sextus *M.* 7.243, 8.147, and 8.317.) Cicero's easy acceptance of Academic ethical 'principles' over and above the Academic's experience may reflect the mitigated sceptical position criticized by Aenesidemus in Photius *Library* 212 170a.17–19 and Sextus in *PH* 1.226. See Brittain 2001, chapter 6.

true impressions, Philo failed to notice something—namely, that the first premise, which he conceded in virtue of an apparent difference between the impressions, was nullified by the second premise, in which he denied that true and false impressions are different. Nothing could be more inconsistent. Which would be right if we Academics did away with truth altogether. Yet we don't, since we discern as many true as false things. But our discerning is a kind of *approval:* we don't find any sign of apprehension.[166]

[**XXXV 112**] "My treatment of the subject still seems too narrow.[167] When there's an open field for my speech to run in, why limit it to the cramped thickets of Stoic arguments? If I were arguing with a Peripatetic, I would deal straightforwardly with a straightforward person. If he said that an <impression> is apprehensible when it is from something true, without adding that significant qualification 'and stamped in a way it couldn't be by something false', I wouldn't contest this very seriously. And even if his reply to my claim that nothing is apprehensible was that the wise person would sometimes hold opinions, I wouldn't rebut his view—especially since even Carneades didn't fight strongly on this issue.[168] But, as it is, what can I do? [**113**] I want to find out what is apprehensible. The reply doesn't come from Aristotle or Theophrastus, or even Xenocrates or Polemo, but from a lesser person: *a true <impression> of a kind a false <impression> couldn't be.**[169]

---

166. See *Ac.* 2.44. Since Philo's disturbance is not reflected in Cicero's standard Clitomachian response, the objection may be read as one that told more strongly against mitigated scepticism—viz., against its increasing reliance on 'persuasive impressions' as evidence for the truth. See pages xxviii–xxx and Brittain 2001, chapter 3.1.

167. *Ac.* 2.112–17 serves as an introduction to the review of the dissensions of dogmatic philosophers in physics (*Ac.* 2.118–28), ethics (*Ac.* 2.129–41), and logic (*Ac.* 2.142–46), which forms the final part of Cicero's speech. The introduction explains that these dissensions undermine Antiochus' claim to the authority of the Academic tradition (*Ac.* 2.112–13) and reveal the intellectual arrogance of dogmatic philosophy (*Ac.* 2.114–17).

168. In this paragraph, Cicero points out that the questions at issue in the dialogue so far have centered on two Stoic epistemological doctrines that Antiochus has foisted on his 'Old Academy'. Cicero in fact accepts these Stoic views, as he says below; but his scepticism does not depend on them, as his review of wider philosophical disagreements will show (see *Ac.* 2.147). Carneades' relative lack of interest in fighting the 'Peripatetic' views on apprehension and opinion is attested in Sextus *M.* 7.402 and *Ac.* 2.59, 2.67, and 2.68. (Cicero refers to this passage in *Fin.* 5.76, without mentioning his acceptance of the Stoic views.)

169. The context suggests that this is Antiochus, the person trying to foist this Stoic

I don't find anything of this kind. It follows, of course, that I will assent to something unknown, that is, hold opinions. The Peripatetics and Old Academics both allow me to do this; but you don't, least of all Antiochus, whose opposition affects me forcefully, whether because I liked the man, as he did me, or because he was, in my estimation, the most polished and sharpest of the philosophers in our time. I want to learn from him first, however, in what sense he belongs to the Academy he professes to belong to. I'll leave out my other objections; but which Old Academic or Peripatetic ever made either of the two claims at stake here—namely, that the only thing that was apprehensible was a true <impression> such that a false <impression> couldn't be just like it, or that a wise person wouldn't hold opinions? None of them, clearly: neither of these views was seriously defended before Zeno.[170] I, on the other hand, think each is true, and this is not just an ad hoc claim, but the position I openly approve.[171]

[**XXXVI 114**] "This is what I can't bear <about Antiochus>: you forbid me to assent to anything unknown, claiming that this is shameful and excessively rash, and yet you take it upon yourself to expound a philosophical system expressing wisdom. So you're going to unveil the nature of the universe, shape my character, determine the ethical ends, set out appropriate actions for me, define the kind of life I should adopt—and, you claim, simultaneously teach me the criteria and methods of argument and understanding. How are you going to manage it so that I never slip up, never form an opinion, while I'm taking on these countless doctrines? And then which philosophical system is it that you're going to take me off to, if you prise me from my own? I'm afraid you'll be rather presumptuous if you say your own—and yet you must say that. And it won't just be you: everyone will rush me off to his own system.

[**115**] "All right. Imagine I resist the Peripatetics, although they claim to have an affinity with orators and that their famous students have

---

doctrine into the Academy (see *Ac.* 2.69–70). But it might refer to Zeno; see below.

170. Zeno is named as the originator of the Stoic definition of apprehension in *Ac.* 1.40–41, 2.18, and 2.77, and of the prohibition on opinion in *Ac.* 2.77. (The qualification is echoed in Augustine *Against the Academics* 2.14. He took it to be an allusion to debates in the Old Academy, though it may refer to the prehistory of scepticism traced in *Ac.* 2.72–76.)

171. Cicero's acceptance of these theses—along with his failure to find anything apprehensible—underpins his adherence to Clitomachus' defence of scepticism; see *Ac.* 2.66, 2.78, and 2.108.

often governed the republic. Imagine I stand firm against the Epicureans, although I know so many of them and they are such good
people and such good friends to each other. What will I do with
Diodotus the Stoic, given that I studied under him as a youth, he has
spent so many years with me, he lives in my house, I admire and love
him—and he spurns these Antiochian views? *It's only our views that are
true,* you say. Yes: only yours, if they are true (since several incompatible views can't be true). Are the Academics really shameless for de-
clining to slip into error? Or is it rather that our opponents are
arrogant in their conviction that they alone have universal knowledge? *I don't claim that I have knowledge, but only that the wise person does,*
he says. Wonderful! But what he knows, of course, are the doctrines
in your system. . . . First, isn't there something odd in wisdom being
explained by somebody who isn't wise?[172] But let's leave ourselves
aside and talk about the wise person, who is, as I've said several times,
the subject of this entire investigation.

[116] "Well, wisdom is divided into three parts by most philosophers,
including yourselves. So first, if you will, let's look at the results of investigations into the nature of the universe. But before we do that, consider this.*[173] Is there anyone so swollen with error that he is convinced
that he *knows* the doctrines in physics? I'm not looking for proofs relying on inductive inference, which are dragged this way and that in
debate and fall short of persuasive necessity. Let's get the geometers
to supply us instead, since they profess to demonstrate rather than
persuade and they prove all their constructions to your satisfaction. I
won't ask them about the basic principles of mathematics—though if
they aren't granted these, they can't get started. *A point is something
with no magnitude, a surface or 'plane' (so to speak) is something with no
depth at all, a line something without any breadth.*[174] Suppose I concede
the truth of these principles. If I ask a wise person to swear an oath
that the sun is *n* times bigger than the earth after Archimedes has constructed in his presence all the proofs to demonstrate this, do you

172. See *Ac.* 2.9 and 2.117. Sextus gives an elaborate series of arguments against the
authority claimed by the dogmatic schools in *M.* 7.314–42 and *PH* 2.37–46; see also
Augustine *Against the Academics* 3.15–17 and fr. 34 below.
173. *Ac.* 2.116–17 serves as an epistemological preface to Cicero's discussion of
physics; the argument of *Ac.* 2.128 plays an analogous role for ethics.
174. See *Ac.* 2.106. Sextus compiles a series of sceptical arguments against these
geometrical principles in *PH* 3.39–44 and *M.* 9.375–417 and 3.1–64. The hypotheti-
cal nature of the principles internal to the mathematical sciences is stressed by
Socrates in Plato's *Republic* 7.533c.

think that he will?[175] If he did, he would show contempt for the very sun he takes to be a god. **[117]** But if the wise person isn't going to believe geometrical proofs, although they apply demonstrative force, as you yourselves say, he won't come close to believing the arguments of philosophers, will he?

"Or, if he will, whose arguments in particular will he believe? We could go through all the doctrines of the physicists, but that's a rather lengthy task. Still, I want to find out which physicist he will follow. Imagine someone who is in the process of becoming wise, but isn't yet: exactly which view or system will he choose? Granted, whichever he chooses, he will choose without wisdom. But assume he has an inspired intellect. Which physicist in particular will he approve (since he won't be able to choose more than one)? I won't press you on unlimited topics: let's just see whose view about the first principles he will approve, since there's a serious disagreement between the leading men about the principles out of which everything is constituted.[176]

[XXXVII 118] "The first physicist was Thales, one of the seven sages (and, we're told, the one to whom the six others conceded primacy): he said that everything was constituted from water.[177] But he didn't convince Anaximander, his fellow-citizen and companion, since the latter said that there was an indeterminate nature from which everything came to be. After him, his student Anaximenes postulated indeterminate air, though he claimed that the things arising from it were determinate, the order of their generation being first earth, water, and fire, and then everything else from them. Anaxagoras proposed indeterminate matter, but he thought that particles came from it, which were minute but internally homogenous, and confused at first, but

175. See *Ac.* 2.82. Archimedes is not known to have worked directly on the size of the sun, though his extant *Sand-reckoner* indicates that he was familiar with Aristarchus' work in this field. He is probably cited just as a famous geometer.

176. Cicero's assimilation of 'first principles' with material constituents reflects the doxographical tradition deriving from Aristotle's *Metaphysics* Bk. 1. Few of the physicists listed in *Ac.* 2.118 would have accepted this interpretation of the function of their 'principles'. (Cicero's source for this list was probably a sceptical doxography compiled by Clitomachus or another student of Carneades; see J. Mansfeld, 'Gibt es Spuren von Theophrasts Phys. Op. bei Cicero?' in W. Fortenbaugh and P. Steinmetz (eds.), *Cicero's Knowledge of the Peripatos*, Rutgers Studies in Classical Humanities 4 (New Brunswick 1989), pp. 133–58.)

177. See the Glossary of Names for further information on the Presocratics listed in this paragraph.

later brought to order by divine mind. Xenophanes, from a slightly earlier period, asserted that everything was one, and that it was unchangeable, and god, not born at any time, everlasting, and in the shape of a sphere. Parmenides chose fire, which put earth in motion and so formed it. Leucippus' first principles were the full and the void. Democritus said much the same on this point, though he was more expansive on others. Empedocles chose the four familiar elements we know. Heraclitus chose fire. Melissus said that whatever there was was indeterminate and unchangeable, and always existed and always would. Plato reckons that the world was made everlasting by god from matter, which receives everything in itself.[178] The Pythagoreans have it that everything starts from numbers and the basic principles of mathematics.

"Your wise person will select one of these physicists to follow, I suppose; the rest of them, the ones he has rejected and condemned despite their numbers and worth, are ruled out of court. **[119]** But whichever view he approves, he will consider his mental apprehension of it just as firm as those he gets from the senses. So he will approve the claim that it is light now no more firmly than, e.g.—since we're dealing with a Stoic—the doctrines that the world is wise, and that it has a mind that constructed itself and the world and orders, moves, and governs everything.[179] (He will also be convinced that the sun and the moon, all the stars and the earth and the sea are gods because a sort of living intelligence inheres in and pervades all of them, though there will be a time when this world will be destroyed by fire.)[180]

[XXXVIII] "Perhaps these doctrines are true (note here that I allow that there are truths); I still don't accept that they are apprehended.

---

178. Cicero's source ascribes only two of the standard three 'principles' seen in Plato's *Timaeus:* he omits the Forms. A similar interpretation probably lies behind Antiochus' account of the Old Academic physical principles in *Ac.* 1.24. (Cicero's doxographical sources for *Ac.* 2.118–43 can be distinguished from Cicero the interlocutor since they often conflict with views he expresses elsewhere in *Ac.* 2.64–146.)
179. These Stoic doctrines are set out in, e.g., Diogenes Laertius *Lives* 7.147 (*SVF* 2.1021) and Cicero *DND* 2.57–78. Cicero's assertion that Antiochus accepted Stoic physics wholesale is questionable; see pages xxxii–xxxiii. (His epistemological argument here is spelled out in *Ac.* 2.128.)
180. A Stoic argument for the intelligence and divinity of the stars is given in *DND* 2.39–44 (*SVF* 2.684). Their periodic destruction—or assimilation into the supreme god—in a universal conflagration (*ekpurôsis*) is attested in, e.g., Origen *Against Celsus* 4.68 (*SVF* 626).

When your wise person, now a Stoic, stops dictating these doctrines to you, Aristotle will turn up, pouring out a golden flood of words to the effect that he's crazy: 'The world never came into being because this wonderful work was never initiated through a new divine resolution; it is so structured on all sides that no force could effect the requisite motions or change, and no process of aging through the lapse of time could occur, such that its order could ever fall apart and collapse.'[181] You'll be obliged to reject his view while defending the Stoic view (above) as if your life and reputation were at stake—although I'm not even allowed to be in doubt. **[120]** Leaving aside the levity manifested in the rash assent of both sides, isn't my freedom from the obligation binding you worth a great deal?

"If god created everything for our sakes (as you have it), why did he create such a supply of vipers and water snakes? Why did he distribute so many deadly or dangerous creatures throughout the land and sea? *These creatures couldn't have been produced with such finished and detailed designs without some divine artistry.*[182] (So you say, though you rather diminish its majesty by having it work out the detailed design of bees and ants, so one ends up with the impression that one of the gods must have been a Myrmecides to construct such miniature works.) **[121]** *Nothing can be created without god,* you say. Well, at this point Strato of Lampsacus will come at you from the opposite side to give your god immunity from this very considerable obligation (though since the priests of the gods have exemptions from public service obligations, it's more than fair for the gods to have them, too!). He says that he doesn't need the gods' labour to construct the world. He explains that everything that exists has been produced by nature—though his explanation is not like Democritus', who claimed that things are compounded from rough, smooth, and hooked or barbed bodies with intervals of void: he takes these to be illusory elements Democritus needs, rather than ones his explanations warrant.*[183] Strato, however, goes through the various parts

<hr />

181. Aristotle *On Philosophy* fr. 20 (Ross). Although the ascription to Aristotle's dialogue on philosophy is questionable, the views in this paragraph are compatible with Aristotle's in *On the Heavens* and *Physics* 8.

182. The Stoic claims that animals were created for human use and by a manifestly intelligent artist are elaborated in considerable detail in Cicero *DND* 2.157–62 and 2.120–33. Chrysippus' general response to objections to providential design based on 'natural evils' was to argue that such things were necessary side effects of well-designed products; see Gellius *Attic Nights* 7.1.7–13 (*SVF* 2.1170).

183. Democritus fr. A80 (DK). The shapes of Democritean atoms are discussed in *DND* 1.66 and, e.g., Aristotle *Metaphysics* 1.4 985b4–22.

of the world explaining that anything that exists or comes into being is or has been produced by natural weights and motions.[184] Doesn't he free god from a considerable task and liberate me from fear in addition? Does anyone have the strength not to quail at the divine power day and night, when he thinks that he is in god's care? Should anything difficult happen (as it does to everyone), can someone with that belief fail to be frightened that it happened deservedly? Yet I don't assent to Strato's view, or indeed to yours: sometimes his view seems more persuasive, sometimes yours does.

[**XXXIX 122**] "All these things are hidden, Lucullus, and shrouded in deep darkness: no gaze of the human intellect is strong enough to penetrate the heavens or enter into the earth. We don't even know our own bodies or the locations or capacities of their various parts. That's why the doctors whose business it was to know them opened up bodies so their parts could be seen (though the Empiricist doctors deny that such parts are thereby better known, since it's possible that they are changed by the process of dissection and uncovering).[185] But is there any such means by which we could cut through, dissect, or split apart the natures of things in order to see whether the earth is attached far below and so held fast, as it were, by its roots, or hangs suspended in midair? [**123**] Xenophanes says that there's life on the moon and that it's a land with many cities and mountains.[186] These claims seem marvelous, but their author could no more swear that it is so than I that it isn't. You even claim that there are people directly opposite us on the other side of the earth, their footsteps standing opposite ours (the people you call 'Antipodeans')![187] So why are you more angry

---

184. Strato fr. 32 (Wehrli); see *Ac.* 1.34 and *DND* 1.35. As his criticism of Democritus indicates, Strato's physical theory was presented as naturalistic rival to reductive atomism. His physical principles were corporeal qualities such as heat, which generated complex entities by their natural movements towards or away from the centre of the world. (In Democritus' theory the atomic 'principles' lacked secondary qualities and their motions were the result of random collisions.)

185. See Celsus *On Medicine* proem 40–44. Empiricist doctors objected to anatomy and vivisection for both epistemological and ethical reasons. (Introductory accounts of medical Empiricism can be found in Celsus *On Medicine* proem 27–44 and Galen *On the Sects.*)

186. Xenophanes fr. A47 (DK). Diogenes Laertius *Lives* 2.8 more plausibly ascribes this view to Anaxagoras, although his view was rather that other worlds are inhabited and have other suns and moons; see Anaxagoras fr. B4 (DK).

187. The Stoics held that the earth was spherical (see Aetius *Doctrines* 3.10.1 [*SVF* 2.648]) and at the gravitational centre of the world; hence they had reason to think

with me, though I don't reject such views, than with those who think you're crazy when they hear them? Hicetas of Syracuse, as Theophrastus reports, thinks that the sky, sun, moon, stars, and all the heavens are stationary, and nothing at all in the world moves except the earth, though since the latter twists and turns itself around its axis with terrific speed it has exactly the same result as if the heavens were moving around a stationary earth.[188] (Indeed, some people think that Plato says the same thing in the *Timaeus*, too, if a bit more obscurely.)[189] What about you, Epicurus? Tell us your view. Do you think the sun is as small as it seems? 'My view? ‡ Surely it seems just the same to you? ‡'*[190] So he mocks you and you make fun of him in turn. Yet Socrates is free from such derision, and likewise Aristo of Chios, because he thinks that no such claim can be known.[191]

[124] "But let me come back to the mind and the body. Do we have sufficient knowledge yet about the nature of the nerves or veins? Do we understand what the mind is, where it is, or even whether it exists or, as Dicaearchus thought, no such thing exists at all?[192] If it does exist, does it have three parts, as Plato thought (the rational, spirited, and appetitive parts), or is it simple and unitary?[193] If it's simple, do

---

that the antipodean parts of the two temperate zones were habitable (see Diogenes Laertius *Lives* 7.156, [*SVF* 2.649]).

188. Theophrastus fr. 240 (Fortenbaugh). Hicetas is ascribed the same view in Diogenes Laertius *Lives* 8.85. Elsewhere, however, he is attested as holding the standard Pythagorean view that there is an 'anti-earth', which seems incompatible with Cicero's claim here; see Aetius *Doctrines* 3.9.1.

189. See *Timaeus* 40c8, where Plato describes the earth by the participle *illomenê*, meaning either that it is 'revolving' or that it is 'conglomerated' around the pole. The passage is discussed in Proclus' *Commentary on the Timaeus* 3.137–38, who cites Aristotle *On the Heavens* 293b31 and Heraclides Ponticus fr. 105 (Wehrli) as examples of the heterodox Galilean interpretation.

190. See *Ac.* 2.82. (The text is corrupt; the translation follows an emendation that gives Epicurus' countermockery some point by alluding to his opponents' failure to 'save the phenomena'.)

191. Socrates and Aristo were famous examples of philosophers who rejected the study of physics. Socrates' view is explained by Varro in *Ac.* 1.15; Aristo's motive is disputed: physics is either 'above us' or 'useless'; see Diogenes Laertius *Lives* 7.160 and Sextus *M.* 7.12 (cf. *SVF* 1.351–57).

192. Dicaearchus fr. 8f (Wehrli); see *Tusc.* 1.24 and 1.41. Cicero's more detailed doxography of differing views about the soul's nature in *Tusc.* 1.18–22 ascribes this view to an interlocutor in Dicaearchus' *Corinthian Dialogue*—though Dicaearchus may also have held it in his own right.

193. Plato argues for the tripartition of the embodied soul in *Republic* 4.436a–41c.

we know whether it's fire or breath or blood, or, as Xenocrates held, an incorporeal number?[194] (Though one can scarcely imagine what that would be like!) Whatever it is, do we know whether it's mortal or eternal? There are many arguments on either side of these questions. One of these views seems certain to your wise person; but the weight of the arguments on either side strikes ours as so equally balanced in most cases that it's not even clear to him which is most persuasive.

[XL 125] "But if you treat me with more self-restraint, and criticize me not for failing to assent to your arguments, but to any at all, I will overcome my reluctance and choose someone to assent to. Who would be best? Democritus, perhaps, since, as you know, I have always been an enthusiast for the first class. Now I'll find myself subject to criticism from all of you: *Do you really think there is any such thing as void, given that everything is so crammed full that ‡ any bodily thing ‡ that is set in motion must yield and where any such thing yields another immediately takes its place?* Or that there are such things as atoms, and that whatever is produced from them is completely unlike them? Or that anything wonderful can be produced without a mind? And that, amazing as the order in this world is, there are innumerable other worlds above, below, to the right and left, before and after it, some of them unlike it, others just like it? That just as we are now in Bauli and looking over at Puteoli, so there are people in innumerable parallel places, with the same names, titles, careers, intellects, figures, and ages, debating the same topics? That if we now (or when we're asleep) seem to 'see' something in our mind, images are bursting into our minds through our bodies from outside? You really shouldn't approve these views or assent to such fictions: it's better not to think at all than to think such perverse thoughts.*[195] [126] So the point isn't that I must assent to *something*, but rather to the same doctrines as you? Be careful: what you're asking may turn out to be shameless (as well as arrogant). Here's one reason: some of your views don't even seem persuasive to me. I don't believe that there is the kind of divination you accept, and I spurn the fate you claim envelops everything. I don't even think that

---

194. Xenocrates fr. 204 (Isnardi Parente); see *Ac.* 1.39 and *Tusc.* 1.20. Xenocrates thought that the soul is a self-moving number; see Aristotle *On the Soul* 1.2 404b.27–28.
195. The criticisms of Democritus in this passage summarize familiar objections to atomism. See, for example, the arguments against void in Aristotle *Physics* 4.7 214a25–32, against anti-teleological reductivism in *Ac.* 2.119–21, against multiple worlds in *Ac.* 2.55–56, and against intromissive theories of thought and imagination in *ad Fam.* 15.16.1, *Div.* 2.137, and *DND* 1.105–10.

this world was engineered by divine thought—though I'm not sure that this may not be right.[196]

[XLI] "But why set *me* up as an object of disapprobation? Do I have your permission not to know what I don't know? Or is it all right for Stoics to disagree amongst themselves but impermissible for us to disagree with them? Zeno and most of the other Stoics think that the aether is the supreme god and endowed with a mind by which everything is governed. Cleanthes, a Stoic of the higher class and Zeno's pupil, thinks that the sun is the master and ruler of things.[197] Thus, dissension among the wise forces us to be in ignorance of our master, since we don't know whether we are the servants of the sun or the aether. You report the size of the sun—I suppose it's the radiance of the sun himself that prompts me to make frequent mention of him. As I was saying, you report the size of the sun as if you'd measured it with a surveyor's rule.[198] Well, I don't believe in your measurement: you are, so to speak, bad surveyors. Is it in doubt, then, which of us is, to put it mildly, more self-restrained?

[127] "And yet I don't think that such physical investigations should be dismissed. The observation or contemplation of nature provides the natural food, so to speak, for our minds and intellects. We rise up, we seem uplifted, we look down on human affairs, and, by thinking about lofty and celestial matters, we scorn our own affairs as small and petty. The process of investigation into the greatest (if also most hidden) matters has its own delight; and if we come across something that strikes us as truth-like, our minds are suffused with a thoroughly humane pleasure. [128] So both your wise person and ours will investigate these questions, but yours to assent, believe, and affirm, ours with the fear of forming rash opinions and the thought that things are going wonderfully for him if he finds something truth-like in questions of this sort.

"Now let's turn to the conception of good and bad. But I have a few words to say first.* When they make firm affirmations about such

196. See *Ac.* 2.119. The general Stoic acceptance of divination is recognized in *Ac.* 2.47 and 2.107. Cicero examines Stoic divination, fate, and providential cosmology in his dialogues *Div.*, *Fat.*, and *DND* 2–3.
197. These conflicting views are ascribed to Zeno in, e.g., *DND* 1.36 (*SVF* 1.154) and to Cleanthes in, e.g., Diogenes Laertius *Lives* 7.139 (*SVF* 1.499), respectively.
198. See *Ac.* 2.82 and 2.128.

physical questions, they don't seem to realize that they lose their warrant for our more evident impressions as well.*[199] For they give their assent and approval equally firmly to the claims that it is light now and that the cawing of a crow prescribes or forbids some action; and, if they measure this statue, they won't affirm that it is six feet tall any more firmly than that the sun, which they can't measure, is more than eighteen times larger than the earth.[200] This gives rise to the following argument:

[1] If the size of the sun is inapprehensible, someone who gives his approval to everything else in the same way as he does to the size of the sun doesn't apprehend them, either.

[2] But the size of the sun is inapprehensible.

[3] So someone who approves that as if he apprehends it doesn't apprehend anything at all.

They will reply that the size of the sun *is* apprehensible. Fine: I won't fight them, as long as they allow that everything else is apprehended in the same sense—since they can't say that one thing is more or less apprehended than another, given that there is one definition of apprehension for everything.

[XLII 129] "But to revert to our new topic: what are the established truths in ethics? Ethical 'ends' are needed, of course, so there's something to determine the highest good and bad. Yet is there any subject where the disagreement between the leading men is greater?[201] I'll set aside the views that now seem abandoned, like Erillus'.** He located the highest good in knowledge and scientific understanding.[202] (Although he was a student of Zeno, you can see how much he disagreed with him and how little with Plato.) The Megarian school was once

199. See *Ac.* 2.116, 2.141, and 2.147. A similar Academic argument that the Stoic theory of apprehension prevents the Stoics from recognizing degrees of epistemic security is found in Sextus *M.* 7.421–22. The point in *Ac.* 2.127–28 (and *Ac.* 2.133–34, 2.141, and 2.146 below) is that the Academics' approval tracks degrees of plausibility and verisimilitude, whereas Stoic assent is always geared only to apprehension.
200. See *Ac.* 2.82. This argument suggests that the view that the sun is eighteen times the size of the earth was advocated by the Stoics.
201. See the Glossary of Names for further information on the philosophers and schools listed in this paragraph and the next.
202. Erillus fr. 1.413 (*SVF*). Erillus' view is set out in Diogenes Laertius *Lives* 7.165 and criticized by Cicero in *Fin.* 2.43, 3.31, 4.40, 5.23, and 5.73. Elsewhere he is known as 'Herillus'.

famous; I see in the record that their leader was Xenophanes (whom I mentioned earlier), who was later followed by Parmenides and Zeno <of Elea>, on whose account these philosophers were called the 'Eleatics'.* A subsequent leader was Euclides, the student of Socrates from Megara; and it was owing to him that the name 'Megarians' was applied to people who maintained that only what is one, alike, and always the same is good.²⁰³ (The Megarians also took a lot from Plato.) The Eretrians received their name from Menedemus, since he came from Eretria: in their view, every good is located in the mind and the mental intuition by which truth is discerned.*²⁰⁴ The Elians held similar doctrines, though, in my view, the latter were more fully and elegantly expounded.*²⁰⁵ **[130]** If we despise these philosophers now, considering them out of date, we should certainly regard the next group with less condescension.²⁰⁶ Aristo, though a student of Zeno, actually accepted the views the latter paid lip service to, that virtue is the only good, and that only what is contrary to virtue is bad: he thought that the practical weights Zeno ascribed to indifferent things were illusory. His highest good is not to be affected on either side by such indifferent things, a state he called *adiaphoria* ['indifference'].²⁰⁷ Pyrrho's, however, was for the wise person not even to experience such things, a state called *apatheia* ['insensibility'].²⁰⁸

203. Euclides fr. 26a (Döring). Diogenes Laertius *Lives* 2.106 reports that Euclides identified the good with wisdom, god, and intelligence. His debt to Plato included an extreme anti-empiricism; see Eusebius *Preparation for the Gospel* 14.17.1 (fr. 27 Döring).
204. Menedemus fr. 17 (Giannantoni). Other sources stress Menedemus' denial of a plurality of goods or virtues; see Diogenes Laertius *Lives* 2.129 (cf. 2.134–36) and Plutarch *Moral Virtue* ch. 2 440e.
205. Diogenes Laertius *Lives* 2.105 records that the Eretrian school was an offshoot of the Elian group. The leader of the latter was Phaedo of Elis, a writer known for his Socratic dialogues. (The text is corrupt. The translation follows Reid's emendation to 'The Elians' rather than Plasberg's suggestion of 'Erillus'; there is no evidence of a connection between Erillus and the Eretrians.)
206. The second group of abandoned views—which usually includes Erillus' elsewhere in Cicero—have the distinction of being useful for discussing and criticizing the function of 'indifferents' in Stoic ethics; see, e.g., *Fin.* 3.31 and 4.40–43 and *Off.* 1.6.
207. Aristo fr. 1.362 (*SVF*). Aristo's view is spelled out in Diogenes Laertius *Lives* 7.160 (*SVF* 1.351). His refusal to recognize Zeno's categories of 'preferred' or 'dispreferred' indifferents (see *Ac.* 1.35–37) is explained in Sextus *M.* 11.63 (*SVF* 1.361) and criticized in Cicero *Fin.* 2.43 and 3.50. (The charge that Zeno's position is inconsistent is set out in *Fin.* 4.68–73.)
208. Pyrrho fr. 69a (Caizzi). 'Undisturbedness' (*ataraxia*) is the end standardly

"So, setting aside all these views, let's look now at the ends that have been defended strongly enough to endure.[209] **[131]** Some promoted pleasure as the end. The earliest of these was Aristippus, a student of Socrates, whose followers became 'the Cyrenaics'. Epicurus, whose school is now better known, came later—though, as a matter of fact, he didn't agree with the Cyrenaics on the subject of pleasure.[210] Next were: pleasure along with what is honourable, which was Calliphon's view; being free from any pain, Hieronymus' view; and the latter along with the honourable, Diodorus' view. (These two were both Peripatetics.) Next was living honourably while enjoying the primary objects nature recommends to human beings: this was the view of the Old Academy, as shown by the writings of Polemo (the Old Academic Antiochus particularly endorses), and the view Aristotle and his friends seem to come closest to as well.[211] Carneades also suggested the view that the highest good is to enjoy the primary objects nature has recommended—but he did so not because he approved it, but in opposition to the Stoics.[212] Last was living honourably, which is derived from the recommendation of nature: this was the ethical end established by Zeno, the originator and leader of the Stoics.[213] **[XLIII 132]** (It's obvious here that the negative ethical ends are the opposites to all the ends I have gone through.)

"Now I'll ask you to tell me which person I should follow, as long as no one gives the extremely uncultured and ridiculous response,

---

ascribed to Pyrrho, but Cicero's term is also attested; see, e.g., Eusebius *Preparation for the Gospel* 14.18.1–4 and 14.18.26, respectively. Cicero's purely ethical interpretation of Pyrrho is clearest in *Fin.* 2.43 and 4.43; he seems to be unaware of Pyrrhonian scepticism.

209. The list of more plausible ends given in this paragraph—and discussed repeatedly in Cicero—derives from Carneades' celebrated 'division of ends'; see *Fin.* 5.16–21 and K. Algra, 'Chrysippus, Carneades, Cicero: The Ethical *Divisiones* in Cicero's *Lucullus*', in B. Inwood and J. Mansfeld (eds.), *Assent and Argument* (New York/Leiden 1997), pp. 107–39.

210. Aristippus fr. 178 (Giannantoni). The differences between Aristippus' and Epicurus' hedonism are elucidated in *Fin.* 2.18–11 and 2.39–41. Epicurus' view is displayed in *Ac.* 2.138 and 2.140.

211. See *Ac.* 1.19–23. Antiochus claimed that the Old Academics and Peripatetics shared a single Platonic system of philosophy (see *Ac.* 2.136, 1.17–18, and 1.22). Cicero agrees that their ethical 'ends' are similar without conceding Antiochus' identification of their views.

212. See *Fin.* 5.20. Carneades is found arguing for a different view in *Ac.* 2.139.

213. See *Ac.* 1.35–39.

'Anyone you like, as long as it's someone.' No reply could be more ill-considered. I want to follow the Stoics. Do I have the permission, I won't say of Aristotle (a rather outstanding philosopher by my lights), of Antiochus himself? (Though he was called an Academic, he was actually an out-and-out Stoic—or would have been with very few changes.) So now there's a determinate question to decide: the wise person is to be either a Stoic or an Old Academic. He can't be both, because their dispute isn't about boundaries but ownership of the whole. Since the order structuring one's whole life is implied by the definition of the highest good, a disagreement about that is a disagreement about the order structuring one's whole life. Hence, since the disagreement between these schools is so wide, the wise person can't belong to both of them, but only to one. If he's a follower of Polemo, the Stoic errs by assenting to something false (and you yourselves say that nothing is more foreign to a wise person); but if Zeno's views are true, the same can be said against the Old Academics and Peripatetics. So is our candidate to assent to neither? ‡ And if I never assent, ‡ which of us is more prudent?* **[133]** Further, when Antiochus himself disagrees with his beloved Stoics on some matters, doesn't he indicate that those are views the wise person won't approve? The Stoics claim that all errors are equal, but this is a view Antiochus disclaims rather forcefully.[214] Permit me to think about which view I should follow, then. *Get on with it! Just pick one now!* he says. Even when I find the arguments on either side acute and of equal weight? Shouldn't I make sure I don't commit a crime? *It's a crime to betray a principle*—that's what you said, Lucullus.[215] So I hold myself back from assenting to something unknown—that's a principle I share with you.

[134] "Here's an even bigger disagreement. Zeno thinks that the happy life is found in virtue alone. What does Antiochus say? *You're right about the happy life, but not the happiest.*[216] The former is a god to believe that virtue lacks nothing. The latter is a mere man, because he thinks that many things are precious to human beings in addition to virtue, and some of them are necessary as well. But in Zeno's case, I

214. The Stoic view is explained in Diogenes Laertius *Lives* 7.120 (*SVF* 3.527) and Cicero *Fin.* 3.32 and 3.48 and *Paradoxa* 3.20–26. Some of Antiochus' grounds for rejecting it can be seen in Cicero's arguments at *Fin.* 4.74–77 and *For Murena* 60–66.
215. See *Ac.* 2.27.
216. See *Fin.* 5.71 and 5.81; Antiochus ascribes the same view to the Old Academics and Peripatetics in *Ac.* 1.22 (1.23). The coherence of the distinction is debated in *Fin.* 3.42–48 and 5.77–86. (Zeno's view is given in *Ac.* 1.35–37.)

worry that he ascribes more to virtue than nature allows, especially in the light of all Theophrastus' learned and eloquent arguments.*[217] And in Antiochus' case, I'm afraid that he is scarcely consistent when he says that there are bad bodily and external circumstances, and yet believes that someone subject to all of them will be happy if he's wise. I am torn: sometimes Zeno's view seems more persuasive to me, sometimes Antiochus'—and yet I think that virtue will utterly collapse unless one of them is right. But such are their disagreements.

[**XLIV 135**] "What about the views they agree on? Can we approve them as established truths? *The wise person's mind is never moved by appetitive desire or transported with pleasure.* Come on! But suppose I allow that this is persuasive; what about the next one? *He is never afraid or feels grief.*[218] Won't the wise person fear his country's destruction or grieve if it is destroyed? That's a harsh view, though one Zeno can't avoid, since he allows nothing except what is honourable to count as a good. But that's far from being the case for you, Antiochus: you accept many kinds of good in addition to what is honourable and many kinds of bad in addition to what is shameful; and the prospect of the latter will inevitably stimulate fear in the wise person, as their occurrence will stimulate grief. But I'd like to know when it became a principle in the Academy to claim that the wise person's mind isn't moved or disturbed.* The Old Academics gave their approval to 'mean-states', taking the view that there was a natural measure for each emotion. (We have all read the Old Academic Crantor's book *On Grief*—it's not long, but it's a golden volume and, as Panaetius advised Tubero, one to learn by heart.) Indeed, they even maintained that nature gave these emotions to our minds for our advantage: they said that fear was given to stimulate caution, pity and distress to stimulate clemency, and even that anger was the whetstone for courage—whether rightly or not we will see some other time.[219]

---

217. Theophrastus fr. 492 (Fortenbaugh); see *Ac.* 1.33 and 1.35. His doubts about the sufficiency of virtue for happiness are set out in *Tusc.* 5.24–25 and *Fin.* 5.77 and 5.85–86.

218. The Stoic claim that (normal) emotions should be eradicated is mentioned in *Ac.* 1.38–39 and defended in *Fin.* 3.35 and *Tusc.* Books 3 and 4. Antiochus' agreement is not attested elsewhere (in *Fin.* 5.32 he allows that the sage is moved by a grievous circumstance, but *Fin.* 5.95 suggests that this is not a full-blown emotion).

219. The Old Academic view is set out in *Tusc.* 4.43–46. Crantor's work *On Grief* argued against the Stoic or a pre-Stoic advocacy of emotional insensibility; see *Tusc.* 3.71 and [Plutarch] *Consolation* ch. 3 102c–d (Crantor fr. 3a–b [Mette]). Panaetius' advice was in a treatise on enduring grief dedicated to Tubero; see *Fin.* 4.43.

[136] "So I don't know how that severity of yours broke into the Academy. But it's the next lot that I can't bear. Not because I disagree with them—most of the Stoic paradoxes (*paradoxa* in Greek) are Socratic—but where did Xenocrates or Aristotle touch on them? It's your idea, after all, that the two schools are nearly identical. But would the latter ever maintain views like these? *Only the wise are kings, rich or handsome. Everything anywhere belongs to the wise. No one except the wise person is a consul, praetor, general*—or even, I suspect, a public commissioner? Or again, *Only the wise person is a citizen, only he is free, while the nonwise are all foreigners, exiles, slaves, and crazed.* And finally, *The writings of Lycurgus and Solon* and our own Twelve Tables *aren't laws, and there aren't any cities or citizen-bodies except those of the wise?*²²⁰ **[137]** If you give your assent to your friend Antiochus, Lucullus, you'll have to defend these doctrines as you would the city walls: I can accept them in fair measure, to the extent I see fit.

[XLV] "I have read in Clitomachus a bon-mot by Aulus Albinus (the Albinus who was consul with your grandfather, Lucullus, and a rather learned man, as the history he wrote in Greek shows). The story goes that in the year of his praetorship, under the consuls Publius Scipio and Marcus Marcellus, when Carneades and Diogenes the Stoic were waiting on the senate in the Capitolium, he quipped: 'So it's your impression, Carneades, that I am not a praetor, this is not a city, and there are no citizens in it?'* But Carneades replied: 'No, that's his, the Stoic, view!'²²¹ Aristotle or Xenocrates—the philosophers Antiochus wished to follow—would never have doubted that Albinus was a praetor or Rome a city or that a citizen-body inhabited it. But, as I said before, our friend Antiochus is clearly a Stoic, though he stammers here and there.

220. The Stoic ethical 'paradoxes' set out the counterintuitive consequences of the basic ethical principles they thought that everyone is committed to. Cicero's first set is reprised in *Fin.* 3.75 (cf. *Paradoxa St.* 6.42–52). The second set is explained in Stobaeus *Eclogues* 2.7.11i p.103.9 (*SVF* 3.328). The final set depends on the Stoic view that only sages can follow the (real) law (see Cicero *Rep.* 3.33) and the definition of a citizen-body as "a body of people living in the same place directed by law"; see Dio *Oration* 36.20 (*SVF* 3.329) and Cicero *Paradoxa* 4.27. (The Twelve Tables recorded ancient laws that formed the basis of the Roman legal system.)

221. Albinus' remark was intended as a criticism of the Academics' refusal to make knowledge-claims; see the similar objections in Epictetus *Discourses* 5.6–7, Aristocles in Eusebius *Preparation for the Gospel* 14.19.3, and Augustine *Against the Academics* 3.22. (The manuscripts mistakenly add the clause "because I am not wise" to Albinus' question. As Reid noted, this would mean that his joke was intended as the criticism of the Stoics Carneades turns it into.)

[138] "As for the rest of you, what advice do you have for me, since I'm worried about slipping into an opinion or giving my approbation and approval to something unknown, which is the last thing you want? Chrysippus often declares that there are only three views on the ethical end worth defending: the end is either the honourable or pleasure or both. He cuts back and thins out the remaining crowd on three grounds: philosophers maintaining that the highest good is for us to be free from all pain may run away from the invidious word 'pleasure', but they don't leave its neighbourhood; philosophers combining that end with the honourable do much the same; and philosophers linking the primary advantages of nature with the honourable aren't really doing anything different. So he keeps three views that he thinks can be defended persuasively.[222] [139] Maybe that's right—though it's not easy to tear myself away from the end adopted by Polemo, the Peripatetics, and Antiochus, and so far I don't find anything else more persuasive. Still, when I see how smoothly pleasure blandishes our senses I find myself slipping into assent to the view of Epicurus or Aristippus. Virtue calls me back, or rather claps her hand on me: she declares that such sensory movements belong to cattle and she links human beings to god.[223] I could take the intermediate position by following Calliphon, given that Aristippus looks only to the body, as if we don't have a mind, and Zeno takes in only the mind, as if we're innocent of bodies. And it's true that Carneades used to defend Calliphon's view so enthusiastically that he even seemed to approve it—though Clitomachus affirmed that he never could work out which view had Carneades' approval.[224] But if I choose to follow this end, won't truth itself and reason—serious, right reason—stand against me?* 'When what is honourable consists in spurning pleasure, are you really going to marry the honourable with pleasure, like man and beast?'

[XLVI 140] "So there's only one pair left to fight it out: pleasure vs. the honourable. This wasn't much of a fight for Chrysippus, as far as

222. Chrysippus fr. 3.21 (*SVF*). Chrysippus' division was the basis for the fuller Carneadian version used in *Ac.* 2.131; see Algra 1997. The six views listed here (*Ac.* 2.138) are identified in *Ac.* 2.131 as those of [1] Zeno (the Stoics), [2] Aristippus or Epicurus, [3] Calliphon, [4] Hieronymus, [5] Diodorus, and [6] Polemo (the Old Academics).
223. See *Ac.* 2.131. A very similar criticism of Aristippus is made in *Fin.* 2.39–41. (Virtue, Zeno's end, is equivalent to the honourable.)
224. See *Ac.* 2.131, where Carneades defended a theoretical view omitted by Chrysippus. (Calliphon's end is the combination of pleasure and the honourable; see *Ac.* 2.131.)

I can see.* 'If you follow pleasure, much of life is ruined, not least fellowship with the human race, love, friendship, justice, and the rest of the virtues, none of which can exist unless it's disinterested. A disposition driven to appropriate action by pleasure as if for profit isn't a virtue, but rather a deceptive imitation or simulation of virtue.'[225] But on the other side you can hear the Epicureans claiming that the term 'honourable' is one they can't even understand—unless, that is, we mean to call what goes down well with the crowd 'honourable'. 'The body is the source of all goods: this is the canon, rule, and ordinance of nature. No one who strays from it will ever have a guide to follow in their life.'[226]

[141] "Do you think that I'm not moved at all when I hear these arguments or countless others? I'm moved as much as you are, Lucullus: you mustn't think that I am any less of a human being than you are. The only difference is that when you're moved by something, you go along with it, assent to it, and approve it; you take it to be true, certain, apprehended, established, stable, and fixed; and you can't be dislodged or moved away from it by any argument.**[227] But I don't think that there are any <impressions> such that if I assented to them I wouldn't often be assenting to something false, because there isn't a differentiating feature dividing true from false <impressions>—especially since the 'criteria' of dialectic don't exist.*

[142] "This brings me to the third part of philosophy.[228] Protagoras gives one criterion, thinking that each person's impression is true for him; the Cyrenaics give another, since they think that there is no criterion except one's internal experience; and Epicurus another, limiting the criteria to the senses, our conceptions of things, and

---

225. Chrysippus fr. 3.21 (*SVF*). Chrysippus is ascribed a similar view in Plutarch *Stoic Contradictions* ch. 15 1040d (*SVF* 3.157), although the rest of Plutarch's chapter indicates that this is a crude summary of his position.
226. Epicurus fr. 400 (Usener). Epicurus' objection to the philosophical use of the term 'honourable' (*kalon*) is cited in *Ac.* 1.7 and further explained in *Fin.* 2.38. The Epicurean view that bodily pleasure is our ethical criterion or 'canon' (*kanôn*) is set out in *Fin.* 1.30; cf. Epicurus' *Letter to Menoeceus* in Diogenes Laertius *Lives* 10.129.
227. See *Ac.* 2.127–28.
228. The section on philosophical disagreements in 'logic' (*Ac.* 2.142–46) is curiously abbreviated in comparison with Sextus' treatment—he devotes *M.* 7 and 8 to epistemology. Cicero implicitly excuses his failure to give a fuller doxography in *Ac.* 2.147.

pleasure.[229] Meanwhile Plato thought that the criterion of truth, along with truth itself, was inaccessible to opinion and the senses: he took it to belong to thought itself and the mind.[230] **[143]** Does our friend Antiochus approve any of these views? No, he doesn't even follow his own predecessors! Where does he follow Xenocrates, who wrote a large number of well-received books on logic, or Aristotle, whose work is sharper and more refined than anyone's? He never strays a foot away from Chrysippus! **[XLVII]** So why are we called 'Academics'?* Have we misappropriated that famous name? Again, why should we be forced to follow philosophers whose views are mutually inconsistent? There is a tremendous controversy even about one of the dialecticians' elementary theorems—namely, how to judge the truth conditions for a conditional in the form exemplified by 'If it is day, it is light.' Diodorus has one view, Philo another, Chrysippus a third.[231] What about all the questions on which Chrysippus disagrees with his teacher Cleanthes?[232] Don't even Antipater and Archidemus, our two leading dialecticians, both rather opinionated men, disagree on a lot of issues?*[233]

[144] So why do you provoke hostility against me, summoning me before the crowd, as it were, and even ordering the workshops to be closed down, as seditious tribunes like to do?[234] What's the point of

229. Cicero gives a standard interpretation of Protagoras' claim that "man is the measure of all things, of those that are that they are and of those that are not that they are not" (fr. B1 DK) cited in Sextus *M.* 7.60 and Plato *Theaetetus* 152a. The Cyrenaic view is expressed in slightly different terms in *Ac.* 2.20 and 2.76. The summary of Epicurus' views (fr. 245 Usener) is paralleled at Diogenes Laertius *Lives* 10.31; cf. Epicurus *Principal Doctrine* 24 (Diogenes Laertius *Lives* 10.147) and Cicero *Fin.* 1.22–23.
230. See Antiochus' similar report in *Ac.* 1.30–32. Cicero's source for this interpretation of Plato's epistemology clearly did not share the sceptical view of Academic history Cicero advocates in *Ac.* 2.74 or 1.46.
231. See Sextus *PH* 2.110–12 and *M.* 8.111–17 and S. Bobzien, 'Logic 2–3.1–7', in K. Algra, J. Barnes, J. Mansfeld, and M. Schofield (eds.), *The Cambridge History of Hellenistic Philosophy* (Cambridge 1999) 83–157, pp. 83–86 and 106–9.
232. See Diogenes Laertius *Lives* 7.179 (*SVF* 2.1). A prominent example is their disagreement over the correct response to Diodorus 'Master Argument'; see Epictetus *Discourses* 2.19.1–5 (*SVF* 2.283) and Cicero *Fat.* 14.
233. The surviving evidence for Archidemus' work on logic (collected in *SVF* 3) is too slight to support Cicero's claim. The two logicians are frequently paired in Epictetus, e.g., in *Discourses* 2.17.40 and 3.2.13.
234. The argument in this paragraph—a second response to the objection in *Ac.*

your complaint that we do away with the systematic arts if not to stir up the artisans? If they come running from all directions, it won't be difficult to rouse them up against you. First I'll relate your invidious paradoxes: by your account, everyone standing in the crowd is an exile, a slave, and insane.[235] Then I'll come to a second charge, which doesn't pertain to the crowd so much as to you, the people who are actually here: Zeno, and Antiochus along with him, denies that you know anything.[236] 'How can that be right,' you'll say, 'when we maintain that even a fool apprehends many things?' [145] Yes, but you deny that anyone *knows* anything, except the wise person. Zeno used to demonstrate this with gestures. When he had put his hand out flat in front him with his fingers straight, he would say: 'An impression is like this.' Next, after contracting his fingers a bit: 'Assent is like this.' Then, when he had bunched his hand up to make a fist, he would say that that was an 'apprehension' or 'grasp'. (This image also suggested the name he gave to it, *katalêpsis* [lit. 'grasp'], which hadn't been used before.) Finally, when he had put his left hand on top, squeezing his fist tight with some force, he would say that scientific knowledge was like that: a state none but the wise enjoyed—though as for who is or ever was wise, even they aren't in a rush to say.[237] It follows then, Catulus, that you don't know that it is light now, or you, Hortensius, that we are in your villa.

[146] "Are these charges any less invidious? I agree that they aren't very sophisticated: my earlier ones were more subtle. Still, just as you argued that the systematic arts were finished if nothing was apprehensible and refused to concede to me that persuasive \<impressions\>

2.22—is restated without the political metaphor in *Ac.* 2.146. The workshops were shut down for political assemblies and legal holidays (*iustitium*). A seditious tribune might exercise this power in contravention of normal procedure in order to amass a pliant crowd to pass controversial laws—this is perhaps what Gracchus did in 133 BCE (see *Ac.* 2.13–15) and certainly what Clodius did when he had Cicero exiled in 58 BCE (see Cicero *On His Own House* 59).

235. See *Ac.* 2.136–37.

236. Sextus gives a similar argument in *M.* 7.432–34.

237. Zeno fr. 1.66 (*SVF*); see *Ac.* 1.40–42 and Sextus *M.* 7.151. The simile may be misleading because the temporal progression does not apply in the epistemological case: assent to a single impression immediately constitutes both an apprehension and a piece of 'scientific' knowledge if the impression is 'apprehensible' and the subject is wise. (The current existence of any Stoic sages is doubted by Chrysippus in Plutarch *Stoic Contradictions* ch. 31 1048e [*SVF* 3.662]; cf. Sextus *M.* 7.432–34 and 9.133–36.)

are adequate for the arts, so I put it to you now that one can't have a systematic art without scientific knowledge. Would Zeuxis, Phidias, or Polyclitus allow that they didn't know anything, for all their incredible skill? And yet if someone had explained to them the force 'knowledge' was supposed to have, they would stop being angry; and they wouldn't be annoyed with us, either, once they had learned that we did away with something that never existed but left them with something adequate for their needs. The care of our ancestors also led them to approve this policy <of forswearing knowledge-claims>.[238] They insisted that people making oaths should swear 'following the view in their mind' and then be held liable 'if they knowingly deceived', on the grounds that there was a lot of ignorance in our lives. They also insisted that anyone giving evidence should report what he 'thought' even about things he had seen first-hand, and that judges under oath shouldn't declare their findings as to the facts, but as to their 'impression' of the facts.*

[XLVIII 147] "However, I should come to a close, Lucullus, since it's time for me to sail, as the west wind's whispers as well as the boatman's signals are telling me, and since I have said quite enough. But next time we think about these questions, let's talk about the remarkable disagreements between the leading thinkers, the obscurity of nature, and the error of so many philosophers about what is good and bad—for, since their ethical views are incompatible and at most one of them can be true, a good number of rather famous schools must collapse. Next time, let's do that rather than talking about the illusions of our eyes or other senses and the paradox of the sorites or the liar, which are traps the Stoics have set for themselves."[239]

General Conclusion

[148] Then Lucullus replied: "I'm not sorry that we discussed these questions: we can debate whatever we see fit at many future meetings,

238. Cicero appeals to the technical terminology of Roman legal practice. The formulae for oaths are exemplified together in Livy *History of Rome* 22.53.10–11 (cf. Cicero *Or.* 2.260); the final formula for evidence and verdicts is deployed in Cicero *For Caecina* 73 and *Against Piso* 97.

239. See *Ac.* 2.112. Cicero suggests that his arguments against Stoic apprehension (*Ac.* 2.64–111) were purely defensive: the fundamental case for scepticism derives from the disagreements of dogmatic philosophers (*Ac.* 2.112–46). The latter were the staple of both Academic and Pyrrhonian sceptical arguments.

particularly at my Tusculan house, I hope." "Wonderful!" I said. "But what does Catulus think, and Hortensius?" Then Catulus said: "What do I think? I am returning to my father's view, which he at least said was Carneades'. That is, while I don't think that anything is apprehensible, I still reckon that the wise person will assent to something he hasn't apprehended—that is, hold opinions—but in such a way that he understands that it is an opinion and realizes that nothing is apprehensible.[240] So, while I ‡ can't accept ‡ that universal *epokhê* ['suspension of assent'], the other Academic view, that nothing is apprehensible, has my vehement approval."*[241] "I'm glad to have your view," I said, "and I don't entirely reject it. But what are your thoughts, Hortensius?" "Away with it," he replied, with a smile. "I'm with you," I said, "since that's a view that suits the Academy."[242] That was the end of our conversation: Catulus stayed behind, while we went down to our boats.

240. Catulus' father is mentioned as a critic of Philo's Roman Books in *Ac.* 2.11–12 and 2.18. His mitigatedly sceptical position—i.e., his acceptance 'opinion'—fits the interpretation of Carneades mentioned in *Ac.* 2.59 and ascribed to Philo and Metrodorus in *Ac.* 2.78. (Cicero's rejection of this view there thus explains Catulus' reservation in the previous sentence.) See pages xxviii–xxx.

241. A corruption in the manuscripts means that it is textually unclear whether Catulus means to accept or reject *epokhê* here. Some scholars assume that Catulus is referring to the distinction between two kinds of assent in *Ac.* 2.104–5; on this view, Catulus would accept *epokhê*. But the previous sentence shows that—unlike Cicero and Clitomachus—he holds opinions and thus rejects *epokhê* in both the senses identified in *Ac.* 2.104–5. See page xxix, n. 48.

242. Hortensius' reply is a pun, meaning either "Away with assent!" or "Away with us (or the boats)!" (The nautical metaphor and its applicability to assent is explained in Cicero *ad Att.* 13.21.3.) Cicero welcomes the pun because he agrees with Hortensius and Lucullus that *epokhê* is the appropriate response to universal inapprehensibility; see *Ac.* 2.59 and 2.78.

Academici Libri
Book 1 *(Varro)*

Introduction

[I 1] The other day, when my friend Atticus was staying with me at my villa in Cumae, we received a message from Marcus Varro reporting that he had arrived from Rome the evening before and would come straight on to us if he was not tired from his journey. On hearing this, we thought we should admit no delay in seeing someone so connected to us by our common pursuits and the length of our friendship. So we immediately set out to meet him; and when we were a short distance away from his villa we saw him on his way to us. When we had embraced him (as friends do), after a decent interval, we took him back to his villa.* **[2]** After we arrived, there was a bit of preliminary conversation while I asked if there was any news from Rome. Then Atticus said: "Stop asking questions we can't ask or have answered without distress, please, and ask him instead whether *he* has any news.[1] Varro's muses have been silent for longer than usual—though I don't imagine he has given up: he must be hiding whatever he's writing." "You're quite wrong," Varro replied; "I consider it a fool's lot to write something you want to keep hidden. In fact, I have a large work on hand I've been working on for some time: I've started on a book dedicated to our friend here," he meant me, "but it's rather large and I'm working it up very carefully."[2] **[3]** "I've been waiting for it," I said, "for quite a while. But I haven't ventured to demand it because I've heard from our friend Libo (you know his enthusiasm: we can't hide anything of this sort from one another) that you haven't stopped work on it. He says you're treating it with such attention that it never leaves your hands.

"However, there *is* something that it never crossed my mind to ask you before. But, now that I've started to put on record the subjects you

---

1. News from Rome in the spring of 45 BCE meant reports of Julius Caesar's success in stamping out the remaining military opposition to his political hegemony.
2. The work in question is Varro's multivolume *On the Latin Language;* its second part is dedicated to Cicero.

and I studied together, by trying to elucidate in Latin the old philosophical system that took its start from Socrates, I will ask you: why is it that, although you write on many topics, you don't cover this field—especially given your skill at it and the preeminence of this pursuit, and the subject altogether, over all the other systematic arts?"[3]

[II 4] Varro replied: "Your question is one that has troubled me a great deal. So I will reply without hesitation: I can respond immediately because, as I said, I have thought long and hard on this subject. As I have seen that philosophy has been very carefully expounded in Greek, I have come to the following view about people from our country who are seriously interested in it. If they have had the benefit of an education in Greek learning, they will read works in Greek rather than in our own language. But if they have taken against Greek arts or disciplines, they won't care for Latin works, either, since the latter can't be understood without knowledge from the Greeks. As a result I have been unwilling to write works that would neither be intelligible to the unlearned nor something the learned cared to read.

[5] "You see, of course, since you've studied the same philosophical doctrines yourself, that *we* can't be like Amafinius or Rabirius.[*4] They argue unsystematically about what's under their noses in ordinary language; they have no recourse to definition, division, or formal argument; and, in fact, they consider the systematic study of speech and argument worthless. For our part, however, we must obey the precepts of the dialecticians and the orators as if they were laws, since our school thinks that dialectic and rhetoric are virtues. So we have no choice but to use novel terms—and since, as I said, the learned will prefer to find these from the Greeks, while the unlearned won't accept them even from us, the whole enterprise is pointless. [6] As for physics, if I approved Epicurus', that is, Democritus' views, I could of course write about it as plainly as Amafinius. Once you've done away with active causes, what's impressive about writing about the chance

---

3. Cicero and Varro had both attended Antiochus' lectures on the Old Academy in Athens in 79–77 BCE (cf. *Ac.* 1.5 and 1.12 below). Unlike Cicero, however, Varro was a convinced Antiochian, as we learn in *Ac.* 1.5–7, and might be expected to have explained his philosophical view in some of his many published works.
4. Amafinius and Rabirius wrote popular works on Epicurean philosophy in Latin; see *Tusc.* 4.6–7 and *ad Fam.* 15.19.2. Varro's dismissal of the Epicureans for their failure to study formal logic and technical rhetoric and the naivety of their physics and ethics is echoed repeatedly elsewhere in Cicero; see, e.g., *Fin.* 1.17–26.

interactions of corpuscles (his term for 'atoms')? You know our physics: since it's constituted by an active cause and the matter that active cause shapes and forms, it can't be done without geometry.⁵ But how is anyone going to be able to do that in Latin? What terms will they express it in, and who are they going to get to understand it?

"As for writing about our lives, ethical dispositions, and what we should seek or avoid, that's easy for them, because they think the good is the same for man and beast. But you're aware, of course, of the remarkable subtlety of our writers on this subject. [7] If you follow Zeno, it's a serious business to get anyone to understand what he means by his true and simple good that can't be divorced from what is honourable—while Epicurus flatly denies that he can even imagine a kind of good that doesn't involve the pleasures that stimulate our senses.⁶ But if you're going to follow the Old Academy, the school I approve, as you know, think how subtly we'll have to expound its position, and how cleverly, even obscurely, we'll have to argue against the Stoics!

"So I fully embrace the pursuit of philosophy for myself, both to make my life as consistent as I can and to delight my mind: as Plato says, I don't believe the gods have given any greater or better gift to human beings.⁷ [8] But I send friends who are interested in it to Greece; that is, I tell them to go to the Greeks so they can draw these doctrines from their original sources rather than pursuing derivative work in Latin.* What I *have* done, however, to the extent that I could—and I'm no great admirer of my books—is to make known to our people subjects no one had yet taught and for which sources weren't available for interested people to consult. These were subjects one couldn't get from the Greeks or even from Latin sources after the passing of our own Lucius Aelius. Still, even in my early *Satires*—the imitations (not translations) of Menippus I spiced up with a dash of humour—there's a good deal of profound philosophy in the mix, and quite a bit of

---

5. See *Ac.* 1.24. Varro is probably referring to the Old Academic study of mathematical astronomy. He may also be alluding to the geometrical basis of the elements in Plato's *Timaeus*, though this seems incompatible with the infinite divisibility of matter noted in *Ac.* 1.27. (Epicurus rejected conventional geometry; see *Ac.* 2.106.)
6. This is a paraphrase of Epicurus *On the Ethical End* fr. 67 (Usener): "As for me, I can't conceive of the good if you take away the pleasures of the throat, the pleasures of sex, the pleasures of sound, or the pleasant motions associated with visual shape." Epicurus' criticism of Zeno's conception of the good is given in *Ac.* 2.140.
7. Plato *Timaeus* 47b1–2.

dialectical language. (I enticed less learned people into reading these parts by a dose of wit, which made them more easily understood.*) And in my *Laudatory Portraits*, and especially in the introductions to my *Antiquities*, I tried to write in a philosophical way, though I don't know how successful I was."[8]

[III 9] Then I replied: "You're quite right, Varro. We were strangers lost in our own city until your books played the role of hosts, leading us home so we could at last recognize ourselves and where we were. You have opened up for us the age and chronology of our country, the laws governing our rites and priesthoods, our domestic and military training, the boundaries of our regions and districts, and the titles, classes, duties, and origins of everything human and divine.* You have also shed a great deal of light on our poets and on Latin literature and language altogether.* And you have yourself written varied and elegant poetry in nearly every metre, as well as introducing the rudiments of philosophy at many points in a way that suffices to stimulate interest, although it's too slight to give instruction.

[10] "Now the defence you offer <for not writing philosophy in Latin> is certainly persuasive: readers will either have the appropriate education and prefer to read Greek works, or they won't and won't read our works, either. But tell me, do you really prove your point?* I don't think so, because people who can't read Greek won't neglect our works, and those who can won't belittle work in their own language. Is there any reason why people educated in Greek literature should read Latin poets but not philosophers? Is it because they take pleasure in Ennius, Pacuvius, Accius, and many others who have reproduced the power, if not the words, of Greek poets? Won't they take considerably more pleasure in philosophers if they model themselves on Plato, Aristotle, and Theophrastus, as the poets have modeled themselves on Aeschylus, Sophocles, and Euripides? (Our orators, at any rate, are praised, I note, when any of them model themselves on Hyperides or Demosthenes.)

[11] "In my own case, Varro—to be completely frank—while I was tied up with many duties imposed by elections, public office, legal

---

8. Varro's vast literary and antiquarian output is lost. But, as Cicero stresses in the next paragraph, his scholarly achievements in the *Antiquities* (47 BCE) had a significant impact on subsequent Roman literature and history. His more philosophical works include the contemporary *On the Latin Language* (43 BCE)—alluded to in *Ac.* 1.2—and later treatises, including the *Disciplines* (on educational theory), and his Antiochian *On Philosophy* (summarized in Augustine, *City of God* 19.1–3).

cases, and even a degree of governance of the republic over and above my solicitude for it, I kept my philosophical interests private and renewed them through reading when I could, to stop them from getting rusty. But now that I have been wounded by a very severe blow from fortune, I am looking for a balm for my sorrow from philosophy; and now that I have been freed from administering the republic, I judge this to be the most honourable relaxation for my time of leisure.[9] Perhaps it is particularly suited to my time of life. Perhaps it is especially consistent with any praiseworthy actions I may have performed. Perhaps it's also true that nothing else is as useful for the education of our fellow-citizens. Or perhaps, if none of these reasons work, I can't see anything else I could do. **[12]** At any rate, our friend Brutus (who is preeminent in every field of merit) is expounding philosophy in Latin so well that you wouldn't feel any need for Greek works on the subjects he treats. And he follows the same philosophical view as you: he studied with Aristus in Athens for quite some time, just as you studied with Aristus' brother, Antiochus. That's why you should dedicate yourself to this branch of literature as well, I think."

[IV 13] Then Varro replied: "I will certainly think this over, though not without your help. But what's this I hear about you?" "In what connexion?" I said. "That you have abandoned the Old Academy," he said, "and are dealing with the New."[10] "What of it?" I said. "Was it more permissible for our friend Antiochus to leave his new home for an old one than for me to switch to the new from the old? Isn't the latest thing always the most up-to-date and corrected? Though Philo, Antiochus' teacher and a remarkable man, as you yourself think, denies in his books—as I heard openly from the man himself—that there were two Academies, and criticizes the mistake of those who thought there were."* "You're quite right," he said, "but I don't think that you're

9. Cicero alludes to the dictatorship of Julius Caesar, which made legal and political work largely impossible, and to the recent death of his daughter Tullia in February 45 BCE.

10. This question (along with Cicero's reply) has been taken as evidence that Cicero had been a follower of Antiochus in the 70s to 50s BCE, before reconverting to Academic scepticism in the mid-40s. But the verb Varro uses is more naturally understood as referring to a recent change of subjects in Cicero's writing and his decision to include openly sceptical interlocutors; see page xi and W. Görler, 'Silencing the Troublemaker: De Legibus I. 39 and the Continuity of Cicero's Scepticism', in J. Powell (ed.), *Cicero the Philosopher* (Oxford 1995), pp. 85–113. (Antiochus' own conversion is discussed in *Ac.* 2.69–71.)

unaware of the riposte Antiochus wrote to Philo's thesis."*11 **[14]** "Actually, I would like you to reacquaint me with this controversy and the whole issue of the Old Academy, if you don't mind, since I have been out of touch with it for quite a while. But if you like that idea," I added, "let's sit down." "I agree with the second suggestion, at any rate," he said, "since I'm rather weak. But let's see whether Atticus is agreeable to my doing what I can see you want me to do." "Me?" Atticus replied. "What else would I rather do than recall the views I heard from Antiochus long ago—and see at the same time whether they can be expressed profitably in Latin?" After this exchange, we sat down facing each other.

Varro's Speech

[15] Then Varro began like this.12 "As I see it, Socrates was the first (this is a point accepted by all) to summon philosophy away from the obscure subjects nature itself has veiled—the questions all his philosophical predecessors had been concerned with—and to direct it towards ordinary life. He set it onto investigating virtue and vice and good and bad in general, considering celestial subjects to be far beyond our knowledge or, even if they were perfectly knowable, still completely irrelevant to the good life.13 **[16]** His manner of argument

---

11. This passage is vital for a reconstruction of the Sosus affair of 88/7 BCE recorded in *Ac.* 2.11–12 and 2.18. We learn there that Antiochus, like Catulus senior (representing mitigatedly sceptical Academics), was enraged by Philo's Roman Books for their historical misrepresentation of 'the Academics'. We can infer from this passage that Philo's historical thesis was a claim about the philosophical unity of the Academy—presumably the suggestion that all the Academics, probably from Socrates on, accepted the epistemological claims of the Roman Books (the target of Antiochus' criticism in *Ac.* 2.18.). See pages xxx–xxxi and xxxvii–xxxviii and Brittain 2001, chapters 4–5.

12. Varro's speech reports Antiochus' views on the history of philosophy. It is divided into two main sections: *Ac.* 1.15–32 records the views of 'the Old Academics and Peripatetics' about ethics (*Ac.* 1.19–23), physics (*Ac.* 1.24–29), and logic (*Ac.* 1.30–32; *Ac.* 1.33–42 explains changes to it made by Peripatetics (*Ac.* 1.33–34) and Zeno, the founder of the Stoa (*Ac.* 1.35–42). Antiochus' own philosophical commitments are not easily read off from this summary, since he accepts some, but not all, of the 'corrections' in the second part; see pages xxxi–xxxv.

13. Socrates' rejection of physics or natural philosophy in favour of an ethics focused on ordinary life is recorded in similar terms in Xenophon *Memorabilia* 1.1.10–16 (cf. Cicero *Tusc.* 5.10); the further claim that physics would be useless even if it were knowable is also found in *Ac.* 2.123 (cf. Xenophon 1.1.13).

is the same in practically all the conversations his students wrote up so eloquently and variously: he makes no affirmation of his own, but refutes other people and says that he knows nothing except just that. This, he says, is his advantage over everyone else: while they think they know what they don't know, he knows just the fact that he doesn't know anything—and that, he thinks, is why he was declared the wisest of all men by Apollo, because not thinking you know what you don't know is the sum of human wisdom.[14] And yet, though he kept making these claims and stuck with this view, every speech of his was taken up with praising virtue and exhorting people to pursue it, as one can see from the books of the Socratics, and especially Plato's.[*]

[17] "Following Plato's complex and eloquent lead, a single and concordant system of philosophy developed under two names: the philosophy of the Academics and the Peripatetics. Despite their difference in name, they agreed in their doctrine.[15] Plato, you see, left Speusippus, his sister's son, as the heir of his philosophy, <but his work was inherited> by two men of outstanding energy and learning: Xenocrates of Calchedon and Aristotle of Stagira. Aristotle's companions were called 'Peripatetics' because they held their debates as they strolled in the Lyceum, while the students who held their meetings and conversations in the Academy (another gymnasium), as Plato had, received their name from there. But since both were raised on Plato's riches, they drew up a fixed system of teaching—a remarkably full and detailed system—and abandoned that Socratic habit of arguing in doubt about everything and without making any affirmation. The result was something Socrates was far from approving: a systematic art of philosophy, an ordering of subjects, and a framework for teaching.

---

14. Varro's portrait of Socrates' method follows Plato's in the *Apology*. (The last clause is an allusion to *Apology* 23b.) The stress on the genuineness of his disclaimer of first-order knowledge and on his aporetic technique contrasts strongly with Lucullus' 'ironic' interpretation in *Ac.* 2.14. Cicero gives a similar view based on Socratic dialogues in *Ac.* 2.74 (though perhaps not in *Ac.* 1.44–45).

15. The essential agreement of the Old Academics and Peripatetics is a fundamental tenet of Antiochus' syncretism (cf. *Ac.* 2.15). The scope of their agreement, however, is left unclear, since Antiochus allows in *Ac.* 1.33–34 that Aristotle undermined the Platonic metaphysics and epistemology and Theophrastus rejected one of Plato's basic ethical doctrines; he also notes several fundamental disagreements about the nature of the mind or soul; see *Ac.* 1.22 and 1.39. (In *Ac.* 1.18, Varro appears to base their unity on their agreement in ethics.)

[18] "Now at first this was, as I said, a single system with two names: there was no difference between the Peripatetics and the so-called Old Academy. True, the fertility of his intellect gave Aristotle the advantage (in my view, at least); but both schools had the same source and the same division of things we should seek or avoid. [V]—But what am I doing?" he said. "It's mad for me to pretend to teach you this! Even if it isn't a case of the proverbial pig teaching Minerva, it's silly for anyone to pretend to teach her!" But Atticus said: "No, no, carry on, Varro! I really love our language and our people, so your story delights me when it's spoken in Latin like this." "Imagine my feelings, then," I said, "since I have declared that I'm going to put philosophy on display to the Roman people!" "Let's go on, then," Varro said, "since you want to.

[19] "Well, they started with a threefold theory of philosophy inherited from Plato, one part dealing with our way of life and ethical dispositions, another with nature and hidden subjects, and the third with argument, i.e., judging what is true or false, correct or incorrect in its expression, and consistent or inconsistent. They derived the first part of philosophy—the pursuit of the good life—from nature. They said that we should obey nature—we shouldn't seek the highest good (which we use to determine everything else) from anything other than nature—and they determined that the goal of appetition, or the ethical end, is to have obtained everything natural in mind, body, and life.[16]

"They located some bodily goods in the whole body and others in its parts: health, strength, and beauty in the whole; in the parts, the soundness of the senses and any excellence of the individual parts, such as speed in the feet, force in the hands, clarity in the voice, and articulate formation of words in the tongue. [20] They considered mental goods to be those enabling our intellects to grasp virtue, and

---

16. The 'Old Academic and Peripatetic' end is redescribed in *Ac.* 1.22 as obtaining all or the greatest primary goods in accordance with nature. Since virtue is the greatest primary good and the source of 'the honourable', this is equivalent to 'living honourably while enjoying the primary objects nature recommends', the end ascribed to Polemo in particular, but also to Aristotle and Antiochus in *Ac.* 2.131–32 and 2.138–39. Antiochus' claim that Polemo anticipated the Stoic appeal to nature and especially their theory of self-appropriation (*oikeiôsis*) is found repeatedly in Cicero—see *Ac.* 1.23 and *Fin.* 2.33–34, 4.14–18, 5.24–33, and 5.74—and perhaps echoed in Plutarch *Common Conceptions* 1069e–f. Its historical accuracy remains controversial; see J. Dillon, *The Heirs of Plato: A Study of the Old Academy, 347–274 BC* (Oxford 2003), pp. 159–66.

these were divided into natural and dispositional goods. They counted quickness at learning and memory (since both belong to the mind or intellect) as natural goods; but they thought that dispositional goods were tendencies or habits. They molded these partly by constant practice and partly by reason—practice and reason being the domain of philosophy. (In the development of philosophy, a stage initiated but not yet completed is called 'progress' towards virtue, but once completed, i.e., once it constitutes a virtue, it is called a 'perfection of our nature', the single best state amongst the mental goods they ascribe to us.) So these are the mental goods. [21] They claimed that the goods belonging to our lives—this was the third kind—were circumstances conducive to the exercise of virtue, on the ground that virtue is manifest in the goods of the mind and body, but also in some circumstances that belong less to nature than to the happy life.* For they considered human beings to be parts of a society and of the human race as a whole, and hence thought that they were bound to other human beings in a humane association.[17] So this is their treatment of the highest and natural good; but they take the other goods, such as wealth, resources, glory, or influence, to be means for increasing or preserving that.* That's how they introduce the tripartite theory of goods.

[VI 22] "These are the 'three kinds of good' most people ascribe to the Peripatetics. Nor are they wrong about that—this division *does* belong to them. The mistake is to think that the 'Academics' of that time differed from the 'Peripatetics'. They shared this theory, and both groups believed that the ethical end was to obtain all or the greatest of the primary objects nature recommends (i.e., the objects sought for their own sake).[18] But the greatest primary objects are precisely the ones in the mind and in virtue. (22) So the unanimous view of that ancient system of philosophy was this: while the happy life depends on virtue alone, it isn't the happiest life without the addition of bodily goods and of the other category described above, i.e., goods

17. The third kind of good includes relational goods such as friendships and membership in a flourishing community; see *Fin.* 5.68. The Stoics construed these goods as psychological states in the good person (see, e.g., Stobaeus *Eclogues* 2.7.11c p. 94.21, *SVF* 3.98); but the Peripatetics and Old Academics regard them as external goods, i.e., as partly contingent on other people or the state of the world.

18. The goods sought for their own sake are the primary goods included in the three categories of the 'highest good', as opposed to the 'other goods' mentioned at the end of *Ac.* 1.21; see *Fin.* 5.68. The status of the latter is left rather unclear here and in *Fin.* 5.

conducive to the exercise of virtue.[19] **[23]** This framework also allowed them to discover the principle of action in life, as well as the principle of 'appropriate action', namely, the conservation of the objects nature prescribes.* This gave rise to the avoidance of idleness and spurning of pleasures, which in turn led people to undertake many serious (and painful) labours for the sake of what is right or honourable (as well as for the objects conforming to the framework laid down by nature). This was the source of friendship, justice, and equity, and of the preference for these over the enjoyment of pleasures and many of life's advantages.[20] So this was their training of ethical dispositions and the system or framework of the part of philosophy I put first.

[24] "Their treatment of nature—the second part of philosophy—led them to divide it into two things, with one active and the other lending itself to it and thus acted on in some manner.*[21] Force was in the active nature, they thought, and just a kind of 'matter' in the nature it acted upon, but both were present in each. For matter couldn't cohere by itself without being contained by some force, nor force without some matter since anything that exists is necessarily somewhere. But it was only the product of both that they called 'body' and, so to speak, 'a quality'.

"(I'm sure you'll allow me to use novel terms in these unfamiliar subjects, as the Greeks themselves—the sources for the material we've

---

19. See *Ac.* 2.134, where this distinction between the happy and happiest lives is also ascribed to Antiochus himself.

20. The status of pleasure in Antiochus' ethics—or in his version of the ancients' ethics—is unclear. In some accounts it ranks as a natural primary object (see *Fin.* 5.45), but the distinction between pleasure and 'advantages' here suggests that Varro disagrees.

21. Varro's exposition of Old Academic physics in *Ac.* 1.24–29 is extremely compressed and, as a result, very controversial; see pages xxxii–xxxiii and D. Sedley, 'The Origins of Stoic God', in D. Frede and A. Laks (eds.), *Traditions of Theology* (Boston/Leiden 2002), pp. 41–83. The metaphysical analysis outlined in this paragraph corresponds to an interpretation of Plato's *Timaeus* given by Theophrastus fr. 230 (ed. Fortenbaugh = Simplicius *Commentary on Aristotle's Physics* 26.7–15) and echoed in *Ac.* 2.118; but it is also very similar to the Stoic view, e.g., in Diogenes Laertius *Lives* 7.134 (*SVF* 2.300). (The text of the last clause in this sentence is disputed. Reid and other editors think that the phrase *efficeretur aliquid*—translated above as 'acted on in some manner'—must mean 'something else is produced' and emend the clause accordingly. This is what the Latin phrase means in *Ac.* 1.28; but its use in the second sentence of *Ac.* 1.24 demands the less usual sense given above.)

been dealing with—do?" [**VII 25**] "Of course," Atticus said, "and you can even use Greek terms, when needed, should Latin fail you." "That's very kind of you, but I'll try to speak entirely in Latin, except when I use terms like 'philosophy', 'rhetoric', 'physics', or 'dialectic', which, like many others, ordinary usage now accepts as Latin. So I used the term 'qualities' for what the Greeks call *poiotêtes*—itself not an ordinary word in Greek, but a philosophical term, like many others.[22] None of the dialecticians' terms, for instance, are in ordinary usage, so they use their own terms. In fact, it is a common feature of nearly all systematic arts that they must either coin novel terms for their new discoveries or use words coined for other things metaphorically. But if this is what the Greeks do when they've been busy with these subjects for so many centuries now, isn't it a good deal more legitimate for us, when we're trying to deal with them for the first time?" [**26**] "Absolutely, Varro," I said, "and I think you'll have done very well by your fellow-citizens if you increase their supply of words as you already have their knowledge of facts." "In that case," he said, "I'll risk using novel terms on your authority, if it proves necessary.)

"Some of these 'qualities' are primary, others are derived from them. The primary qualities are uniform and simple; the derivatives are differentiated and, as it were, 'multiform'. Thus air (another Greek word we use in Latin), fire, water, and earth are primary, while the species of living things and the products of the earth are derived from them. Hence the former are called 'principles' or, to translate the Greek term, 'elements'; and among them, air and fire have the function of imparting motion or being active, while the remaining parts—water and earth, I mean—of receiving or, as it were, 'undergoing'.[23] (Aristotle imagined that there was a unique fifth kind from which stars and minds are made, i.e., something different from the four elements I mentioned above.)[24]

22. The Greek term *poiotês* ('quality') was introduced by Plato in *Theaetetus* 182a.

23. Varro makes it sound as if earth and water were wholly inert and passive, like matter, and are thus the 'things' acted on and moved by air and fire. But since all of the elements are 'qualities', all are active to some degree. The Stoic view is remarkably similar; see Nemesius *On Human Nature* 5 p.164.15–18 (Matthaei; *SVF* 2.418) and Plutarch *Common Conceptions* ch. 49 1085c–d (*SVF* 2.444).

24. Aristotle argued for a fifth element to explain the eternal circular motion of the heavens in his work *On the Heavens,* but he did not suggest that it was the material basis for the mind or soul (though see *Generation of Animals* 736b36). Cicero's error (repeated in *Tusc.* 1.22) is probably due to later Peripatetic elaborations of Aristotle's scattered remarks on the role of *pneuma* (fiery air) in human psychology, and a subsequent conflation of *pneuma* with the fifth element.

[27] "But underlying everything there is a kind of 'matter', they think, without any form, and lacking any of those qualities (let's keep using this term and make it more familiar and gentler on the ear). Everything has been produced or brought about from this, because matter as a whole can receive everything and change in every way and in every part. Matter thus 'perishes' into its parts rather than into nothing; and these parts can be infinitely cut or divided since there is no smallest unit in the nature of things, i.e., nothing that can't be divided. Moreover, everything that is moved is moved through intervals, and these intervals can likewise be infinitely divided.

[28] "Now because the force we called 'quality' moves in this way, i.e., because it passes to and fro <through matter> like this, they think that matter as a whole is completely changed, producing what they call 'qualified things'.[25] From these a single world has been brought about in the totality of <material> nature when it coheres and is continuous in all its parts.[26] No portion of matter, and no body, is outside this world: everything in it is a part of the world, and all its parts are held together by a sentient nature possessed of perfect reason (which is eternal since there is nothing stronger to make it perish).

[29] "This force is the mind of the world, they claim; it is also an intelligence, the perfect wisdom they call 'god', and a kind of 'providence' over all the things subject to it, which exercises forethought primarily over celestial affairs, but also over terrestrial matters of relevance to human beings. Sometimes they call this 'necessity', because nothing can be other than as it is determined in the 'fated' (if I may) and immutable sequence of its eternal order."[27] But occasionally they

25. In *Ac.* 1.24 'quality' referred to the conjunction of 'force' and 'matter', but here it is identified with 'force', and in *Ac.* 1.29 with god. (The new distinction between 'quality' and 'qualified things' may correspond to the primary and derivative 'qualities' of *Ac.* 1.26.) The reference to the manner in which force moves through matter probably alludes to all the interactions of the two natures described in *Ac.* 1.24–27. The idea that the oscillation of force in matter produces individual things is close to the Stoic doctrine of 'tonic force'; see Nemesius *On Human Nature* 2 p.71.1–4 (Matthaei; *SVF* 2.451) and Alexander *On Mixture* p. 224.23–26 (*SVF* 2.442).

26. The 'nature' in this sentence must be matter, the second of the two natures identified in *Ac.* 1.24. The contribution of force, the first 'nature', is explained in the next sentence.

27. Plasberg marks a lacuna in this sentence, and some editors have wanted to add 'fate' as another term for god or force (it is one the Stoics could use in this context, though see Cicero *DND* 1.39). But the sentence makes sense as it is.

call it 'chance' because it brings about many things we find unforeseen and unexpected owing to the obscurity of their causes (or our ignorance of them).[28]

[**VIII 30**] "Next is the third part of philosophy, which dealt with reasoning and argument. Both schools treated it as follows.[29] The criterion of truth was not in the senses, they maintained, although it took its start from the senses: the mind was the judge of things.[30] They believed that this was the only faculty deserving our trust, because it alone discerned what was always simple, uniform, and same as itself. (*Idea* was the term they used for this, the name Plato had already given it; but we can rightly call it a 'Form'.)[31] [**31**] The senses were all blunt and feeble, in their view, and quite unable to apprehend the things people thought were subject to perception, because the latter were either so small that they were undetectable by the senses or moving so rapidly that nothing was one or constant or even self-identical because everything was continually slipping or flowing away. For this reason, they called this whole domain 'subject to opinion'.[32] [**32**] Knowledge, they believed, existed only in the conceptions and reasoning of the mind. Accordingly, they approved the use of definitions of things and applied them to all the subjects they discussed. The analysis of words was another practice they approved, i.e., investigating the explanations for the names things had been given (which they called *etumologia* ['etymology']). They went on to use certain signs or 'marks' of things as guides to arrive at proofs or demonstrations

28. The titles and attributes of force in this paragraph are those the Stoics customarily ascribe to their god; see Diogenes Laertius *Lives* 7.147 and 7.149 (*SVF* 2.1021 and 2.1132) and Cicero *DND* 1.39 (*SVF* 2.1077). If the Old Academics accepted universal determinism and regarded the 'world-soul' as the highest god, as Antiochus (or Varro) implies here, their position anticipated the Stoics' very precisely in its major departures from the Platonic views advocated in the *Timaeus* and *Republic* 10.

29. Varro's exposition of the logic of the two schools in *Ac.* 1.30–32 is thoroughly Platonic (with the exception of the final reference to Peripatetic rhetoric), as he implicitly recognizes in *Ac.* 1.33.

30. Elsewhere *orietur*, 'took its start from', is translated as 'derived from', which implies a form of empiricism accepted by Antiochus (see, e.g., *Ac.* 2.21–22 and 30–31), but apparently incompatible with the Platonic view given here and in *Ac.* 1.31. The phrase here may allude to the role of perception in the process of 'recollection'; see Plato *Phaedo* 73c.

31. The term *idea* became the technical term for transcendental 'Platonic Forms' in the Platonic tradition. Plato's forms are ascribed similar qualities, e.g., in *Phaedo* 78d.

32. See Plato *Timaeus* 28a; cf. *Republic* 5.477–79.

of the thing they wanted to explain. This was their teaching of the whole method of dialectic, i.e., speech used in formal argument.* Its counterpart, as it were, was the ability to use rhetoric, i.e., the development of continuous speech adapted for persuasion.[33]

[33] "Such was the original system of philosophy they inherited from Plato. If you would like me to, I'll go on to explain the changes it underwent to my knowledge."*[34] "We would certainly like you to," I said, "to answer for Atticus, too." "It's the right answer," Atticus said. "This is an outstanding exposition of the tradition upheld by the Peripatetics and Old Academy!" [IX] "Well, the first to change things was Aristotle, who undermined the Forms I mentioned a bit earlier— though Plato had been so astonishingly keen on them that he claimed that there was an element of the divine in them.[35] The next was Theophrastus. He was a charming speaker and of such a good disposition that he serves as a showcase for honesty and candour. But in one sense he shattered the authority of the old tradition with even more violence: he stripped virtue of its beauty and rendered it weak by denying that the happy life depended only on it.[36] [34] As for Strato, his pupil, he should definitely be removed from the tradition, for all his sharpness of intellect. He abandoned the most necessary part of philosophy—the part treating virtue and ethical dispositions—dedicating himself entirely to the study of nature, and then disagreed extensively with his teachers even in that part of philosophy.[37] Speusippus and Xenocrates, however, who were the first people to take over Plato's theory and authority, and after them Polemo and Crates, along with Crantor—all fellow-Academics—diligently preserved the doctrines they had received from their predecessors.[38] Next came Zeno and Arcesilaus, who had been dedicated students of Polemo. [35] But Zeno—Arcesilaus' senior in age and a very subtle disputant as well as

33. The phrase translated by 'counterpart' is a gloss on the Greek term *antistrophos*, used in this context by Aristotle in *Rhetoric* 1.1.
34. Antiochus' reaction to the 'corrections' set out in *Ac.* 1.33–42 is not clear from Varro's report; see pages xxxi–xxxiv.
35. Some notable examples of Aristotle's criticisms of the Platonic Forms (or at least some versions of them) are in *Nicomachian Ethics* 1.6, *Metaphysics* 1.9, and the fragmentary *On the Ideas*.
36. Theophrastus fr. 497 (Fortenbaugh). See *Ac.* 2.134.
37. Strato fr. 13 (Wehrli). See *Ac.* 2.121.
38. Varro underplays the originality of the Old Academics and their often radically divergent elaborations of Platonic suggestions, as his remark on Xenocrates and his predecessors in *Ac.* 1.39 lets slip. See Dillon 2003.

a razor-sharp thinker—tried to correct the tradition. If you agree, I'll set out his corrections as well, as Antiochus used to." "I do," I said, "and you can see that Atticus is signaling his assent, too."

[X] "Well, Zeno was not at all the sort of person to hamstring virtue, as Theophrastus had. Quite the reverse: his position was that everything belonging to the happy life depends on virtue alone. He admitted nothing else into the category of goods, and gave the name 'honourable' to the uniform, unique, and only good there was.[39] [36] But, though everything else was neither good nor bad, he claimed that some of these <indifferent> things were in accordance with nature and others contrary to nature—and in between the latter two he added a further class of intermediates. He taught that those in accordance with nature were worthy of selection and assigned them a degree of value, and the reverse for the opposite class, while those that were neither he left in the intermediate class, to which he ascribed no practical weight at all. [37] But among those worthy of selection <or disselection> some were assigned considerable value or disvalue; he called the former 'preferred' and the latter 'dispreferred' <indifferents>.[40]

"So this was one case in which he had changed not so much the doctrines as the terms.[41] The next was his classification of 'appropriate' and 'inappropriate' actions as intermediate between right action and error. Since he classed only actions performed rightly as good and only actions performed perversely, i.e., errors, as bad, he considered the <unqualified> performance or omission of appropriate actions intermediate, as I said.[42]

39. See *Ac.* 2.131–32 and 2.134 on Zeno's definition of the end and his disagreements with the Old Academics and Theophrastus about goodness.
40. The Stoic theory of value and its relation to goodness is set out in more detail in Diogenes Laertius *Lives* 7.101–7 and Cicero *Fin.* 3.16–25 and 3.50–54. (The two supplements in the translation are necessary to make sense of Cicero's rather rapid summary.)
41. Antiochus regarded the Stoic doctrine of value as merely a restatement of the Old Academic and Peripatetic view of the relative insignificance of bodily and external goods in comparison with virtue or honourable states and action; see *Fin.* 4.68–72 and 5.72–75. The general claim that Zeno's differences from 'the ancients' were merely terminological is a leitmotif of Antiochus' theory of the history of philosophy; see *Ac.* 2.15–16 and 1.43 below.
42. Zeno thought that actions such as preserving one's health or paying back debts were normally 'appropriate' for any agent. But the action-type is morally 'indifferent' as such, and every individual action is either a case of virtuous action (and

[38] "<Zeno also made four further corrections in ethics.> While his predecessors claimed that not every virtue belonged to reason, but that some were brought to perfection through natural dispositions and habit, he considered all of them to be rational.*43 While they thought that the nonrational kinds of virtue I just mentioned were separable, he argued, first, that this was quite impossible; second, that what was intrinsically excellent wasn't just the exercise of the virtues, as his predecessors had claimed, but the disposition itself; and third, that all the same no one actually had virtue without exercising it continually.44 While they didn't try to eradicate emotion from human beings—they allowed it to be in our nature to grieve, have appetitive desires, be frightened, and be transported with pleasure—but tried to diminish it and narrow its range, his view was that the wise person should lack these morbid passions altogether.45 [39] While the ancients claimed that such emotions were the products of our nonrational nature and ascribed nonrational desire to one part of the mind and reason to another, he disagreed even with these doctrines. He thought that emotions were voluntary, i.e., brought about by the judgment of opinion, and that the source of all emotions was a sort of wild lack of self-control.46 This is more or less where Zeno stood in ethics.

---

hence good) or vicious action (and hence bad); see Diogenes Laertius _Lives_ 7.107–10 and Cicero _Fin._ 3.58 (_SVF_ 3.493–98), and Brennan 2003. Antiochus took this to be a misleading restatement of the Platonic doctrine of the primacy of virtue; see, e.g., _Republic_ 4.443d–e.

43. The Stoic doctrine is set out in Plutarch _Moral Virtue_ ch. 2 441 (_SVF_ 3.255); Lucullus presents it as Antiochus' view in _Ac._ 2.31. The 'ancient' (primarily Aristotelian) view is mentioned in _Ac._ 1.20. In _Fin._ 5.34 Antiochus accepts the natural but not the dispositional virtues of _Ac._ 1.20.

44. These Stoic doctrines about virtue are explained more fully in Diogenes Laertius _Lives_ Bk. 7; see 7.125 (_SVF_ 3.295) on the inseparability of the virtues, 7.94–97 on the intrinsic excellence of the disposition itself, and 7.128 (_SVF_ 1.569) on its continual exercise. Antiochus' agreement with the Stoics in the former two cases, at least, is shown by _Fin._ 5.66–67. (Plato and Aristotle argue for the Socratic thesis of the inseparability of the virtues in, e.g., _Republic_ 4.443d–444c and _Nicomachian Ethics_ 6.13; but they acknowledge the separability of lower kinds of 'virtues'.)

45. See _Ac._ 2.135, which notes Antiochus' agreement with the Stoic view.

46. Zeno thought that emotions were voluntary because they derive from opinion—i.e., our own weak assent to impressions; see _Tusc._ 4.14 and _Ac._ 1.41. The relevant opinion is the false belief that something sufficiently good or bad is happening or going to happen to you that you should get worked up about it; see _Tusc._ 3.24–25, and _Tusc._ 4.22 on the source of emotion (cf. _SVF_ 3.379–85).

[IX] "His position on the natural principles was as follows. First, he didn't accept the addition to the four elements of that fifth nature his predecessors imagined as the source of the senses and the mind: he declared that fire was the nature that brings everything into being, and also the mind and the senses.*[47] A second disagreement with them was his belief that it was quite impossible for anything to be acted on by something entirely without body (which is what Xenocrates, along with his predecessors, had claimed the mind to be): neither what acts nor what it acts on could be noncorporeal.[48]

[40] "The alterations he made in the third part of philosophy were more extensive.[49] The first change here was his innovative set of claims about sense-perception itself. He considered sense-perceptions to be compounds of a kind of externally induced 'impact'—he called this a *phantasia,* but we can call it an 'impression' (and let's hold on to this term, since we're going to need it rather often in the rest of our conversation).*[50] But, as I was saying, he conjoined these—the impressions 'received' by the senses, so to speak—with the assent of our minds, which he took to be voluntary and have its source in us.[51]

47. See *Ac.* 1.26. Zeno defined god as an intelligent fire constituting nature; see Cicero *DND* 1.39 and 2.57–58 (*SVF* 2.1077). As *pneuma* (or fiery air) it also constitutes our minds or natures; see Diogenes Laertius *Lives* 7.156 (*SVF* 2.774).

48. Zeno's disagreements on physics are limited to questions about the mind or soul because, in Antiochus' account, the Old Academics anticipated his major physical doctrines. But Varro recognizes here that Plato and at least the early Old Academics held that the mind was incorporeal (Xenocrates' definition is given at *Ac.* 2.124).

49. Antiochus' response to Zeno's radical innovations in epistemology is demonstrated in *Ac.* 2.17–60: in this case, at least, he accepted the corrections to the Platonic tradition without reservation.

50. Zeno fr. 1.55 (*SVF*). Zeno defined an impression as a 'printing (*tupôsis*) on the soul'; see Diogenes Laertius *Lives* 7.50 and Sextus *M.* 7.228–41 (*SVF* 2.55–56), where the psychological implications of this metaphor are disputed by Cleanthes and Chrysippus. But the stress here is on the external cause of perceptual impressions; see *Ac.* 2.34 and *Fat.* 42–43.

51. Zeno fr. 1.61 (*SVF*); see *Ac.* 2.37–39. The Stoics thought that our rational acceptance or rejection of externally induced impressions allowed us to play active and individual causal roles in the world; see Diogenes Laertius *Lives* 7.85–86 (*SVF* 3.178). But they were compatibilists: our assent is voluntary or 'up to us' because it is determined by our own characters or beliefs rather than external circumstances; see *Fat.* 39–43 and Gellius *Attic Nights* 7.2 (*SVF* 2.1000). (Zeno in fact reserved the term 'perception' for the conjunction of '*apprehensible*' perceptual impressions and assent, as Cicero explains in *Ac.* 1.41.)

[41] "He didn't put his trust in all impressions but only in those that revealed their objects in a special way. Since this kind of impression could be discerned just by itself, he called it 'apprehensible'.⁵²—Can you bear this?" "Of course," Atticus replied, "how else could you translate *katalêpton* [lit. 'graspable']?"—"But once it had been received and approved, he called it an 'apprehension' or 'grasp', like something grasped by one's hand. (In fact, that was his source for this term, since no one had used this word for that kind of thing before. Zeno used a lot of novel terms, but what he was saying was new, too.) He called an impression that had been apprehended by one of the senses a 'perception' itself. And if it had been apprehended in such a way that it couldn't be dislodged by reason, he called it 'scientific knowledge', if not, 'ignorance'.⁵³ The latter was also the source of opinion, which was a weak condition covering false as well as unknown <impressions>.⁵⁴

[42] "But to the 'apprehension' I mentioned he assigned a position in between scientific knowledge and ignorance, counting it as neither good nor bad, though he said it alone warranted our trust. Owing to it he also rated the senses as trustworthy, since, as I said before, he thought that an apprehension caused by the senses was true and

52. Zeno fr. 1.60 (*SVF*); see *Ac.* 2.18, 2.77, and 2.112–13. The self-warranting nature of 'apprehensible' impressions is stressed in similar terms in Sextus *M.* 7.252 and, by the Younger Stoics, 7.257. This passage explains Cicero's curious choice of passive phrases to describe 'apprehensible' impressions despite the active term standardly used in Greek, i.e., 'cataleptic', *kataléptikê*, which means 'providing' or 'enabling apprehension'. He clearly thinks that the relevant Greek term is the related passive form 'apprehensible', *katalêpton*—and his literal translation here, using *comprehendibile*, is an accurate rendering of the passive term. See pages xxxix–xliii.
53. See *Ac.* 2.145. Assent to a perceptual 'apprehensible' impression is an apprehension constituting a veridical 'perception' (see *Ac.* 1.40 and Diogenes Laertius *Lives* 7.52 [*SVF* 2.71]). But the apprehension or perception itself constitutes either a case of 'scientific' knowledge in the sage or a case of 'ignorance' in the fool; see Sextus *M.* 7.151–53 (*SVF* 2.90).
54. The sage's knowledge is secure because his belief-set is entirely constituted by apprehensions; see *Ac.* 2.23. But even the apprehensions of ordinary people are insecure (or cases of 'ignorance') because their belief-sets do not prevent them from assenting to 'inapprehensible' impressions, i.e., from forming true or false opinions; see Plutarch *Stoic Contradictions* 1056f (*SVF* 2.993). (Some sources also employ 'opinion' in a second sense, meaning 'weak supposition', which is an epistemic state roughly equivalent to 'ignorance' as defined here; see Stobaeus *Eclogues* 2.7.11m pp. 112.2–4 [*SVF* 3.548], Sextus *M.* 7.151, and E. Arthur, 'The Stoic Analysis of the Mind's Reactions to Presentations', *Hermes* 111 (1983), pp. 69–78.)

reliable—not because it apprehended all the features of its object, but on the ground that it omitted nothing detectable by it.[55] Another reason was that nature had given apprehension as a standard and starting point for scientific knowledge of the world: it was the source from which our conceptions of things were later stamped on our minds, which in turn give rise not just to the starting points but to certain broader paths for discovering reason.[56] But error, rashness, ignorance, opinion, supposition, and, in a word, everything foreign to stable and consistent assent, he excluded from virtue and wisdom.[57] These were pretty much all the changes marking Zeno's disagreement with his predecessors."

Interlude

[XII 43] When he had finished, I said: "Well, Varro, that was certainly a succinct and lucid exposition of the theory of the Old Academy and the Stoics—though I think it's true, as Antiochus believed, that the latter should be considered a correction of the Old Academy rather than a new system."[*58] Varro replied: "Since you have defected from the theory of the ancients and approve Arcesilaus' innovations, it's your job now to explain how and why the break occurred, so we can see whether this defection was adequately justified."

55. The Stoic view about the range of features represented in 'apprehensible' impressions is unclear. In *M.* 7.248–51 Sextus insists that they reproduce "all the characteristics (*idiômata*)" of their objects; but this may mean 'all their *distinctive* features'. See Frede 1999, pp. 305–8.
56. See *Ac.* 2.21–26 and 2.30–31. Perceptual apprehension generates the (pre-) conceptions or 'starting points' from which reason develops. (The function of perceptual apprehension as the 'standard' or criterion for nonperceptual knowledge is distinct from the criterial role of self-warranting 'apprehensible' impressions; see G. Striker, 'The Problem of the Criterion', in S. Everson (ed.), *Epistemology* (Cambridge 1990), pp. 143–60.)
57. See *Ac.* 2.77 (cf. 2.66–68) and pages xxii–xxiii. The cognitive failings of ordinary people listed here include false belief ('error') and premature assent to insufficiently warranted impressions ('rashness'), which results in unwarranted true or false belief ('opinion'). The precise meaning of the remaining terms here is unclear. 'Ignorance' [*inscientia*] was defined above as the ordinary person's disposition to assent to false or unwarranted impressions; but Varro uses an alternative Latin term here [*ignorantia*], which may refer to culpable lack of belief.
58. Cicero's agreement here with the principal thesis of Antiochus' history (see *Ac.* 2.16) conflicts with his position in *Ac.* 2. In the earlier book, he consistently used the disagreements between the Old Academics and Stoics to undermine Antiochus; see, e.g., *Ac.* 2.69, 2.112–13, and 2.143 and Brittain 2001, chapter 4.ii.

Cicero's Speech

[44] Then I said: "This is how we understand it. It wasn't a spirit of intransigence or rivalry (in my view, at any rate) that gave rise to Arcesilaus' extended disagreement with Zeno, but the obscurity of things that had previously led Socrates to his confession of ignorance—as even before him, it had led Democritus, Anaxagoras, Empedocles, and virtually all the early philosophers to say that nothing could be cognized, apprehended, or known, because the senses were limited, our minds weak, and the course of our lives brief, while the truth had been submerged in an abyss (as Democritus said), everything was subject to opinion and custom, no room was left for truth, and consequently everything was shrouded by darkness.*59 [45] That's why Arcesilaus used to deny that anything could be known, not even the residual claim Socrates had allowed himself, i.e., the knowledge that he didn't know anything.60 He thought that everything was hidden so deeply and that nothing could be discerned or understood. For these reasons, he thought that we shouldn't assert or affirm anything, or approve it with assent: we should always curb our rashness and restrain ourselves from any slip.61 But he considered it particularly rash to approve something false or unknown, because nothing was more shameful than for one's assent or approval to outrun knowledge or apprehension. His practice was consistent with this theory, so that by

59. See *Ac.* 2.14 and 2.72–74. The catchphrases summarize the Presocratics' sceptical pronouncements; they are attributed specifically to Democritus (fr. B117 DK cited in *Ac.* 2.32), Empedocles, Xenophanes, and Anaxagoras by Lactantius in his *Divine Institutes* 3.28.10–13 and 3.30.6. See Brittain and Palmer 2001.

60. This account of Socrates' views seems to be inconsistent with Cicero's earlier version in *Ac.* 2.74 (responding to *Ac.* 2.15) as well as Varro's in *Ac.* 1.15–16. Socrates is represented there as the aporetic questioner of Plato's Socratic dialogues, whose confession of ignorance is the consequence of his method. But here his aporetic method is explained as a consequence of his acceptance of inapprehensibility for theoretical reasons set out by the Presocratics. The earlier version gives the precedent for his own position to which Arcesilaus appeals in *Or.* 3.67, *DND* 1.11, and *Fin.* 2.2.

61. Cicero grounds Arcesilaus' suspension of assent on his acceptance of universal inapprehensibility and of a theory of rationality here. This explanation of his motivation conflicts with the less dogmatic accounts in *Ac.* 2.66–67 and 2.77, where both views derive from 'agreements' with Zeno, and with the more clearly sceptical interpretations in Sextus *PH* 1.232–33 and Diogenes Laertius *Lives* 4.28. See pages xxiii–xxv and J. Cooper, 'Arcesilaus: Socratic and Sceptic', in J. Cooper, *Knowledge, Nature, and the Good: Essays on Ancient Philosophy* (Princeton 2004), pp. 81–103.

arguing against everyone's views he led most of them away from their own: when arguments of equal weight were found for the opposite sides of the same subject, it was easier to withhold assent from either side.[62]

[46] "They call this the 'New Academy', though I think it's old, assuming we count Plato as part of the Old Academy. In his books nothing is affirmed, there are many arguments on either side, everything is under investigation, and nothing is claimed to be certain.[63] Still, let's call the position you expounded the Old and this the New Academy. It stuck with Arcesilaus' position right down to Carneades, the fourth in line after Arcesilaus. Carneades had expertise in every area of philosophy; he was also—as I heard from people who had studied with him, and particularly from the Epicurean Zeno, who radically disagreed with him, but admired him beyond all other philosophers—a person of incredible ability in . . ."[64]

---

62. A tempting emendation by Madvig would replace the phrase *de sua*, 'away from their own <view>', with *in eam*, 'to his own <position of *epokhê*>'.

63. See *Ac.* 2.74 (responding to *Ac.* 2.15). This is Cicero's response to Varro's account in *Ac.* 1.17. Evidence for other sceptical interpretations of Plato's dialogues is found in the anonymous *Commentary on the Theaetetus* col. 54.38–55.13 and *Prolegomena to Plato's Dialogues* chapter 10. See pages xxxv–xxxviii and J. Annas, 'Plato the Sceptic', *Oxford Studies in Ancient Philosophy*, suppl. vol. (Oxford 1992), pp. 43–72.

64. The manuscripts break off here. Cicero's lost report on Carneades may have indicated how he strengthened the sceptical Academy by introducing 'persuasive' impressions as a 'practical criterion'; see *Ac.* 2.16 and 2.32 and Augustine *Against the Academics* 2.12.

Fragments from the
Academici Libri[1]

Book 1

1.   What makes Mnesarchus so splenetic? Why does Antipater cross swords with Carneades in so many books?[2] (cf. *Ac.* 2.69)

2.   . . . he thought their views were in harmony owing to the similarity of the terms.

Book 2

3.   Does anything seem as flat as the sea? That's why the poets even call it the 'level <deep>'. (cf. *Ac.* 2.105)

4.   People who begin to love political office too late are rarely admitted to it and cannot find adequate acceptance from the populace. (cf. *Ac.* 2.70?)

5.   . . . to do away with greed, dismiss wickedness, and set up one's life as a model for youth . . . (cf. *Ac.* 2.114)

---

1. The translation follows the order of Reid's collection of fragments (omitting the incoherent fr. 17 *malcho in opera adfixa*). Most of the fragments assigned to specific books are from the grammarian Nonius Marcellus (fr. 1–15, 18–28, and 30–31). Since Nonius' interest in the work was limited to odd grammatical forms—such as the phrase 'cross swords' in fr. 1—he does not always supply a whole sentence and he never gives the context of the fragments. Fr. 18–31 are almost identical to sentences in the first edition. In these fragments, minor changes between the two editions are marked with square brackets for supplements in the second edition and angle brackets for omissions from the first edition. See pages xviii–xix.
2. Fr. 1–15 are cited in Nonius Marcellus' *Compendious Erudition* pp. 65; 43; 65; 69; 104; 121; 162; 162; 394; 474; 545; 65; 65; 123; and 419. (The page numbers refer to the pagination in the early edition by J. Mercerus. The standard Teubner edition by W. Lindsay's from 1903 has a different pagination but still records Mercerus'.)

6. What about the moon? Can you really say what shape it is? Its horns appear blunter at one time and sharper at another, as it waxes and wanes. (cf. *Ac.* 2.75–82)

7. What about the sea? Isn't it blue? But when a wave is churned by oars, it turns purple and <the surface> of the water is somehow tinged or contaminated . . . (cf. *Ac.* 2.105)

8. But if we believed that, we wouldn't need plumb lines, builders' squares, or rulers.

9. There are different complexions in adults and youths, the sick and the healthy, the sober and the drunk . . . (cf. *Ac.* 2.88)

10. When we submerge ourselves, like divers plunging in the water, we can't see what's above, or only a little, obscurely. (cf. *Ac.* 2.80–81)

11. . . . some people even find a box of unguent disgusting.

Book 3

12. But who wouldn't say that it is quite miserable and extremely stupid to spend all one's time crossing swords or fighting with desperate criminals?

13. . . . just as we are now sitting at the Lucrine Lake, watching the tiny fish leap.

14. . . . to think that in all the diversity of living things it is only humans who are endowed with the desire for knowledge and understanding.

15. . . . he should have a right, he should claim his freedom . . .

16. . . . but if people who have followed the wrong path in life were allowed to correct their error by remorse, like people who have taken a wrong turn on a journey, their rashness would be easier to correct.[3]

---

3. Lactantius *Divine Institutes* 6.24. Augustine makes considerable use of the simile of a wrong turn as an anti-sceptical argument in his *Against the Academics* 1.10–14 and 3.34–36.

18.   . . . we will just say that perspicuity—which is the thing we must keep a very tight grip on—is missing.[4] (= *Ac.* 2.51)

19.   . . . who used to rear a great number of hens for their living; well, when these men had inspected an egg, they could usually tell which hen had laid <it>. (= *Ac.* 2.57)

Book 4

20.   But the Stoics, with Antiochus in agreement, thought that . . . (= *Ac.* 2.67)

21.   . . . seek the shade of the Maenian balconies, so, when things got hot, Antiochus sought the [path] of the Old Academics. (= *Ac.* 2.70)

22.   He isn't sculpted from stone or hewn from wood . . . (= *Ac.* 2.101)

23.   . . . because it looked green to us a moment ago, and will look gray < . . . >, and the patch that < . . . > is glittering in the sun . . . (= *Ac.* 2.105)

24.   . . . and I believe Clitomachus when he writes that Carneades had accomplished an almost Herculean labour . . . (= *Ac.* 2.108)

25.   That seemed a bit rich even to Antiochus, as well as self-contradictory! (= *Ac.* 2.109)

26.   But he didn't convince Anaximander, his fellow-citizen and companion, since the latter said that there was an indeterminate . . . (= *Ac.* 2.118)

27.   . . . (as you have it), <why has> he created such a supply of vipers and water snakes . . . (= *Ac.* 2.120)

28.   . . . though his explanation is not like Democritus', who claimed that things are compounded from rough, <smooth,> and hooked or barbed bodies . . . (= *Ac.* 2.121)

29.   All these things are hidden, [Varro], and <shrouded> in deep darkness . . .[5] (= *Ac.* 2.122)

---

4. Fr. 18–28 are cited in Nonius *Compendious Erudition* pp. 139; 117; 69; 65; 99; 164; 107; 163; 122; 65; and 189 (Mercerus).
5. Martianus Capella *The Marriage of Philology and Mercury* 5.157.

30.   . . . than I that it isn't. You even claim that there are people directly opposite us on the other side of the earth, their footsteps standing opposite ours . . .[6] (= *Ac.* 2.123)

31.   . . . clearly a Stoic, though he stammers here and there. (= *Ac.* 2.137)

Unassigned Fragments

32.   *These are your words, <Cicero>:* But in my view we aren't just blind to wisdom, but blunt or dull even to the things that seem partially discernible.[7] (cf. *Ac.* 2.80–82)

33.   *The Academic says:* I take everything I decided to call 'persuasive' or 'truth-like' to be like this. But if you want to give them another name, I don't object in the slightest. It's enough for me that you now understand properly what I'm saying, i.e., that you understand which things I am giving this name to: a wise person should be an investigator of nature, not a creator of terms. . . . *Do you think that Cicero, whose words these are, lacked the knowledge of Latin to be able to find suitable terms to express his thoughts?*[8] (cf. *Ac.* 2.98–105 and 2.32–36)

34.   *There's a passage in the books Cicero wrote to defend this view [viz., the Academic view] <which says that>* . . . the second prize is given to the Academic wise person by all the self-declared sages from the other schools, since they must obviously claim the first prize for themselves. A persuasive conclusion one can draw from this is that he is right to take the first place in his own judgment given that he has the second place in the judgment of all the others.[9] (cf. *Ac.* 2.114–15)

35.   *Cicero says in that book that* it was their custom to hide their views and that they were not in the habit of revealing them to anyone who had not lived with them right up to their old age.[10] (cf. *Ac.* 2.60, 2.139)

---

6. Fr. 30–31 are cited in Nonius *Compendious Erudition* pp. 102 and 80 (Mercerus).

7. Lactantius *Divine Institutes* 3.14.

8. Augustine *Against the Academics* 2.26. It is not clear that this passage—or either of the next two excerpts—gives a 'fragment' of Cicero's Latin; the last sentence could quite naturally be taken to mean only that Cicero used the terms *probabile* and *verisimile* ('persuasive' and 'truth-like'). The fact that the Academic protagonists say something in Augustine does not itself imply that they are quoting Cicero; and since Augustine has just given a mistaken definition of these Academic terms, it seems unlikely he has Cicero's text before him here.

9. Augustine *Against the Academics* 3.15.

10. Augustine *Against the Academics* 3.43.

36.   *In fact, Cicero himself gives a similar plaudit to <Varro> in his* Academic Books *when he says that the dispute there was one he had had* with a person who was easily the sharpest of men and without any doubt the most learned.[11] (cf. *Ac.* 1.1–3)

Concordance of fragments[12]

Reid	Plasberg	Reid	Plasberg	Reid	Plasberg
1	1	13		25	
2	11	14	17	26	
3	4	15	20	27	
4	14	16	18	28	
5	13	17		29	
6	3	18		30	
7	6	19		31	
8	2	20		32	21
9	7	21		33	12
10	8	22		34	15
11	9	23		35	16
12	19	24		36	22

11. Augustine *City of God* 6.2.
12. Plasberg cites the unnumbered fragments in his apparatus under the relevant parallel passages in *Ac.* 2.

Textual Appendix

This appendix lists significant departures from Plasberg's Teubner text, marked with an asterisk at the end of the relevant sentence in the translation. Authorities are cited as they are given in Plasberg's apparatus (or, when necessary, Reid's); the translator's own conjectures are cited under 'Brittain'. (Plasberg's Greek letters for the manuscripts of the *Academici Libri* are anglicized here.)

Text translated here	Manuscript or editorial authority
Lucullus (*Ac.* 2):	
2.7 contra omnis dicere quae	Reid
2.7 in utramque partem dicendo eliciant	dett. (Reid)
2.8 quae praescripta a quibusdam et	dett. (Reid)
2.9 ut potuerint potuerunt omnibus rebus	Madvig
2.9 Iudicaverunt autem re semel audita atque	Lambinus
2.10 totam enim rem Lucullo integram	dett.
2.11 cum quo Antiochum	A1V
2.12 tum et illa dixit Antiochus	A2V2B2
2.43 quoniam vel illa vera definitio	AVB
2.48 non numquam, veri simile <est>	A2, corrected by Madvig
2.50 Ut, si lupi	V2
2.50 quod de suo genere	A2B2
2.53 inter visa nihil interesset	V2
2.54 ut si sint	Baiter
2.55 [et eo quidem innumerabiles]	Reid
2.56 potiusque refello propter	V2
2.58 nihil . . . magis adsentiri <par> est	V2, corrected by Davies
2.58 hoc illud esse, quasi	Madvig
2.63 tantum enim te non modo	AVB
2.76 Quid tibi Cyrenaei videntur	Durand
2.77 quod est, ut eius<dem> modi	V2, corrected by Davies

2.79 Manent . . . , iacet . . . dicit.	Reid
2.80 et importunitate insistere	David Mankin (per litteras)
2.80 Sit hic quidem	dett. (Reid)
2.80 audiret quam . . . male ageret	Reid
2.80 et e regione, Pompeianum non cerno	Reid
2.81 dicet me acrius	dett. (Reid)
2.82 mentiantur aut non multum	V2
2.84 quae falsa esse non posset	dett. (Reid)
2.88 experrectus sit eum somnia ea putare	Brittain (after Halm)
2.88 illa visa putare, ut erant, somnia	Madvig
2.89 laeva innixus, Diana facem iacit a luna	anon. (Reid)
2.94 progredi; inlustribus igitur rebus	AVB
2.95 mentiris et verum dicis	A3
2.95 sequendas esse alias, alias inprobandas	Reid
2.99 contra naturam esset probabile nihil esse	Christ
2.102 quod tamen . . . probabilia, non videtur hoc	Reid's punctuation
2.104 Etenim cum placeat . . . relinqui	Reid
2.107 et id quidem perspicuum est	Reid
2.108 in quo est etiam adsensus	Reid
2.108 scripta multa, sed	Manutius
2.109 in navigando in conserendo	Manutius
2.109 ut hoc ipsum quidem decretum sapientis esse	Reid
2.113 sed qui minor est	dett. (Reid)
2.116 at illud ante	Reid
2.116 liniamentum sine ulla latitudine	Reid
2.121 nec ut ille qui ex asperis	Reid
2.123 Egone? nonne vobis idem tantum	David Mankin (per litteras)
2.125 ut quidquid movebitur corporeum	Reid
2.128 at paulum ante dicendum est	Reid
2.128 cum physica ista	Aldina
2.129 Omitto illa	Madvig
2.129 ut Erillum qui in cognitione	Davies
2.129 ambo ex Elea itaque ab is Eleatici	Brittain (after Plasberg)
2.129 quod is ex Eretria fuit	dett. (Reid)
2.129 Elii similia, sed opinor	Reid
2.132 adsentietur? Sin ego numquam	Brittain

2.134 sed ille vereor	ANB
2.135 ab Academia vetere	Halm
2.135 decreta	F2
2.137 [quia sapiens non sum]	Reid
2.139 ipsa [se]veritas	dett. (Reid)
2.139 et gravis et recta ratio	ANB2
2.140 Chrysippo fuit . . . non magna contentio	A2B2
2.141 adquiescis adsentiris adprobas	A2B2
2.141 fixum vis esse	Reid
2.141 nullo discrimine	A2NB2
2.143 Quid ergo Academici	Manutius
2.143 opiniosissimi homines	N
2.146 cognovissent, ea non ut esse facta	Reid
2.148 qua re *epokhên* . . . non probans	Madvig

Academica **Book 1:**

1.1 satis eum longo intervallo	D
1.5 Vides autem—eadem enim ipse didicisti—	Davies
1.8 ut ea a fontibus	GD
1.8 quae facilius	Brittain
1.9 tu sedem regionum	GD
1.9 plurimumque idem	Gruterus
1.10 sed da mihi nunc: satisne probas	D
1.13 negat in libris	Davies
1.13 quae contra ea Philonis	Reid
1.16 tamen in virtute laudanda	s
1.21 Nam virtus	Reid
1.21 aut [ad] tuendum	s
1.23 conservatione earum rerum	GD
1.24 eoque efficeretur aliquid	Brittain
1.29 inter quasi fatalem	GD
1.32 in quo tradebatur	Manutius
1.33 quas acceperim immutationes	Halm
1.38 quasdam virtutes natura	Reid
1.39 etiam mentem atque sensus	Reid
1.40 et teneamus hoc	D
1.43 verum esse autem arbitror	GD
1.44 ut iam ante Socratem	Reid

Glossary of Names

All dates are BCE. Cicero's references to the people listed here are given in the general Index.

Academics: followers of Plato or members of his school, the Academy. There were three principal groups of Academics: Old Academics, i.e., Plato and his dogmatic successors before Arcesilaus (c. 390–c. 275); New Academics, i.e., sceptical Academics from Arcesilaus to Philo (c. 275–c. 40); and Antiochians or (revived) 'Old Academics' (c. 95–c. 40).

Accius: Lucius Accius was a poet from Umbria (170–c. 86) who wrote more than forty tragedies as well as other poems.

Aelius: Lucius Aelius Stilo (or Praeconinus) was a Roman Stoic and scholar from Lanuvium (c. 150–50?). He wrote a treatise on Stoic 'assertibles'. Varro was his student and rival in the range of his learning.

Aeschines: a sceptical Academic philosopher from Naples (c. 160–c. 90). He was a student of Carneades and later Melanthius and was regarded as a leading Academic in 110.

Aeschylus: the Athenian tragic poet from Eleusis (c. 525/4–456/4), whose plays included the *Oresteia*.

Africanus: see Scipio Africanus.

Ajax: the protagonist of a play of the same name by Ennius, adapted from a Greek original by Sophocles. Ajax was a leading Greek warrior at Troy who went mad after failing to win the weapons of Achilles in a contest with Ulysses. In his madness he slaughtered a herd of cows under the impression that they were his fellow-Greeks and friends. He committed suicide from shame.

Albinus: Aulus Postumius Albinus was praetor in 155 (and consul in 151). He wrote a history of Rome in Greek.

Alcmaeon: the protagonist in a play of the same name by Ennius, adapted from a Greek original (probably the *Alcmaeon at Psophis* by Euripides). In the play, Alcmaeon is driven mad by the Furies after killing his mother Eriphyle to avenge her betrayal of his father

Amphiarus. Apollo and Diana eventually purify him and secure his acquittal at a trial for matricide.

Alexander: 'the Great', king of Macedon and conqueror of Persia (356–323).

Alexinus: a dialectician from Elis (c. 340–c. 270) who was a student of Eubulides. Eubulides and his students seem to have abandoned the metaphysics of the Megarian school to which they originally belonged in favour of logical investigations, including work on paradoxes. They were later known as 'Eristics'. Alexinus is also reported to have founded his own school in Olympia.

Amafinius: Gaius Amafinius was a Roman Epicurean who popularized Epicurean philosophy in Latin in the early first century BCE. He and Rabirius are the only Roman Epicurean writers Cicero mentions (other than the poet Lucretius); one of his correspondents adds Catius.

Anaxagoras: a 'Presocratic' natural philosopher from Clazomenae (c. 500/499–c. 428/7) who may have taught Pericles and Euripides. He is known for his 'homoiomerous' physical first principles—which may refer to stuffs like bone and flesh, but are probably material qualities like hot and cold—and for positing that the world was ordered by divine intellect (see Plato's *Phaedo*). There are no traces of scepticism in the surviving fragments of his work.

Anaximander: a Presocratic natural philosopher from Miletus (c. 610–c. 540) who was the student of Thales and teacher of Anaximenes.

Anaximenes: a Presocratic natural philosopher from Miletus (c. 565–c. 525) who was the student of Anaximander. Doxographers (including Cicero's source) make him the teacher of Anaxagoras, despite the chronological difficulties this entails.

Andromacha: the title of a play by Ennius, adapted from a Greek original (possibly the *Trojan Women* by Euripides). Andromacha was the wife of the Trojan prince Hector; in Ennius' play she is portrayed as a captive after the fall of Troy, reacting to the murder of her young son Astyanax.

Antiochus: an Academic philosopher from Ascalon (c. 130–c. 68). Antiochus was a sceptical Academic student of Philo for many years but defected to found his own dogmatic school of (revived) 'Old Academics' [here called 'Antiochians'], probably in c. 95. He advocated a return to Old Academic and Peripatetic views but accepted Stoic ethics and epistemology as a largely valid 'correction' of the older tradition.

He wrote the *Sosus* in response to Philo's Roman Books while in Alexandria (87/6–84/3) and later taught in Athens, where Cicero heard him lecture in 79. He accompanied Lucullus both in Alexandria and later in the Second Mithridatic War (74–69). His other books included a work on epistemology and a treatise *On the Gods.* His school continued under his brother Aristus.

Antiopa: the title of a Latin play by Pacuvius, probably adapted from Euripides' Greek original *Antiope.* Antiope suffered many travails after giving birth to Amphion and Zeuthus, illegitimate sons of Zeus (Jupiter).

Antipater: a Stoic philosopher from Tarsus (c. 210–130) who was a student of Diogenes of Babylon and later succeeded him as scholarch in 150. His work to defend Stoic logic and epistemology against its Academic and dialectical detractors (most notably, Carneades) was much admired by later Stoic authors; but he also wrote on ethics and theology. His students included Panaetius and Dardanus.

Apollo: a god associated with the sun, and the brother of Diana (Artemis in Greek). Despite Alcmaeon's fear of them, Apollo and Diana eventually cured him.

Aratus: a poet from Soli (born c. 315), celebrated for his extant astronomical poem, *The Phaenomena.* He was a student of Zeno of Citium and his Stoic leanings are evident in his poem, which Cicero translated into Latin (see *Ac.* 2.66).

Arcesilaus: a sceptical Academic philosopher from Pitane (316/5–241/0) who was the student of Polemo, Crates, and Crantor and became scholarch of the Academy at Crates' death in 268/7. (Arcesilaus had previously studied with Theophrastus and may have learned dialectic from Diodorus Cronus.) Arcesilaus was responsible for the sceptical turn in the Platonic Academy. His motives in championing inapprehensibility and the suspension of assent are controversial but seem more likely to be connected to his revival of the Socratic method—responding to his interlocutors' views rather than arguing for any of his own—than the positive doctrines Cicero suggests they were in *Ac.* 1.44–45. His students included Lacydes, his successor, and, perhaps, Chrysippus.

Archidemus: a Stoic philosopher from Tarsus (c. 180–c. 110) who was a student of Diogenes of Babylon and later of Antipater. He set up a Stoic school in Babylon (perhaps in c. 145). He is known only for his work in logic.

Archimedes: a mathematician and inventor from Syracuse (288/7–212/11). His astronomical works are lost, but an extant work offers a method for calculating the size of the sun.

Aristippus: a student of Socrates from Cyrene (c. 420–c. 350) who endorsed a form of hedonism and was regarded as the founder of the Cyrenaic school (q.v.). His hedonism is distinct from Epicurus' in seeing no place for the virtues and in concentrating on the pleasures of the moment. He was probably innocent of the qualified epistemological scepticism of the later Cyrenaics.

Aristo (*Ac.* 2.12): an Antiochian philosopher from Alexandria (c. 110–c. 30) who was a student of Antiochus and his brother Aristus. Like Cratippus (another student of Aristus), Aristo later abandoned the revived 'Old Academy' for the Peripatetics. He may have written commentaries on Aristotle's *Categories* and *Prior Analytics.*

Aristo of Chios: a Stoic philosopher (c. 320–c. 240) who was a student of Zeno and a contemporary of Cleanthes. Aristo came to be regarded as a heterodox figure when his theories of virtue and psychology were undermined by Chrysippus. But before that he was a leading Stoic figure, despite his differences with Zeno and Cleanthes, and prominent in the defence of Stoic epistemology against Arcesilaus. He wrote on ethics and at least two works against dialecticians.

Aristotle: a student of Plato from Stagira (384/3–322) who founded the Peripatetic school in the Lyceum after Plato's death (335/4). Although Antiochus, like later Platonists, regarded Aristotle as a follower of Plato (if one with serious reservations about the Platonic Forms), much of his work is a critical revision of Platonic thought. He invented the discipline of formal logic, and his works on ethics and metaphysics remain influential. He and his school also began the systematic study of politics, poetry, and biology. (Since his technical works were not widely known until Cicero's old age, Cicero's knowledge of his philosophical views is derived from his lost dialogues and from later Peripatetic sources.)

Aristus: an Antiochian philosopher from Ascalon (c. 110–c. 40). He was a student of his brother Antiochus and later succeeded him as leader of the revived 'Old Academy'. He was a friend of Brutus, and Cicero heard him lecture in 51–50 in Athens. Since several of his most prominent students (including Aristo and Cratippus) defected to the Peripatetics, the revived 'Old Academy' seems to have collapsed with his demise.

Atticus: Titus Pomponius Atticus (110–32) was a Roman Epicurean and the great friend and correspondent of Cicero. He lived in exile in Athens from 85 to 65, where he savoured the nonpolitical life of the Epicureans. He studied under Phaedrus (an Epicurean) in Rome in the 90s, and heard Antiochus' lectures in Athens in the 70s. Although he did not write philosophical works, he contributed to Cicero's dialogues through his work on the historical chronology of Rome.

Avianius: Gaius Avianius Flaccus was a corn-trader and friend of Cicero; he died in 46.

Brutus: Marcus Iunius Brutus (c. 85–42) was a nephew of Cato minor and one of the Liberators or assassins of Julius Caesar. He studied philosophy in Athens with Aristus, Antiochus' brother, as well as with Cratippus the Peripatetic. He wrote at least three philosophical works advocating Antiochian ethics: *On Endurance, On Virtue,* and *On Appropriate Action.* He was a friend of Cicero's and the dedicatee of several Ciceronian works.

Calliphon: a Greek philosopher, probably of the third century known only for his view on the ethical end. He is sometimes mentioned in connexion with Deinomachus, who is also unknown.

Carneades: a sceptical Academic philosopher from Cyrene (214/3–129/8) who studied with Hegesinus and later took over as scholarch of the Academy. Cicero does not mention that he retired in 137/6 and was replaced by two short-lived successors (another Carneades followed by Crates of Tarsus, both obscure figures to us) before his student Clitomachus won the position. Carneades was notorious in Rome for his display arguments for and against natural justice, given in the course of an embassy on behalf of Athens to Rome led by him, Diogenes of Babylon, and the Peripatetic scholarch, Critolaus, in 155. According to Clitomachus he revived Arcesilaus' scepticism and reinvigorated it with his 'theory' of persuasive impressions; but other students, including Metrodorus of Stratonicea, claimed that he advocated a mitigated form of scepticism. Like Socrates and Arcesilaus, he did not write any philosophical books.

Cassius: Lucius Cassius Longinus Ravilla (second century) was a lawyer and judge (and consul in 127). He passed a populist law providing for secret ballots in legal cases tried before the people.

Cato maior: Marcus Porcius Cato (234–149) was a Roman orator and politician from Tusculum. He was consul in 195 and became notorious for his stern moralism as censor from 184, and later for his insistence that Carthage be destroyed. He projected a traditional Roman anti–Greek intellectual image, but was a sophisticated writer. His works included a historical work *Origins* and the extant *On Agriculture.*

Cato minor: Marcus Porcius Cato (95–46) was a tribune in 63—possibly the anti-sceptical tribune joked about in the *Academica*—and consul in 51. He was a determined Stoic and a Republican opponent of Julius Caesar, and his principled suicide made him into the archetypal Roman Stoic martyr. Cicero found him difficult to deal with politically but admired his learning (portrayed, e.g., in Cicero's *On Ethical Ends* 3) and celebrated his life in a lost work, *Cato*—to which Caesar replied in his *Anti-Cato* (also lost).

Catulus senior: Quintus Lutatius Catulus (149–87) was consul in 102. Cicero regarded him as a model orator whose success depended in part on his literary and philosophical knowledge (see Cicero, *On the Orator*). His sceptical Academic affiliation and familiarity with Philo's Roman Books are probably fictional.

Catulus: Quintus Lutatius Catulus (c. 115–61) was consul in 78. His career was less successful than his father's and his philosophical credentials more plainly fictional. He died in 61, shortly after the fictional date of the first edition of Cicero's work. Following his father, he advocates the mitigated sceptical Academic position of Philo and Metrodorus in the first edition, while Cicero represents Clitomachus' radical scepticism. The lost first book of the first edition, the *Catulus,* was dedicated to him.

Censorinus: Lucius Marcius Censorinus was consul in 149 and took part in the Third Punic War against Carthage, which resulted in the total destruction of that city. Clitomachus' dedication of his book to him (perhaps c. 140) is notable both because Clitomachus was a Carthaginian and because it is the earliest Greek philosophical work known to have been dedicated to a Roman.

Charmadas: a sceptical Academic philosopher (c. 168/7–c. 95) and a student of Carneades, also known as Charmides. Charmadas was celebrated in antiquity for his mnemonic theory, which was part of a larger interest in rhetoric. He contributed to the changes in Academic scepticism that led to Philo's transformation of it in his Roman Books.

Chrysippus: a Stoic philosopher from Soli (c. 281–c. 208) and a student of Cleanthes, who later became the third scholarch of the Stoa (in 230/29). He wrote more than seven hundred books on all areas of philosophy, but is most celebrated for his elaboration of the Stoic propositional logic and their theory of compatibilism. His impact on the formulation of Stoicism was so great that Stoic views not explicitly ascribed to Zeno or other named Stoics are usually assumed to be his. He is the original source for many of the anti-sceptical arguments deployed by Antiochus.

Cicero: Marcus Tullius Cicero (106–43) was a brilliant orator and leading Roman politician, as well as a remarkable philosophical writer and thinker. His forensic oratory allowed him to became consul in 63, when he crushed the Catalinarian conspiracy (cf. *Ac.* 2.62–63). He lost political influence under the hegemony of Pompey and Caesar and was exiled for a year in 58. After Julius Caesar's assassination, he tried to marshal the opposition to Antony but failed, and was eventually murdered in the proscriptions of 43. His philosophical studies began in Rome, where he studied under Philo in the mid-80s, but he also heard Posidonius and Antiochus (the latter in Athens in 79–77), as well as many other leading philosophers. He was probably a convinced sceptical Academic throughout his life, though his works on political theory and rhetoric from the 50s play it down. His great series of Latin philosophical works on theology, divination, fate, ethics, and epistemology was written in 46–44. In the dialogue, he advocates the radical scepticism of Clitomachus.

Cimmerians: in Homer (*Odyssey* 11.14), the mythical inhabitants of a land untouched by the light of the sun, where Odysseus (Ulysses in Latin) met and interviewed the spirits of some notable dead people. Some people believed that the Cimmerians had lived in the area in which the dialogue is set.

Cleanthes: a Stoic philosopher from Assos (331/0–230/29) and student of Zeno, who later became the second scholarch of the Stoa (in 262/1). He wrote more than fifty works in all areas of philosophy, but his work was later overshadowed by the systematization and reworking of his and Zeno's views by his student Chrysippus. His celebrated *Hymn to Zeus* is still extant. It was probably Cleanthes and Aristo, rather than Zeno, who met the brunt of Arcesilaus' sceptical arguments.

Clitomachus: a sceptical Academic philosopher from Carthage (187/6–110/9) and student of Carneades, who later became scholarch of the Academy (in 129/8). Clitomachus advocated a radically sceptical interpretation of Carneades' scepticism, in opposition to Metrodorus of Stratonicea. His works presenting Carneades' views were widely cited by later philosophers, including Cicero, Plutarch, and Sextus

Empiricus. His dedication of philosophical books (in Greek) to Censorinus and Lucilius suggests that he was familiar with Roman literary circles; he also wrote a *Consolation* to his fellow-citizens on the destruction of Carthage by the Romans.

Cotta: Gaius Aurelius Cotta (124–74) was consul in 75. His philosophical interests were reinforced by a period of exile in Athens (90–82), where he studied with Philo. Cicero knew and admired him as an orator and thinker and made him the chief Academic interlocutor in his dialogue *On the Nature of the Gods.*

Crantor: an Old Academic philosopher from Soli (c. 340–276/5) who was a student of Xenocrates, Polemo, and Crates. Crantor was a significant figure in the Old Academy who wrote an influential commentary on Plato's *Timaeus* (the first commentary on a Platonic dialogue) as well as the widely cited work *On Grief.* He brought Arcesilaus to the Academy in c. 295.

Crassus: Publius Licinius Crassus Dives Mucianus (c. 180–131) was consul in 131. He was the brother of Scaevola and father-in-law of Gracchus' younger brother. He supported Gracchus' populist reforms.

Crates: an Old Academic philosopher from Athens (c. 340–268/7) and student of Polemo, who later became the fifth scholarch of the Academy (270/69–268/7). Very little is known about his philosophical views. Arcesilaus studied with him.

Cyrenaics: philosophers belonging to the school founded by Aristippus, or advocating its hedonism and dogmatic scepticism about the apprehensibility of the external causes of our impressions.

Dardanus: a Stoic philosopher from Athens (c. 170–c. 90). Dardanus was a pupil of Diogenes of Babylon and of Antipater. Cicero's report that he and Mnesarchus were leading Stoics at the time of Antiochus' conversion from scepticism (c. 95) exhausts our knowledge of his work.

Democritus: a 'Presocratic' philosopher from Abdera (c. 470/69–c. 380/79) who was a more or less exact contemporary of Socrates. Democritus wrote many works on ethics, mathematics, music, and the arts, but he is best known as the chief proponent of atomism before Epicurus. (His relation to Leucippus, his atomist forerunner, is unclear.) Cicero's sceptical reading of Democritus' epistemology is supported by some fragments but is probably exaggerated.

Demosthenes: a celebrated orator and anti-Macedonian politician from Athens (384–322).

Diana: a goddess associated with the moon (Artemis in Greek) and the sister of Apollo. Despite Alcmaeon's fear of them, she and Apollo eventually cured him.

Dicaearchus: a Peripatetic philosopher from Messene (c. 375–300) who was a student of Aristotle. Dicaearchus wrote on a wide range of subjects including geography, ethics, and politics, but he was later best known for his Pythagorean-influenced works on the soul. Cicero probably misascribes to him the view that the soul does not exist at all, which seems to have been advocated by a character in one of his dialogues.

Dio: an Antiochian philosopher from Alexandria (c. 110–57) who studied with Antiochus and his brother Aristus. Dio later led an embassy to Rome to plead against the reinstatement of Ptolemy Auletes as ruler. Ptolemy had him poisoned there in 57.

Diodorus: a Peripatetic philosopher from Tyre (c. 170–c. 110) who was a student of Critolaus and succeeded him as scholarch of the Lyceum.

Diodorus (Cronos): a dialectician (c. 350–c. 283) belonging to the Dialectical school, a rival offshoot of the Megarian school. Diodorus' lectures were attended by Zeno (early 300s) and perhaps Arcesilaus (290s). He was notorious for his development of logical paradoxes such as the sorites and for his arguments against the processes of motion and change.

Diodotus: a Stoic philosopher (c. 120–59) who taught Cicero Stoic logic and later lived in his house as his pensioner.

Diogenes: a Stoic philosopher from Babylon (c. 240–150) who was a student of Chrysippus and later became scholarch of the Stoa (c. 170–150). He was an influential writer on the theory of music and of rhetoric, as well as on psychology and ethics. He participated in the Athenian embassy to Rome in 155 with Carneades, as well as teaching him Stoic logic.

Dionysius: a Stoic philosopher from Heraclea (c. 330–c. 250) who was a student of Zeno of Citium. He was known as 'the Renegade' owing to his rejection of Stoic ethics. It is unclear whether he adopted an Epicurean or Cyrenaic form of hedonism, though the criticism of the Stoics in Cicero's report is an Epicurean one.

Eleatics: the group of philosophers—usually Xenophanes, Parmenides, Zeno, and Melissus—who supported (or were often taken to support) Parmenides' monism and denial of change. Cicero's reports are curious in two respects. First, he ascribes a pluralistic physics to Parmenides (from the second part of his poem) and presents monism as Melissus' view in *Ac.* 2.118. Second, he lists Xenophanes as the founder of the Megarians in *Ac.* 2.129, rather than of the Eleatics, although he died a century before the former group arose. (The Megarians are, however, often considered an offshoot of the Eleatic school.)

Elians: a short-lived group of Socratic philosophers started by Phaedo of Elis (c. 430–c. 350?), which turned into the Eretrian school at the time of Menedemus (c. 300). Phaedo was a student of Socrates who wrote Socratic dialogues, though he is now known mainly from Plato's *Phaedo.*

Empedocles: a 'Presocratic' philosopher from Acragas (c. 495–c. 435?) who advocated the system of four material elements that later became a standard feature of most ancient physics. (In his case, however, it was managed by Love and Strife, which Cicero omits.) He also held a vaguely Pythagorean doctrine of transmigration of souls. His philosophical poetic technique was admired by Lucretius, as well as by Cicero.

Empiricists: a group of medical doctors, and later philosophers, who rejected the speculative physics and theoretical basis of 'rationalist' Greek medicine and developed a sophisticated notion of experience instead. The movement began in the third century and became an influential philosophical position by the first century BCE.

Ennius: Quintus Ennius (239–169) was a Roman poet, originally from southern Italy. He was brought to Rome by Cato maior, where he wrote many works, including tragedies such as the *Alcmaeon* and *Andromacha,* an epic historical poem called the *Annales,* and other works including the *Epicharmus,* a didactic poem on physics. His *Annales* began, after an invocation, with the dream cited by Cicero, in which he met Homer.

Epicharmus: a comic poet from Sicily (c. 540?–c. 480?), later regarded as a Pythagorean and ascribed an interesting set of philosophical works derived from the Platonic dialogues but said to have been plagiarized by Plato. Ennius' *Epicharmus* apparently set out a physical system involving four elements.

Epicureans: the followers of Epicurus (q.v.). Their 'home institution' was the Garden in Athens, but other schools were set up throughout the Graeco–Roman world. Cicero's stress on their mutual friendship emphasizes an important ethical doctrine they held.

Epicurus: the Athenian philosopher from Samos (342/1–271/0) who founded the Epicurean school (311/0 in Mytilene, 305 in Athens). He advocated revised versions of atomism and hedonism, founded on the radically empirical epistemology that Cicero mocks.

Eretrians: a short-lived group of post-Socratic (or sub-Platonic) philosophers who formed a successor school to the Elians in Eretria c. 300. The only Eretrian we have any knowledge about is Menedemus.

Erillus: a Stoic philosopher from Carthage (c. 330–c. 270), known elsewhere as Herillus. He was a student of Zeno but was later regarded as heterodox owing to Chrysippus' criticism of his views on ethics. His position is Platonic in its single-minded stress on cognitive achievements; its perceived flaw was that while he (unlike Aristo) did offer a subsidiary criterion for action, he assigned no value to it.

Euclides: a philosopher from Megara (c. 450–c. 365) who was a student of Socrates and later founded the Megarian school. By making Xenophanes the school founder, Cicero endorses the Eleatic interpretation of his (obscure) views.

Euripides: the tragic poet from Athens (c. 485–c. 405) who wrote ninety plays, many of which were adapted into Latin by Pacuvius, Accius, Ennius, and other Roman writers.

Eurystheus: a mythical king of Argos and the setter of Hercules' twelve labours.

Evandrus: a sceptical Academic philosopher (c. 250–c. 165) who was a student of Lacydes and acted as co-scholarch of the Academy with Telecles during Lacydes' terminal illness (216/5–206/5). Although Cicero appears not to know of it, he and Telecles were joint scholarchs until 167/6, when the latter died. Evandrus remained scholarch until his death a few years later, when Hegesinus succeeded as scholarch. His work is unknown.

Fannius: Gaius Fannius (second century) was a student of the Stoic Panaetius and a contemporary historian of the time of Scipio and the Gracchi. Cicero was uncertain whether he and the consul of 122 of the same name were identical (see *Letters to Atticus* 12.5b).

Flaminius: Gaius Flaminius was a Roman general and politician. He was elected consul in 223 and in 217, when he was killed by Hannibal. His populist measure was to introduce more equitable land distribution as a tribune in 232.

Galba: Servius Sulpicius Galba was a Roman general and politician who became consul in 144.

Geminus: see Servilius.

Gracchus: Tiberius Sempronius Gracchus (c. 170–133) was tribune in 133. He attempted a widespread reform in Roman governance, centered on land redistribution, but was murdered by his fellow-aristocrats.

Hagnon: a sceptical Academic philosopher from Tarsus (c. 170–c. 110) who was a student of Carneades. Little is known of his philosophical activity, except the title of a work, *Prosecution of Rhetoric.*

Hegesinus: a sceptical Academic philosopher (c. 200–c. 160), who succeeded Evandrus as scholarch in c. 165. He was the teacher of his successor Carneades. Nothing else is known about him.

Heraclitus (*Ac.* 2.11–12): a sceptical Academic philosopher from Tyre (c. 120–c. 50?) who was present in Alexandria when Antiochus learned of Philo's Roman Books in 87/6. Cicero's report suggests that he had been a student of Philo in Athens, when the latter advocated the mitigated scepticism the Roman Books disavowed. His arguments with Antiochus show that he remained a sceptical Academic, but nothing further is known of his life.

Heraclitus: the Presocratic philosopher from Ephesus (c. 540–c. 480?), famous for his enigmatic style. The role of fire in his physics is disputed; he probably intended it to be a symbol for the process of change, rather than the basic constituent of material things.

Hercules: the Greek hero and demi-god, best known for the twelve tasks or 'labours' set for him by the usurper Eurysthenes. Among these tasks was the elimination of several monstrous beasts, which became a paradigm of human strength and endurance. In Euripides' version of the story in *The Madness of Hercules,* he returned home on completion of his labours, but was stricken with madness and killed his children under the impression that they were Eurysthenes'.

Hermarchus: a prominent Epicurean philosopher from Mytilene (c. 325–c. 250) who was the student of Epicurus and succeeded him as scholarch of the Garden in 271/0.

Hicetas: a Pythagorean philosopher from Syracuse (fifth century). Elsewhere he is credited with the view that there is an 'anti-earth', which may imply that he in fact accepted the standard Pythagorean view that the planets and the earth revolve around a 'central fire'.

Hieronymus: a Peripatetic philosopher from Mytilene (c. 330–c. 250?) who was a student of Theophrastus. Little is known of his philosophical work beyond his adoption of a remarkably un-Aristotelian ethical end, some moralistic criticism of Arcesilaus, and the title of a work *On Self-restraint* (which was probably an anti-sceptical work, but might have been against consumerism).

Homer: the Greek poet (probably from the eighth century) who composed the *Iliad* and *Odyssey.*

Hortensius: Quintus Hortensius Hortalus (114–49) was consul in 69. He was Cicero's principal rival as an orator in the early part of his life. Cicero converted him to philosophy in his fictional *Hortensius,* but he was perhaps less successful in reality.

Hyperides: a Greek orator and anti-Macedonian politician from Athens (389/8–322/1).

Iliona: the daughter of Priam of Troy and protagonist of a play by Pacuvius of the same name, probably adapted from a lost Greek original. She saved her brother Polydorus by switching him for her son Deiphilus, who was then mistaken for Polydorus and murdered by her husband Polymestor. (Hence the dream-interlocutor Cicero cites is her dead son.)

Lacydes: a sceptical Academic philosopher from Cyrene (c. 280–206/5), who was a student of Arcesilaus and succeeded him as scholarch of the Academy in 241/0. He is credited with 'stabilizing' the sceptical Academy, which he may have done by explicitly adopting and advocating universal inapprehensibility and suspension of assent. (Arcesilaus' consistent practice of the Socratic method made his attitude to these theses hard to discern.) In the last ten years of his life, he was too ill to fulfill the duties of the scholarch and effectively gave control of the Academy to his students Evandrus and Telecles.

Leucippus: the Presocratic philosopher, probably from Miletus (c. 490–c. 440?) who invented atomism as a naturalistic response to Eleatic monism. His views were rapidly overshadowed by Democritus' formulation of atomism.

Libo: Lucius Scribonius Libo (c. 90–c. 20) was a Roman politician. He was the father-in-law of Pompey and brother-in-law of Octavian (later Augustus), and became consul in 34.

Lucilius: Gaius Lucilius (c. 180–102/1) was a Roman poet from Campania. He was a friend of Scipio and a celebrated writer of satire, often with philosophical themes.

Lucullus: Lucius Licinius Lucullus was a Roman general and politician (c. 115–57/6). Cicero describes his career in *Ac.* 2.1–3: he won fame as a youth in the 90s by prosecuting Servilius, the prosecutor who had forced his father into exile; thereafter he was quaestor in 88, proquaestor under Sulla in the 80s, aedile in 79, praetor in 78, and consul in 74. His campaign against Mithridates was successful but too long, so he lost control over it to Pompey in 68/7. His triumph was delayed by Pompey's faction until Cicero's consulship in 63. Cicero suggests elsewhere that he had rather less knowledge and interest in philosophy than he is credited with here. (Hence Cicero's repeated reminders that his speech merely reports Antiochus' arguments.)

Lycurgus: the probably mythical early law-giver of Sparta.

Lysippus: a sculptor from Sicyon (c. 370–c. 320) famous for his statues of Alexander.

Manilius: Manius Manilius was consul in 149, with Censorinus.

Marcellus: Marcus Claudius Marcellus was a Roman general and consul in 166, 155, and 152. Cicero refers to his consulship in 155, with Scipio Nasica Corculum.

Marius: Gaius Marius was a Roman general and politician from Arpinium (c. 157–87). He was consul seven times between 107 and 87. His radical politics were mainly aimed at retaining his legionaries' support.

Megarians: philosophers associated with the school founded by Euclides in Megara in the early 390s. The Megarians were interested in dialectic, initially as a tool for metaphysical investigation, like Plato, but later increasingly for its own sake. (The school seems to have split, leaving Euclides and Stilpo as its principal representatives. Eubulides and Alexinus were later known as 'Eristics'; Clinomachus and Diodorus Cronus were independent 'Dialecticians'.)

Melanthius: a sceptical Academic philosopher from Rhodes (c. 180–c. 130) who was a student of Carneades and a teacher of Aeschines. Nothing further is known about him.

Melissus: a 'Presocratic' philosopher from Samos (c. 490–c. 430) who argued for a form of Eleatic monism roughly similar to Parmenides'.

Since Cicero ascribes positive physical views to Parmenides, his characterization of Melissus' position has to serve as his take on the monists. Melissus' dates are known only from his naval victory over the Athenians in 441.

Menedemus: an Eretrian philosopher and politician (345/4–261/0) who studied under Stilpo before joining the Elian school and transferring it to Eretria (hence its name). Menedemus was a significant and controversial philosophical figure at the time of Arcesilaus. His philosophical position is largely unknown but seems to have had much in common with the early Megarians—i.e., an extreme form of rationalism.

Menippus: a satirical poet from Gadara (c. 300?–250?) of Cynic affiliation. His satires were a model for Lucilius and Lucian, as well as for Varro.

Metrodorus: (*Ac.* 2.73) an atomist philosopher from Chios (c. 420?–c. 340?), regarded as a student of Democritus by Cicero and clearly indebted to his views. Despite its Academic-sounding formulation, his scepticism seems to have depended on a dogmatic theory of atomism.

Metrodorus: a sceptical Academic philosopher from Stratonicea (c. 180–c. 105) who had been an Epicurean but became a prominent student of Carneades. Metrodorus' close connection with Carneades is stressed in several sources, presumably to underline his claim that the other Academics, notably Clitomachus, had misunderstood their teacher. His view was a minority one in his lifetime (he probably taught outside of the Academy during Clitomachus' scholarchate from 129/8 to 110/9), but gained prominence after its adoption by Philo in the form of mitigated scepticism (see *Ac.* 2.78 and 2.148) c. 100.

Minerva: a Roman name for Athena, the goddess of wisdom.

Mithridates: Mithridates VI was king of Pontus (120–63). He fought against the Romans more or less continuously from 89 onwards. In the First Mithridatic War (89–85) his armies overran Asia and Greece and posed a serious threat to Roman hegemony. He was successfully opposed by Sulla, Murena, and Lucullus and beaten decisively by Pompey.

Mnesarchus: a Stoic philosopher (c. 170–c. 90). Cicero's report that he and Dardanus were leading Stoics at the time of Antiochus' conversion from scepticism (c. 95) exhausts our knowledge of his work.

Murena: Lucius Licinius Murena was a Roman general, elected praetor in 88. He fought Mithridates in the First and Second Mithridatic Wars through the 80s.

Myrmecides: a Greek artist of the sixth century. He was celebrated as a miniaturist sculptor. Cicero, probably correctly, takes his name to be a pun, meaning 'ant-like' or 'ant-likener'.

Neptune: the sea god (Poseidon in Greek).

New Academics: philosophers belonging to the Platonic Academy during its sceptical phase (c. 275–c. 40). Our sources distinguish various subgroups, classified inconsistently as the Middle and New Academies, or as the Second, Third, and Fourth Academies. The most significant philosophical distinctions between sceptical Academics are those between radical sceptics (Arcesilaus, Carneades according to Clitomachus), mitigated sceptics (Carneades according to Philo and Metrodorus), and fallibilists (Philo in his late Roman Books). After Philo's death, the Academy probably ceased to function as an institution; but we continue to hear of a few sceptical 'Academics' until the late first century BCE.

Old Academics: philosophers belonging to the Platonic Academy during its initial, dogmatic phase (c. 390–c. 275). These include Plato and his successors as scholarch—Speusippus, Xenocrates, Polemo, Crates—as well as Crantor. Under Polemo, Crates, and Crantor, Plato's views were systematized to some extent, especially in ethics. When Antiochus renounced scepticism c. 95, he cited their authority to back up his claim to be reverting to genuine Academic (or Platonic) views. The sceptical Academics rejected his dogmatic interpretation of Plato and Socrates and hence did not classify them as Old Academics.

Pacuvius: Marcus Pacuvius was the nephew of Ennius and a poet from Brindisium (c. 220–c. 130). His plays included tragedies adapted from Greek originals, such as *Antiopa* and *Iliona.*

Panaetius: a Stoic philosopher from Rhodes (c. 185–110/9) who probably succeeded Antipater as scholarch of the Stoa in 130/29. He is credited with a shift in emphasis in Stoic ethics, but his admiration for Plato and Crantor did not extend to accepting an irrational 'part' of the soul. (His doubts about divination stem from his understanding of physics rather than agnosticism: he was a priest in Rhodes.) His friendship with Scipio, with whom he traveled in 140–38, gave him celebrity in Rome.

Parmenides: a Presocratic philosopher from Elea (c. 515–c. 450) who is elsewhere celebrated as the champion of Eleatic monism. Cicero's reports are curious, because he or his source lists him as a straightforward physicist (relying on the second part of his poem, rather than his *Truth*) and suggests that he advocated an ethical end without specifying what it was. It was presumably the rational a priori knowledge that is the goal of the first part of his poem.

Penelope: the wife of Ulysses celebrated in Homer's *Odyssey*, who had to fend off suitors during her husband's twenty-year absence at and after the Trojan War. One stratagem she used was deferring her response until she had finished weaving a shroud, which she systematically unplucked at night.

Peripatetics: the followers of Aristotle, including Theophrastus, Strato, Dicaearchus, and Hieronymus, as well as later neo-Aristotelians like Aristo and Cratippus. Cicero's knowledge of the Peripatetics was quite extensive, but in this work he is mainly concerned with setting out (and, in his own speech, undermining) Antiochus' historical thesis of the essential doctrinal unity of the Peripatetics and Old Academics.

Phidias: a Greek sculptor (c. 465–c. 425) famous for his gold and ivory statue of Athena in the Parthenon in Athens.

Philo: (*Ac.* 2.143) a dialectician and philosopher, probably from Megara (c. 340?–c. 260?), who was connected with Diodorus Cronus and was perhaps his student. He is known for his interpretation of conditionals (material implication), definition of possibility, and five dialectical daughters.

Philo: a sceptical Academic philosopher from Larissa (159/8–84/3) who was a student of Clitomachus and succeeded him as (probably) the last scholarch of the Academy in 110/9. In the 90s he adopted a form of mitigated scepticism (based on Metrodorus' interpretation of Carneades; see *Ac.* 2.78), which was subsequently regarded as the orthodox position of the New Academics. (It was against this view that Aenesidemus, a former student, reacted by founding or 'reviving' Pyrrhonian scepticism.) But he later adopted a third view, set out in his Roman Books—written in 88/7 while in exile in Rome during the First Mithridatic War—which advocates a fallibilist position on knowledge and hence rejects scepticism. Antiochus, a former student, disputed both the novel epistemological claims of the Roman Books and their historical claim to represent what the Academic tradition from Plato onwards had believed (see *Ac.* 2.18 and 1.13). Cicero does not discuss the Roman view in any detail in the extant books, though he may have done so in the lost *Catulus.*

Plato: the philosopher from Athens (428/7–348/7) and student of Socrates who founded the Academy. The controversy between Antiochus and the Academics over his general philosophical position is part of an institutional battle to claim his authority. The underlying dispute over how to interpret his dialogues has yet to be settled.

Polemo: an Old Academic philosopher from Athens (c. 350–270/69) who was a student of Xenocrates and later succeeded him as scholarch of the Academy. Antiochus regarded him as the systematizer and principal advocate of Platonic ethics and physics in the Old Academy. His students included Crates, Crantor, Zeno, and Arcesilaus.

Polyaenus: an Epicurean philosopher from Lampsacus (c. 330–278/7) who had been a geometer before he met Epicurus. (Epicurus rejected abstract geometry as incompatible with both empirical reality and atomism.) He was one of the four authoritative 'leaders' of the early Garden.

Polyclitus: a sculptor from Argos (c. 480–c. 410) famous for his sculpture *The Spear-bearer* and for a treatise on his art called *The Rule.*

Pompeius: Quintus Pompeius was consul in 141. He was a popular orator and politician and an opponent of Scipio—though he also opposed Gracchus' reforms. It is not clear why Lucullus lists him as a populist legal innovator.

Protagoras: a roving philosopher or sophist from Abdera (c. 490–c. 420). He was celebrated for his agnosticism about the gods and his claim that 'man is the measure of all things'. Plato interpreted the latter to imply that one's impressions are always true and criticized it in his *Theaetetus.*

Pyrrho: a philosopher or ascetic from Elis (c. 365–c. 270) who later came to be regarded as the initiator of Pyrrhonist scepticism. Cicero was unaware of the 'revival' of Pyrrhonism in his lifetime by Aenesidemus (an Academic who became disenchanted with Philo's mitigated scepticism). But the source of Pyrrho's ethical goal was apparently a dogmatic scepticism about the apprehensibility of the world.

Pythagoreans: followers of Pythagoras of Samos (c. 570–c. 500?) who initiated a religious brotherhood in southern Italy. Pythagoras' own teachings are difficult to ascertain, but he seems to have been mainly concerned with ethics and reincarnation. Most of his original follow-ers were murdered, but a few survived and fled to mainland Greece. The latter introduced the metaphysical interest in numbers first recorded in Philolaus (in the fifth century) that was later retrojected onto Pythagoras.

Rabirius: a Roman Epicurean who popularized Epicurean philoso-phy in Latin in the early first century BCE. He and Amafinius are the only Roman Epicurean writers Cicero mentions (other than the poet Lucretius); one of his correspondents adds Catius.

Rogus: Tetrilius Rogus is known only from Cicero's mention of him as a scholar who had heard Philo in Rome and was visiting Alexan-dria in 87/6.

Saturninus: Lucius Appuleius Saturninus was a tribune in 103 and 100. He supported Marius' land distributions to his veterans and set up a new tribunal for offences against the state, aimed at aristocrats. He lost Marius' support and was killed under the senate's authority in a riot in 100. Lucullus' family's hostility to him was due to his prosecution of Lucullus' maternal uncle, Quintus Caecilius Metellus Numidicus.

Scaevola: Publius Mucius Scaevola was a jurist and consul in 133. He was suspected of giving legal advice to Gracchus about his proposed reforms (which his brother Cassius supported), but he did not prose-cute Gracchus' murderers.

Scipio: Publius Cornelius Scipio Aemelianus Africanus (185/4–129) was consul in 147 and 134. He was a successful general who destroyed Carthage in 146. He was also a cultured man who numbered Panaetius and the historian Polybius amongst his friends, taking the former with him on his embassy to various eastern kingdoms in c. 140.

Scipio: (*Ac.* 2.137) Publius Cornelius Scipio Nasica Corculum was consul in 155, with Marcellus.

Selius: Publius and Gaius Selius are only known from Cicero's men-tion of them as scholars who had heard Philo in Rome and were vis-iting Alexandria in 87/6.

Servilius: Publius Servilius Geminus was consul in 252 and 248. His near identical twin Quintus is otherwise unknown.

Siron: an Epicurean philosopher of the first century BCE who worked in Italy. Aside from Cicero's acquaintance with him, we know only that he worked with Philodemus in Naples and was perhaps the teacher of the poet Virgil.

Socrates: the philosopher from Athens (469–399) who inspired Plato and the Socratics, as well as later philosophers including Zeno of Citium and Arcesilaus.

Socratics: followers of Socrates in the fourth century, especially those who wrote about him, including, most notably, Aeschines of Sphettos, Plato, and Xenophon. Many writers and philosophers were inspired by Socrates; their portraits of his philosophical activity and interpretations of his views were widely divergent.

Solon: a poet and politician from Athens (c. 640–c. 560) who reformed Athenian law and political institutions. He was regarded as one of the seven sages.

Sophocles: the tragic poet from Athens (c. 495–406) who wrote 120 plays, including *Antigone* and *Oedipus the King.*

Speusippus: an Old Academic philosopher from Athens (c. 408–339/8) who was the nephew of Plato and succeeded him as the second scholarch of the Academy in 348/7. His metaphysical speculations and theory of pleasure were criticized by Aristotle and went rapidly out of fashion. Antiochus seems to have regarded his role in the 'Platonic tradition' as relatively insignificant.

Stilpo: a Megarian philosopher from Megara (c. 350–c. 270) whose students included Menedemus and Zeno of Citium. Cicero's mention of him highlights his interest in dialectical argument, but he is reported elsewhere as a moralist and metaphysician (and a rationalist opponent of Platonic Forms).

Stoics: followers of Zeno of Citium and his successors, most notably Chrysippus. Antiochus' (or Lucullus') anti-Academic epistemology and arguments are drawn almost entirely from preexisting Stoic arguments. The relation between Antiochus' Stoicism and his Old Academic pretensions is challenged in Cicero's speech in Book 2 and explained (to some extent) in Varro's speech in Book 1.

Strato: a Peripatetic philosopher from Lampsacus (c. 335–220/19) who was a student of Theophrastus and succeeded him as the third scholarch of the Lyceum in 288/7. As Cicero reports, he limited his work to the more scientific interests of his predecessors, including philosophical physics.

Thales: a Presocratic philosopher from Miletus (c. 624–c. 548?), often regarded as the first natural philosopher. His interests seem to have been largely astronomical (he predicted an eclipse in 585). His postulation of water as the first principle probably amounted to a claim about the origin rather than the constitution of things.

Themistocles: a general and politician from Athens (c. 525–459) who defeated the Persian navy at the battle of Salamis. He was later exiled and ended his life as the Persian governor of Magnesia.

Theophrastus: a Peripatetic philosopher from Eressos (372/1–288/7) who was a student of Aristotle and succeeded him as scholarch of the Lyceum in 322/1. Like Aristotle, he was remarkable for the breadth of his scientific interests, from biology to rhetoric, as well as for his philosophical work in metaphysics and ethics. Arcesilaus was one of his many students.

Timagoras: an Epicurean philosopher of uncertain provenance and date. He may be identical with Timasagoras of Rhodes (second century), whose work on perception and anger is criticized by Philodemus.

Tubero: Quintus Aelius Tubero was a Roman jurist and Stoic (second century). He was a friend of Scipio Africanus, as well as of Panaetius; the Stoic Hecato dedicated a treatise on ethics to him.

Tuditanus: Sempronius Tuditanus was the grandfather of Fulvia, Mark Antony's wife (first century BCE). Elsewhere Cicero reports that he used to dress up as a Greek actor and shower the crowd in the forum with money.

Ulysses: the Latin name for the Greek hero Odysseus, the protagonist of Homer's *Odyssey*. Ajax was maddened by the award of Achilles' arms to Ulysses and hence tried to kill him, but in his madness he mistook a cow for Ulysses.

Valerius: Publius Valerius Poplicola was believed to have been the first consul after the expulsion of the kings of Rome in 509. He is supposed to have created the first right to appeal magistrates' decisions to the people (under the Valerian law).

Varro: Marcus Terentius Varro (116–23) was a follower of Antiochus from Reate. He was the most learned and wide-ranging scholar of the Republican age, and wrote on many topics (as Cicero reports in *Ac.* 1.8–9), including the partially extant *On the Latin Language* (alluded to in *Ac.* 1.3). His teachers included Aelius Stilo and Antiochus. Cicero was less friendly towards him than his dialogue suggests, though his admiration for his work is genuine.

Xenocrates: an Old Academic philosopher from Chalcedon (379/8–314/3) who was a student of Plato and became the third scholarch of the Academy after Speusippus' death in 339/8. His metaphysical speculations were criticized by Aristotle and went rapidly out of fashion; but his work was very influential in the Platonist revival that began shortly after Cicero's death.

Xenophanes: a poet and Presocratic philosopher from Colophon (c. 570–c. 475). The claim that he taught Parmenides is probably false, although the latter may have been influenced by his rationalistic theology. The dogmatic scepticism ascribed to him by the Academics is supported by a surviving fragment disclaiming knowledge (but not rational belief), probably about physics and theology.

Zeno: the philosopher from Citium (334/3–262/1) who founded the Stoa c. 300. Zeno's ethics can be seen as an attempt to give a systematic version of Socrates' ideas in Plato's Socratic dialogues (especially the *Protagoras*). His empiricizing epistemology was perhaps a more radical innovation, though it, too, can be traced back to Platonic antecedents (notably, in the *Theaetetus*). Antiochus emphasizes Zeno's Platonic heritage (e.g., by stressing his study with Polemo) in order to recruit him as a 'corrector' of the Old Academy rather than as the radical and original philosopher his contemporaries, including Arcesilaus, saw in him.

Zeno (*Ac.* 2.129): a Presocratic philosopher from Elea (c. 490–c. 430?) who was a student of Parmenides. Plato suggests that his paradoxical arguments about change and motion were designed to support Parmenides' monism.

Zeno (*Ac.* 1.46): an Epicurean philosopher from Sidon (c. 150–c. 75) who succeeded Apollodorus ('the tyrant of the Garden') as scholarch c. 110. Cicero knew him in Athens in 79/8.

Zeuxis: a Greek painter from Heraclea in southern Italy (c. 450–c. 380?) famous for the verisimilitude of his painting.

Select English–Latin– Greek Glossary

References are to notable uses or to Greek glosses in Cicero; further references are given in the Index. Explicit Greek glosses are in bold; the remaining Greek terms are indicative of the dominant Stoic terms (and in brackets where the correspondence is uncertain).

active (cause)	effectio (1.6), efficiens (1.24)	*poiêtikos dunamis*
appetition	[expetendum] (2.29)	*(orekton)*
appetitive desire	cupiditas (2.135)	*epithumia*
apprehend	percipere [comprehendere] (2.17)	*katalambanein*
apprehensible	quae percipi posse (2.17)	*katalêptikos*
	comprehendible (1.41)	**katalêpton**
apprehension (*see* grasp *and* knowledge)	perceptio, comprehensio (2.17)	**katalêpsis**
appropriate action	officium (1.37)	*kathêkon*
approval (*see* assent)	approbatio (2.37; 2.104)	**sunkatathesis**
approve	(ap)probare (2.104)	*peithesthai*
artistry (*see* skill *and* systematic art)	artificium (2.30)	*tekhnê*
assent (*see* approval)	adsensio (2.37)	**sunkatathesis**
assertible	enuntire, effatum (2.95)	**axiôma**
canon (*see* rule)	norma (2.140)	*kanôn*
clear	clarus (2.17)	*dêlos, enargês, tranês*
come to rest	quiescere (2.93)	**hêzukhazein**
conception	notitia (2.21–22)	**ennoia**
control (in our)	in nostra potestate (2.37)	*eph'hêmin*
criterion (*see* judgment)	iudicium (2.18)	*kritêrion*
critical ability	intellegentia (2.18)	*(kritikos)*
disposition	mores (1.19)	*diathesis*

dispreferred indifferents	reiecta (1.37)	*apoproêgmena*
dissimulation ('irony')	dissimulatio, ironia (2.15, 2.74)	**eirôneia**
distinctive	proprium (2.43)	*idion*
disvalue	aestimatio minor (1.37)	*apaxia*
element	elementum (1.26)	*stoikheion*
emotion	permotio (1.38)	*pathos*
end (ethical)	finis (bonorum)	*telos*
error	error (2.66, 1.42)	*hamartia*
etymology	explicatio verborum (1.32)	**etumologia**
evidence	argumentum (2.36)	*tekmêrion*
evident (*see* plain evidence)	evidens (2.18)	*enarges*
examination	circumspectio (2.36)	*diexhodeuein*
experience (ordinary)	consuetudo (omnis, 2.42)	*sunêtheia*
experience	usus (2.22)	*empeiria*
fate	fatum (2.126)	*heimarmenê*
form	forma (2.58)	*eidos*
Form	species (1.32)	**idea**
formal argument	oratio accurata (2.44)	
goal	extremum (2.29)	*telos*
good	bonum (2.129)	*agathon*
grasp (*see* apprehension)	comprehensio (2.17)	**katalêpsis**
happy life	beata vita (2.134)	*eudaimonia*
honourable	honestum (2.71)	*kalon*
ignorance	inscientia (1.41), ignorantia (1.42)	*agnoia, aphrosunê*
imagination	cogitatio (2.48)	*phantastikon, phantasma*
immutable	immutabilis (2.23)	*ametaptôpton*
impede	impedire (2.33)	*perispan*
impressed	signatum (2.18)	*enapomemagmenon*
impression	visum (2.18, 1.40) [(ea quae) videri]	**phantasia**
imprint	signari (2.71)	
impulse	appetitio (2.24)	**hormê**
inapprehensible	[quae percipi non posse (2.18)]	**akatalêpton**

indeterminate	infinitum (2.118)	*apeiron*
indifference	[non movere] (2.130)	**adiaphoria**
inductive inference	coniectura (2.42)	*(stokhasmos* or *epilogismos)*
insensibility	[non sentire] (2.130)	**apatheia**
intellect	ingenium (2.1)	*(nous)*
intelligence (living)	intellegentia animalis (2.119)	*(noeros)*
intelligence (vs. senses) (*see* mind)	mens (2.34, 1.29)	*dianoia*
judgment (*see* criterion)	iudicium (2.19)	*krisis*
kind	genus (2.50)	*genos, eidos*
know	scire (2.14, 1.45)	*eidenai, katalambanein*
knowledge (*see* apprehension)	cognitio (2.129, 1.15)	
known (adj.)	cognitum (2.18)	*katalêptos*
mark	nota (2.33)	*(idiôma)*
marking	notio (2.85)	
matter	materia (1.24)	*hulê, ousia*
mind (vs. body)	animus (2.21)	*psukhê, hêgêmonikon*
mind (vs. senses) (*see* intelligence)	mens (2.30)	*dianoia*
molded	effictum (2.18, 2.77)	*enapotetupômenon*
nonexistent	nullum (2.23), nihil (2.39)	*anhuparkton*
obstacle	[obstare] (2.19)	*enstêma*
opinion	opinio (2.59)	*doxa*
paradox	mirabilia (2.136)	**paradoxa**
peculiar	insignis (2.101)	
perception	sensus (2.108, 1.41)	*aisthêsis*
perspicuity (*see* plain evidence)	perspicuitas (2.17)	**enargeia**
persuasive	probabile (2.32)	*pithanon (eulogon* 2.100)
plain evidence (*see* perspicuity)	evidentia (2.17)	**enargeia**
pleasure	voluptas (2.138)	*hêdonê*
power	vis (1.24)	*dunamis*
practice	exercitatio (2.20)	*(empeiria, askêsis)*
preconception	notitia (2.30)	**prolêpsis**
preferred (indifferents)	praeposita (1.37)	*proêgmena*

primary object	res prima (2.131, 1.22)	*prôton*
principle (first)	principium (2.117)	*arkhê*
principle (philosophical)	decretum (2.27)	**dogma**
proof	argumenti conclusio (2.28)	**apodeixis**
property (individual)	proprietas (singula, 2.56)	*idiotês*
providence	[procurans] (1.29)	*pronoia*
quality	qualitas (1.24)	**poiotês**
rashness	temeritas (2.66, 1.42)	*propeteia*
reason	ratio (2.26)	*logos*
restrain (*see* suspend assent)	sustinere (2.48)	*epekhein*
right action	recte factum (1.37)	*katorthôma*
rule (*see* criterion)	regula (2.32)	*kanôn, kritêrion*
scientific knowledge	scientia (2.23)	*epistêmê*
secure	stabilis (2.23)	*asphalês*
shameful	turpis (1.45)	*aiskhros*
shared	communis (2.33)	*koinos, aparallakton*
sign	signum (2.36)	*sêmeion*
skill (*see* artistry *and* systematic art)	ars (2.20)	*tekhnê*
sophism	fallaces conclusiunculae (2.75)	**sophismata**
stable	firmus (2.43)	*bebaios*
stamped	impressum (2.18)	*enapesphragismenon*
strength of mind	firmitas (2.66)	*aneikaiotês*
suited to its nature	accommodatum ad naturam (2.38)	**oikeion**
suspend assent (*see* restrain)	sustinere (adsensiones, 2.104)	*epekhein*
suspension (of assent)	retentio (2.59)	**epokhê**
systematic art (*see* artistry *and* skill)	ars (2.22)	*tekhnê*
truth-like	veri simile (2.32)	*eikos*
unclear	incertum (2.54)	**adêlon**
unimpeded	[impedire] (2.33)	*aperispaston*
unknown	incognitum (2.18)	*akatalêptos*
vacuous	inanis (2.34)	*diakenos*
value	aestimatio (1.37)	*axia*

vice	vitium (2.39)	*kakia*
virtue	virtus (2.1)	*aretê*
void	inane (2.125)	*kenon*
voluntary	voluntarium (1.39)	*hekousion*
weak	imbecillus (1.41)	*asthenês*
what is	quod est (2.77)	*huparkhon*
wisdom	sapientia (2.23)	*phronêsis*
wise (person)	sapiens (2.27)	*phronimos*
world	mundus (1.28)	*kosmos*

Index

Note that subentries under 'Stoic' include Antiochian material borrowed from the Stoics.

and Socrates and Plato 2.74; as
consul 2.3, 2.62–63; as
philosophical writer 2.5–7, 1.3,
1.10–12, 1.18; as dialogue
participant 2.9, 2.13, 2.30,
2.61–63, 2.64–147, 2.79
(yesterday), 2.148, 1.1–3, 1.14,
1.18, 1.33, 1.35, 1.43, 1.44–46
Cimmerians: 2.61
Cleanthes (Stoic): 2.73, 2.126, 2.143
Clitomachus (Academic):
Carneades' views: wise no
opinions 2.78; persuasive
impressions 2.98–101, 2.102–5;
two kinds of assent 2.104;
Herculean resistance of assent
2.108, fr. 24; on Stoic ethical
paradoxes 2.137; on
Calliphon's ethical end 2.139.
Other: books dedicated to
Lucilius and Censorinus
2.102; and Academic
succession 2.11, 2.16, 2.17
colour: of snow 2.72, 2.100;
inapprehensible (Cyrenaics)
2.70, (Academics) 2.105;
Academics do not deny
existence of 2.103; fr. 7, 9, 23
conception: source of 2.21, 1.42; if
false 2.22; of truth and falsity
2.32; assent 2.38; gives rise to
reason 1.42; an Epicurean
criterion 2.141; Old Academic
source of knowledge 1.32
conditional: 2.96, 2.98; disputed
truth conditions for 2.143
conjunction: judged by dialectic
2.91
consistency (compatibility): 2.22;
judged by dialectic 2.91, 1.19
constancy: depends on
apprehension 2.23; of life 2.31;
assent 2.39; of wise 2.53
Cotta (Academic): 2.84, 2.85
Crantor (Old Academic): 2.135,
1.34

Crassus: 2.13
Crates (Old Academic): 1.34
crime: betraying a principle 2.27,
2.132
criterion (of truth or knowledge):
Stoic: 2.18, 2.29, 2.33, 2.53,
2.114; persuasive and
unimpeded impression cannot
be 2.59; Academics cheat us of
2.60. *Old Academic:* the mind
1.30. *Academic:* no Stoic
criterion 2.84–85; no criterion
for Stoic 'insoluble arguments'
2.95, or for dialectic 2.141;
dispute over (Protagoras,
Cyrenaics, Epicurus, Plato,
Old Academics and Peripa-
tetics, Stoics) 2.142–43. *See
also:* persuasive *and* truth-like
Cyrenaics: 2.20–21, 2.76, 2.131,
2.142

Dardanus (Stoic): 2.69
definition: presupposes
apprehension 2.43; not used
by Epicureans 1.5; used by
Old Academics 1.32
Democritus (Presocratic): no
apprehension 2.14, 1.44; truth
hidden 2.32, 2.73; identical
worlds 2.55–56; atomism
2.118, 2.121, 2.125, 1.6, fr. 28
Demosthenes: 1.10
dialectic: arbiter and judge of truth
and falsity 2.91; undermined
by sorites paradox 2.92–94;
undermined by liar paradox
2.95–98; basic principle:
assertibiles are either true or
false 2.95; Epicurus rejects
excluded middle 2.97;
Carneades learned from
Diogenes (Stoic) 2.98; criteria
of nonexistent 2.141; Aristotle,
Xenocrates, and Chrysippus
wrote on 2.143. Old